BECOMING READERS AND WRITERS

Centered around the idea that literacy teaching is more than the transmission of strategies and skills, this volume serves as a foundation for approaching literacy from an identity perspective. Through incisive and accessible chapters from top scholars, it introduces readers to the concept of literate identities, examining them across ages and grade levels to present an overview of how scholars and educators can use this concept in their research and teaching.

Organized by developmental level with sections on early childhood, middle childhood, adolescence, and cross-age research, contributors reveal how literacy can be framed as an identity practice to engage students and support their development. Applying a range of theoretical perspectives and frameworks, each chapter identifies the identity theory used, explains the relevant methodology and research questions, covers implications for practice, and includes questions or prompts for discussion. The volume reveals how understanding literate identities is at the heart of effective and inclusive literacy instruction by addressing key topics, including culturally relevant pedagogy, intersectionality, and transnationalism, among others. Illuminating multiple pathways to understanding students as readers and writers, this book is essential for teachers, scholars, and researchers in literacy education, research methods, and multicultural education.

Christopher J. Wagner is an Associate Professor of Elementary and Early Childhood Education at Queens College, City University of New York, USA.

Katherine K. Frankel is an Associate Professor of Literacy Education at Boston University, Boston, USA.

Christine M. Leighton is an Associate Professor of Education at Emmanuel College, Boston, USA.

BECOMING READERS AND WRITERS

Literate Identities Across Childhood and Adolescence

Edited by Christopher J. Wagner, Katherine K. Frankel, and Christine M. Leighton

NEW YORK AND LONDON

Designed cover image: © Getty Images

First published 2024
by Routledge
605 Third Avenue, New York, NY 10158

and by Routledge
4 Park Square, Milton Park, Abingdon, Oxon, OX14 4RN

Routledge is an imprint of the Taylor & Francis Group, an informa business

ISBN: 978-1-032-22170-0 (hbk)
ISBN: 978-1-032-20204-4 (pbk)
ISBN: 978-1-003-27140-6 (ebk)

DOI: 10.4324/9781003271406

Typeset in Bembo
by SPi Technologies India Pvt Ltd (Straive)

CONTENTS

ILLUSTRATIONS

Figures

Tables

EDITOR BIOGRAPHIES

Katherine K. Frankel is an Associate Professor of Literacy Education at Boston University, Boston, USA. Her research in partnership with youth and teachers focuses on understanding how adolescents' multiple literacies and identities intersect with the literacy practices of their schools.

Christine M. Leighton is an Associate Professor of Education at Emmanuel College, Boston, USA. She works with teachers and students in multilingual and multicultural classrooms with the aim of ensuring meaningful and equitable learning opportunities that foster language and literacy development.

Christopher J. Wagner is an Associate Professor in the Department of Elementary and Early Childhood Education at Queens College, City University of New York, USA. His research focuses on early literacy, identities, and multilingual learners.

CONTRIBUTOR BIOGRAPHIES

Kewsi Burgess is a doctoral candidate in the Department of Educational Theory and Practice at the University at Albany, State University of New York, USA. He examines the literacy identities of African American males in school, through a culturally sustaining and humanizing lens.

Catherine Compton-Lilly holds the John C. Hungerpiller Chair at the University of South Carolina, USA. She engages in longitudinal qualitative research. Her interests include time as a contextual factor as children progress through school and construct literate identities. Compton-Lilly publishes widely in academic and practitioner literacy journals.

Laura C. Dacus is an Assistant Professor in the School of Education at the University of Tennessee at Chattanooga, USA. She researches how students experience and conceptualize writing within secondary and postsecondary school contexts.

Grace Enriquez is a Professor of Language and Literacy at Lesley University in Cambridge, MA, USA. A former ELA teacher and literacy staff developer, she engages collaborative, humanizing, ethnographic, and critical research in high-needs urban populations to focus on reader response; children's literature for social justice; critical literacies; intersections of literacies, identities, and embodiment; and the teaching of writing. Her work has been published in books and articles for national and international audiences.

Chantal Francois (she/her/hers) is an Assistant Professor in the Department of Instructional Leadership and Professional Development in Towson University's

College of Education. She is a former urban public school teacher and leader. Her work explores humanizing literacy pedagogies for Black, Latinx, and Indigenous populations.

Katherine K. Frankel is an Associate Professor of Literacy Education at Boston University, Boston, USA. Her research in partnership with youth and teachers focuses on understanding how adolescents' multiple literacies and identities intersect with the literacy practices of their schools.

Kierstin Giunco is a doctoral student at Boston College, USA. Her research interests include nurturing students' agency and literate identities. In addition, she works with teachers in the field to support their professional agency as they explore questions about their teaching practices.

Leigh A. Hall is the Director of Research at Merlyn Mind. Previously she held the Wyoming Excellence Endowed Chair in Literacy Education at the University of Wyoming.

Elisabeth Johnson is an Independent Education Consultant who facilitates the design, implementation, and evaluation of formal and informal learning environments. Her work centers on cultures, curriculum, and continuous learning. Liz recently published in *Critical Digital Literacies: Boundary Crossing Practices* (2021), *English Teaching: Practice and Critique* (2020), and *Australian Journal of Language and Literacy* (2018).

Bobbie Kabuto is a Professor at Queens College, City University of New York. She was the 2019 Recipient of the United Kingdom Literacy Association (UKLA)/Wiley Research in Literacy Education Award. Her research interests include bi/literacy and socially constructed identities. Bobbie is the author and editor of seven books and has published over 30 journal articles and book chapters.

Stavroula Kontovourki is an Associate Professor of Literacy and Language Arts Education at the University of Cyprus in Cyprus. Her work focuses on literacy and embodiment, multimodality, and literacy teachers, curricula, and educational policy. She co-edited *Literacies, Learning and the Body* (Enriquez, Johnson, Kontovourki, & Mallozzi, 2016) and recently published in *Literacy* (2022), *Reading Research Quarterly* (2022), *English Teaching: Practice and Critique* (2020), and in edited volumes.

Julie E. Learned is an Associate Professor in the Department of Educational Theory and Practice at the University at Albany, State University of New York, USA. She researches adolescent literacy. By examining how secondary schools position readers and writers and how young people experience, resist, and help construct school contexts, she investigates issues of equity in literacy education.

Christine M. Leighton is an Associate Professor of Education at Emmanuel College, Boston, USA. She works with teachers and students in multilingual and multicultural classrooms with the aim of ensuring meaningful and equitable learning opportunities that foster language and literacy development.

Tisha Lewis Ellison is an Associate Professor in the Department of Language and Literacy Education at the University of Georgia. Dr. Lewis Ellison's research explores the intersections of family literacy, multimodality, and digital and STEAM literacy practices among Black and Latina/é/x families and youth.

Lindsey Moses is an Associate Professor of Literacy at Arizona State University in the Mary Lou Fulton Teachers College. She is the program coordinator for the M.A. in Literacy Education. Her research interests include early literacy, bilingual learners, identity, and instructional practices to support language and literacy in diverse contexts.

Lisa M. O'Brien is an Assistant Professor of Education at Merrimack College. Her research focuses on examining ways to reduce the opportunity gaps underlying educational inequities and fostering preservice teachers' racial literacy.

Tairan Qiu is an Assistant Professor of Literacy Education in the Department of Curriculum and Instruction at the University of Houston. Her research agenda is oriented around exploring the myriad language and literacy practices of transnational youth to advocate for more educational opportunities to sustain their entire cultural, linguistic, and literacies repertoires.

Bradley Robinson is an Assistant Professor in the Department of Curriculum and Instruction at Texas State University. Dr. Robinson's research examines the relations between literacy and technology in formal and informal learning spaces, with a dual focus on novice video game design and the platformization of a literacy.

Allison Skerrett is a Professor in the Department of Curriculum and Instruction in the College of Education at The University of Texas at Austin. She studies the literacy practices of youth of color, including transnational youth, across myriad social contexts, and considers the implications of those practices for secondary literacy education.

Per Henning Uppstad is a Professor of Special Needs Education at the Norwegian Reading Centre, University of Stavanger. He holds a PhD in general linguistics, with research interests in technology-enhanced learning, reading, and writing; educational assessment; and early literacy intervention.

Christopher J. Wagner is an Associate Professor in the Department of Elementary and Early Childhood Education at Queens College, City University of New York, USA. His research focuses on early literacy, identities, and multilingual learners.

Bente Rigmor Walgermo is an Associate Professor at National Centre for Reading Education and Research in Norway. She specializes in research on reading and writing motivation, and assessment. She is leading large research and development projects where the aim is to develop motivating assessments.

INTRODUCTION

Approaching Literacy from an Identity Perspective

Christine M. Leighton, Christopher J. Wagner, and Katherine K. Frankel

Introduction

This book arose from a series of discussions we, the three editors, had around literate identities and what can be learned about literacy development and instruction when literacy is framed as an identity practice. To shed light on the field of identity studies and to help others see the complexity in research on literate identities, we start this book by explaining how this volume came to be and the questions that emerged as we engaged with this work.

I, Christine, had been engaged in practitioner inquiry with a fifth-grade teacher, Kierstin, around her literacy instruction (see Chapter 5). As Kierstin was designing her literacy instruction, she was focused on her students' development of literacy skills and strategies. However, she was perceiving that this focus alone was inadequate to engage students in her curriculum and support their literacy development. The students were telling her important information about who they were as readers and writers, the literacy events and practices they found relevant and meaningful, and how they negotiated these understandings with her and with others. As we recognized the information students were sharing with us, we began to center their literate identities in Kierstin's literacy instruction and in our research.

As our work took this turn toward students' literate identities, I reached out to two other researchers, Chris and Kate (the other editors of this volume), who also approach their work from identity perspectives. We engaged in discussions and eventually collaborated on a research symposium on the broad topic of literate identities. We approached these discussions from our various perspectives as teacher educators and researchers interested in literate identities among children

DOI: 10.4324/9781003271406-1

and youth. Our conversations coalesced around several key questions, that while not new to the field, remain important to interrogating literate identities. These included: What are literate identities? Why do they matter in the field of literacy teaching and research? What theories and methods are used to study literate identities and why do they matter? Do answers to these questions vary as we look across childhood and adolescence?

As we talked and presented together, we found that other scholars had similar questions. Yet we did not know of a resource we could direct others to that could provide a helpful starting point for those trying to make sense of these complexities. This book represents our attempt to provide scholars, both emerging and established in the field of identity studies, with a starting point and a site for discussion about literate identities in all their complexity. To that end, we invited scholars who ground their research within a diversity of perspectives on literacy and identity to share how their work responds to the questions above, with a goal of providing ourselves and others with a resource to better understand and grapple with the complexities of literate identity research. The result is the 12 chapters included in this book that each present a different approach to theorizing and studying the literate identities of children and adolescents.

The 12 chapters illustrate the diversity of ways that scholars answer questions about literacy and identity, as well as the nuance and complexity of adopting an identity perspective in literacy research. Together they help us consider possible answers to the questions we posed, and to explore ongoing questions in the field that have the potential to shape how we understand literacy and learning. In the next sections, we briefly take up the core questions that drove our conversations and that frame this book. In doing so, we aim to introduce the reader to the conversations, topics, and issues that are central to this volume, and that are addressed by the authors in each chapter.

What Are Literate Identities?

As we began our work together, we broadly defined literate identities as the ways people construct the self as a reader and writer across contexts and time as they engage in literate practices. In other words, literate identities are the views people have about what literacy is and who they are as readers and writers. This definition stems from the view that reading is not just about learning skills, but that it also involves the ways readers and writers interact and negotiate their literate identities in contexts where culture, institutional norms, and power are at play (Gee, 2000; Lewis et al., 2007). This is a perspective that has been taken up by many researchers in diverse ways, leading to what Moje and Luke (2009) have characterized as an "identity turn" in literacy research.

Though we offer this definition as a starting place, there is variation in how the term literate identities is constructed and used in literacy research.

These nuances in how researchers define literate identities create both small and large differences in how they study identity (Wagner, 2021). Previous scholars have taken up the work of synthesizing aspects of this field, and offer readers various ways to understand the theoretical and conceptual foundations of studying identities. For example, Moje and Luke (2009) offer five metaphors for thinking about how different perspectives shape views of identity. Norton (2013) reviews how poststructural theory has informed the construct of identity in ways that underlie much of the work in the field today. Wagner (2021) outlines how definitions of identity change depending on the theoretical framing that researchers use while also identifying commonalities found in contemporary research on literate identities. Readers may find any of these reviews helpful if they wish to better understand the broader contours and history of this field.

In this volume, we aim to put these different perspectives on literate identities in conversation. In doing so, this volume offers readers various ways to approach the study of literate identities, and various ways to find connections to their own research on literacy. Below we offer a few of the ways readers may approach the chapters in this volume, and we offer examples of chapters readers may consider as starting points.

Within this book, the reader will find chapters focusing on differing contexts and dimensions of literacy. For example, several chapters focus on how literate identities are negotiated and enacted in classroom and school contexts (e.g., Hall, Chapter 6; Learned et al., Chapter 7; Moses, Chapter 1). Other chapters explore the ways literacies are used as part of the lived experiences of participants outside of formal school contexts (e.g., Lewis Ellison et al., Chapter 9). Some chapters explore ways to balance literacy skills as taught and assessed in schools with sociocultural dimensions of learning (e.g., Giunco et al., Chapter 5), while others consider broader concepts of literacy ranging from multimodality to embodiment (e.g., Compton-Lily, Chapter 10; Enriquez et al., Chapter 12).

In addition, the chapters in this volume include children and youth from a range of communities and lived experiences, including Black and Latinx youth (e.g., Francois, Chapter 4; Giunco et al., Chapter 5; Lewis Ellison, Chapter 9), immigrant youth (e.g., Compton-Lilly, Chapter 10), children from outside the United States (e.g., Walgermo & Uppstad, Chapter 2), transnational youth (e.g., Skerrett, Chapter 8), youth with learning disabilities (e.g., Kabuto, Chapter 11), and multilingual children (e.g., Wagner, Chapter 3).

Ultimately, the goal of this book is not to provide a rigid definition of literate identities but rather to open space to consider the various ways researchers use identity perspectives to interrogate and understand literacy learning and literate practices. To this end, the reader will find that this book offers varying ways to conceptualize literate identities and that authors situate their approach within a diversity of theories that inform their work.

Why Do Literate Identities Matter in Literacy Teaching and Research?

There are many reasons why literate identities matter in literacy pedagogy and research and how they reflect the nuances and complexity of literacy (McCarthey & Moje, 2002). Broadly speaking, identities matter because reading and writing are complex acts that connect to who we are as human beings. Literacy scholars and professionals across research traditions and theoretical paradigms widely acknowledge the ways that "learning is far beyond just a cognitive function, but is deeply embedded in the racial, cultural, historical, socioeconomic, and gendered identities of language and literacy users" (Yaden & Rogers, 2022). Indeed, as Nasir and Hand (2008) have argued, learning and schooling are about "the very definition of who one is and who one is in the process of becoming" (p. 78). In this way, an identity perspective centers the ways that literacy, learning, and identities are intertwined processes (Lave & Wenger, 1991).

Identity perspectives provide ways to think about literacy that integrate cognitive, sociocultural, and other dimensions of reading. Various chapters in this book take up this aim to approach literacy learning as dynamic and multifaceted. For example, Francois (Chapter 4) uses a culturally relevant pedagogy framework to examine Latinx and Black youths' experiences in school. Lewis Ellison et al. (Chapter 9) draw on intersectionality to consider the "literate intersectional identities" of an adolescent Latina in a STEAM workshop. Kabuto (Chapter 11) uses a critical sociocultural framework to consider the construction of a learning disability over time. Enriquez et al. (Chapter 12) use embodiment to examine bodily intra-actions in children of varying ages. These authors each consider aspects of literate identities in relation to questions of power and social structures, race, gender, immigration status, and other social identity categories.

Given current discourse that has framed literacy through the lens of the "science of reading" (Goodwin & Jiménez, 2020), we also seek to position literate identities as an alternative framework to approaching literacy that provides a more holistic view of literacy learning. Popular discourse on reading and literacy that draws from the science of reading is often dominated by oversimplifications of reading and literacy that reduce these complex activities to a narrow set of skills, including a focus on decoding and phonics. These debates are not new, and over the past several decades various stakeholders in the literacy field have engaged in regular and at times contentious exchanges around literacy approaches that too often take all-or-nothing stances that leave insufficient room for the complexity of reading and literacy.

In reality, most contemporary literacy researchers understand the merit and importance of teaching discrete skills such as decoding, while also acknowledging that there is more to reading than these skills alone. Put another way, decoding and similar literacy skills are necessary but insufficient to prepare children and adolescents to be readers and writers. Literate identities provide a productive framework for bridging these divides in how literacy is conceptualized in popular and academic discourse, and for recentering conversations on literacy learning around the complex and intersecting needs of literacy learners as they are becoming readers and writers. Given the current climate of discourse on schooling and literacy learning, we hope that readers will consider how an identity framework might lead toward healthier, more nuanced, and more diverse research and discourse on literacy.

What Theories and Methods Are Used to Study Literate Identities?

As researchers take up the study of literate identities, the theories they adopt shape not only how they conceptualize identities and literacy but also the questions they attempt to answer and the methods they use to do so. Other reviews (see Wagner, 2021) identify and describe broad "families" of theories (e.g., psychological, social, poststructural, critical, integrative). As we have noted above, we do not aim to provide a single definition of literate identities or to impose a rigid structure on the field and the different theoretical approaches to studying literate identities. We instead see the ways that the boundaries between theoretical traditions are often blurred, and how it is common for identity researchers to draw across theoretical perspectives in their research. Our approach here is to honor and embrace the complexity and richness of research that treats theories as complex, interconnected, and malleable tools for exploring identities.

In creating this book, we have aimed to bring together researchers whose work reflects the diversity of viewpoints and theoretical lenses currently used in the field. This book includes researchers who draw on social perspectives such as communities of practice, ideological approaches, and figured worlds (e.g., Hall, Chapter 6; Moses, Chapter 1; Wagner, Chapter 3); poststructural perspectives that include positioning theory and transnationalism (e.g., Learned et al., Chapter 7; Skerrett, Chapter 8); psychological or cognitive perspectives that include motivation and self-concept (e.g., Walgermo & Uppstad, Chapter 2); critical perspectives that include culturally relevant and sustaining pedagogies, intersectionality, and critical disability studies (e.g., Compton-Lilly, Chapter 10; Francois, Chapter 4; Kabuto, Chapter 11; Lewis Ellison et al., Chapter 9); and posthumanist perspectives such as assemblage and embodiment (Compton-Lilly, Chapter 10; Enriquez et al., Chapter 12).

Though we aim to be representative of a range of theories and methodologies used in the field of identity studies, we also recognize that not all theories and methodologies used by identity researchers are represented in this book. At the same time, many of the authors in this volume integrate theoretical perspectives in unique ways that help to more fully explore their research questions. Many of the authors likewise draw across multiple methodological approaches in an attempt to construct more complex views of identities. By drawing on multiple theories and methodologies that span paradigms, the work in these chapters reflects the complexity and range of approaches to identity research that can be found in the broader field.

These chapters likewise provide opportunities for readers to consider how various identity theories can connect to or extend theories that may be salient in their own work. For example, in Chapter 10 Compton-Lilly shows how the application of different theories yields different insights and presentations of literate identities. In Chapter 3, Wagner considers how existing theories may be revised and extended to more fully account for multilingualism. These chapters similarly provide opportunities for readers to consider ways to apply or combine existing methodologies to study identities. For example, in Chapter 1 Moses provides extensive details of her decision-making processes that led to her methodological approaches in two studies with young children.

We encourage readers to consider ways that theories and methods build on one another to support explorations of the complexities and nuances of literate identities. We likewise encourage readers to take up and consider theoretical and methodological directions that are needed in identity research and that are raised in the chapters in this book. This includes considering how current approaches and paradigms can be built upon to extend and deepen what can be learned about literacy from an identity perspective.

Do Answers to These Questions Vary Across Childhood and Adolescence?

Though researchers have examined literate identities in various contexts and among different groups of learners, individual studies on literate identities have tended to focus on specific populations of readers, often looking at students in a narrow grade or age range. This tendency toward studying literate identities in narrow developmental time periods has contributed to more limited understandings of how literate identities change and develop over time and as children grow as readers and writers. In addition, researchers have not often been in conversation across age and developmental levels, exacerbating the often-siloed approach to the study of literate identities across childhood and adolescence. Our collaboration as editors began as an attempt to bridge conversations across age and developmental levels to spur conversations about what can be learned by collaborating and looking across the field of identity studies.

Accordingly, a primary aim of this volume is to bring together authors that work across ages to explicitly put research with young people of different ages in conversation. This volume attempts to look across age and context to consider how children and youth construct and express reading identities, with particular attention to how reading identities vary and are similar across ages. Together, the collected chapters in this volume provide an overview of research across ages and grades (early childhood, middle childhood, adolescence, and cross-age research).

Though this book is organized by broad age groups, we encourage readers to consider both how these categories are helpful in directing attention to specific developmental concerns that shape literacy experiences and learning, and in what ways it may be appropriate to question and deconstruct these categorizations by age and grade. The last section of this book includes three chapters that specifically explore identities across time. These chapters both consider time as a factor in identities and work to deconstruct notions of time. We likewise encourage readers to consider what can be learned by attending to developmental perspectives on identities, and what can be learned by critically questioning rigid notions of development and time.

How This Book Is Structured

This book is structured to help the reader consider each of the questions we have outlined in this chapter. This book is divided into four sections by developmental levels. The first three sections include chapters that address literate identities in early childhood, middle childhood, and adolescence, respectively. The fourth section includes chapters that consider identities for children and youth across these age groups, and that include cross-sectional or longitudinal data that provide ways of looking at identities across time.

Each section of this book begins with a section introduction that provides an overview of important developmental considerations that inform literate identities at that age level, a review of theoretical and methodological considerations in identity research, and an overview of how each chapter approaches these topics. We highlight connections and divergences in how the authors ground their work theoretically, as well as how these perspectives inform authors' methodological choices. Readers who are interested in more information on theory and methods may want to look to these section introductions for more specific discussions of these topics.

In each chapter, the authors provide an explanation of the theory or theories they use to guide their research, explain their research methodology with attention to how theories of identity shaped the research questions and the collection and analysis of data, explain findings from the research, and provide implications for future research and practice. Each chapter concludes with questions for discussion that can be used to guide conversation on these chapters or to prompt readers to consider on their own what they may take from these chapters.

This volume ends with a conclusion that explores themes from across the chapters and provides implications for the future of the identity field. We offer guidance for researchers to suggest directions and needs in theory and methods for identity research, for practitioners to provide ways an identity perspective can inform the practice of teaching, and for policy-makers to guide decision-making on learning and schooling. We hope that readers likewise draw their own conclusions and find ways that the work shared in this volume can inform their own thinking and practice as literacy researchers and teachers, and that they do so in ways that continue to center children and adolescents in the practice of literacy.

References

Gee, J. P. (2000). Identity as an analytic lens for research in education. *Review of Research in Education, 25*, 99–125. https://doi.org/10.3102/0091732x025001099

Goodwin, A. P., & Jiménez, R. T. (2020). The science of reading: Supports, critiques, and questions. *Reading Research Quarterly, 55*, S7–S16. https://doi.org/10.1002/rrq.360

Lave, J., & Wenger, E. (1991). *Situated learning: Legitimate peripheral participation.* Cambridge University Press. https://doi.org/10.1017/cbo9780511815355

Lewis, C., Enciso, P., & Moje, E. B. (Eds.). (2007). *Reframing sociocultural research on literacy: Identity, agency, and power.* Lawrence Erlbaum. https://doi.org/10.4324/9781003064428

McCarthey, S. J., & Moje, E. B. (2002). Conversations: Identity matters. *Reading Research Quarterly, 37*(2), 228–238. https://doi.org/10.1598/RRQ.37.2.6

Moje, E. B., & Luke, A. (2009). Literacy and identity: Examining the metaphors in history and contemporary research. *Reading Research Quarterly, 44*(4), 415–437. https://doi.org/10.1598/RRQ.44.4.7

Nasir, N. I. S., & Hand, V. (2008). From the court to the classroom: Opportunities for engagement, learning, and identity in basketball and classroom mathematics. *Journal of the Learning Sciences, 17*(2), 143–179. https://doi.org/10.1080/10508400801986108

Norton, B. (2013). *Identity and language learning: Extending the conversation* (2nd ed.). Multilingual Matters.

Wagner, C. J. (2021). Literacy and identities. In G. Noblit (Ed.), *Oxford research encyclopedia of education.* Oxford University Press. https://doi.org/10.1093/acrefore/9780190264093.013.990

Yaden, D., & Rogers, T. (Eds.). (2022). Literacies and language. *International encyclopedia of education* (4th ed.). Elsevier.

SECTION I

Literate Identities in Early Childhood

Introduction to Literate Identities in Early Childhood

Christopher J. Wagner

Introduction

Early childhood is a unique period in children's development of literacy and the self. Generally regarded as the period from birth to age eight (about grade three in US schools), the early childhood years are characterized by both rapid changes in development and the learning of foundational literacy practices. In the early childhood years, children move through significant milestones in the development of language. Among these, children generally:

- Learn to use and communicate with oral language;
- Develop understandings of print literacies;
- Learn foundational reading and writing skills;
- Transition into schooling as a site for literacy learning; and
- Learn to manage differences in home and school literacies.

Together these represent remarkable changes in the ways and complexity of how children communicate and express themselves in a rather brief period of time.

At the same time that young children are developing as users of language and print literacies, they are constructing literate identities. Young children often co-construct literate identities through participation in literacy practices with adults, and the development of these identities can help to facilitate the acquisition of early literacy skills (Gee, 2002). By the age of four, children generally develop both specific and general ideas about their literate identities and the ability to communicate about the self as a reader and writer in complex and context-specific ways (Cimpian, et al., 2017; Rogers & Elias, 2012; Wagner, 2018, 2021). From this early age, literate identities develop in tandem with and

DOI: 10.4324/9781003271406-3

support children's literacy learning in ways that are foundational to their growth as readers and writers.

Theorizing Identities in Early Childhood

In theories used to study literate identities, the historical centering of identity as an adolescent and adult phenomenon has been commonplace. This has both arisen from and been sustained by the cultural prevalence of identity as a coming-of-age process in adolescence and the popularity of models like Erik Erikson's (1980) psychosocial theory of human development. These models have perpetuated the view that identities do not start to develop until the end of childhood and the start of adolescence, and are largely developed in the adolescent and early adult years (Compton-Lilly, 2006). These views have been bolstered by a common assumption that young children lack the cognitive ability to reflect on the self (Brummelman & Thomaes, 2017; Harter, 2012).

In more recent years, views toward identity processes in young children have shifted as research on cognition and human development has challenged assumptions that young children are limited in their ability to construct complex identities. As early as preschool, children have intuitive theories about personal identities and share many adult intuitions about the self (Starmans, 2017). Rather than being inconsistent or lacking coherence with past identity experiences, young children show continuity in their constructions of the self (Cimpian et al., 2017). An emerging body of research has begun to convincingly show that children's ability to construct identities is largely stable across childhood, and though children do refine the content of their beliefs about who they are, their underlying ability to construct identities exists from a young age.

Most current theories have not yet caught up to these changes in how researchers understand young children's identity development. For the most part, whether young children require different identity theories than those used for teenagers and adults has largely not been asked by researchers in the field. With limited exceptions, there has not been an explicit development of theories or models of identities in early childhood (Harter, 2012; Wagner 2020). This poses a problem for researchers of young children when common theories in the field neglect aspects of young children's development or literacy practices. For example, not all theories that explain identities as socially negotiated look beyond verbal communication to consider how embodiment, affect, and nonverbal modes of communication are used by young children to position the self in social interactions.

When selecting theories for identity research in early childhood, researchers must critically consider whether a theory is appropriate for studying identities in young children. This requires considering whether a selected theory imposes existing tendencies toward developmental bias, language-based explanations of identity construction, or outdated models of cognition and growth. When theories that adopt these perspectives are used in research with young children, they can undermine the validity of research and perpetuate problematic and limiting assumptions about identities in early childhood. Researchers may likewise consider opportunities to create space for young children in identity theory. This can include refining existing theories or developing new theories that may more fully explain identity processes in younger learners.

Research Methods in Early Childhood

Researchers collecting data about young children and their literate identities are likely to encounter specific methodological challenges. These arise from children's developing ability to verbally communicate about their identities, sometimes shorter attention spans for formal research procedures, and other differences that make young children unique when compared to adolescent or adult research participants (Compton-Lilly, 2006; McCarthey & Moje, 2002; Wagner, 2018, 2021). Despite these methodological challenges, young children are a vital source of data on their own literate identities, and navigating research methods with young children is essential to research in this area.

As a source of information about their literate identities, young children are capable meaning-makers. Research with children as young as ages two and three has shown how these children can provide information about and participate in the interpretation of their identities as readers and writers (Kabuto, 2011; Choi, 2021). Constructing valid interpretations of children's literate identities requires the use of developmentally accessible data collection methods and appropriate opportunities for reflection (Albon & Rosen, 2013; Genishi & Dyson, 2009; Wagner, 2018, 2021). This often requires turning to more flexible, open-ended, and participatory research methods that create spaces for children to share and enact different ways of being readers and writers.

Researchers can often look to the activities children already participate in as spaces for exploring their literate identities. For many children, who they are as readers and writers surface in the narratives of their play, the arts they create, and the conversations they have with others in informal interactions (Compton-Lilly, 2006; Genishi & Dyson, 2009). Observing and interacting with children through play and other "child-like" activities can tell us much about who children are as readers and writers. When working from this stance, common approaches to gathering and interpreting data with young children include observations of literacy activities, conversations during reading or writing, drawing or art-based interviews, and retrospective discussions of literacy artifacts (Angell et al., 2015; Kendrick & McKay, 2004; Wagner, 2018, 2021).

Other data sources on young children's literate identities can include reports from knowledgeable adults (Gutierrez-Clellen & Kreiter, 2003; Orellana & Peer, 2012). As regular observers of children's literacy practices in the classroom, teachers can provide information on the routines, instruction, and literacy practices in which children participate. Teachers often develop trusting relationships with children that make them well-positioned to report on aspects of children's identities that they may not share or enact in the presence of researchers. While teachers often work with a child for only one year, parents and other caregivers are uniquely positioned to have a long-term view of their child's identity development and history. In both cases, these adults can provide information that can corroborate or extend understandings of young children's identities.

For many children, the literacy practices they learn in the home and community differ from those they may learn or be asked to use in school. This is particularly common for Black, Latinx, indigenous, immigrant, multilingual, and other groups whose home language practices differ from school norms (Kabuto, 2011; Langer-Osuna & Nasir, 2016; Wynter-Hoyte & Boutte, 2018). These differences can be particularly salient for young learners for whom the majority of their language and literacy histories have occurred in out-of-school spaces. Collecting data beyond school settings to include literate practices in the home and community spaces is particularly important if research aims to be inclusive of diverse language and literacy practices. Accordingly, studies that rely solely on data collected in school settings are more likely to yield incomplete and partial pictures of young children's literate identities.

Chapters in This Section

This section includes three chapters on literate identities in early childhood. Section IV, which gives attention to the development of literate identities across childhood and adolescence, includes examples of longitudinal and cross-sectional research that begin with children in the early childhood years. Readers interested in research on early childhood should look to the chapters in both of these sections for examples of the theories and methods that can be used to study the literate identities of young children. Across the three chapters in this section, the authors draw on a diverse range of theoretical and methodological approaches to conceptualize literate identities and their relation to teaching and learning in early childhood.

In Chapter 1, Moses looks at data across two studies to consider how students in a first-grade classroom negotiated accepted literate identities and exerted agency to redefine accepted literate identities in the classroom. This chapter highlights the impacts of curriculum and schooling practices on young learners and draws attention not only to negative outcomes for children in the early years but also to instances of positive positionings of students. Moses calls on researchers not only to examine the systems and practices that often oppress and marginalize certain young readers and writers but also to interrogate the systems and practices that support positive identity negotiations and honor the identity work of children.

Moses shows how multiple theories (communities of practice, cultural tools, and positioning) can be brought together in complementary ways to understand identity as a complex social process in which even young children have agency. Moses likewise shows how varied data sources and the use of robust qualitative data analysis methods can be used to produce complex portraits of young children's identities and reveal the processes through which they are constructed in social spaces. By describing the decision-making processes involved in this research, Moses also shows how decisions about theory and research methods shape the interpretation of data and understandings of children's literate identities.

In Chapter 2, Walgermo and Uppstad present a study of an assessment designed to simultaneously identify learners in need of literacy support and promote literacy interest and self-concept as students are assessed. The authors show how assessments can be reimagined to be inclusive of literate identities, and they call for assessments that have stronger motivational qualities. In doing so they not only point to common concerns about literacy assessments raised by both researchers and teachers, they also point a way forward to more meaningful assessment practices. Walgermo and Uppstad offer direction on how assessments can be reenvisioned to value literate identities as equal to literacy skills and be more closely integrated with instruction.

Through their use of assessment data, Walgermo and Uppstad show how literate identities can be studied at a large-scale and how quantitative methods can contribute to understandings of literate identities. This offers readers a different methodological approach that contrasts with the qualitative methods that are more common in the field. Walgermo and Uppstad weave together concepts of motivation and identity that tie into reading and literacy as meaning-making practices. The authors use these theories to consider the correspondence between motivation, self-concept, and self-efficacy, and show how conceptual models can be modified through research to more fully capture the links between related constructs that inform identities and learning.

In Chapter 3, Wagner looks at data across two studies on multilingual learners in prekindergarten and kindergarten to explore the roles of language and multilingualism in children's literate identities. The author shows how literate identities are not only connected to reading and writing, but are profoundly connected to language, particularly as young children are beginning to learn to read and write. Wagner shows how a monolingual view of literate identities has led to an overlooking of the more expansive set of language practices, skills, and dispositions that shape the literate identities of multilingual learners. Wagner likewise shows how multilinguals can construct literate identities that differ across home, school, and community spaces.

By using a broader sociocultural and poststructural framework to understand identities, Wagner seeks to sidestep theories that were developed to attend to monolingual adults. By doing so, Wagner aims to open spaces to consider how the identities of young multilingual learners may differ based on both children's development and their language histories. Wagner likewise shows how the use of varied data sources, including data sources that draw across different contexts for language use and include families, can produce more complex portraits of young children's identities. The author highlights the particular salience of looking beyond school spaces when researching multilingual learners to understand the roles of home and community language practices in young children's literate identities.

Together, these chapters highlight a range of approaches that each add to our collective understanding of literate identities in early childhood. At the same time, differences in the theories and research methods used across these chapters show how the ways identities are studied and conceptualized matter in research on young children. For example, Walgermo and Uppstad are able to construct hierarchical relationships between concepts like global self-concept, academic self-concept, and reader or writer self-concept. In contrast, Moses considers constructs like cultural tools and communities of practices, but presents the relationship between these constructs as less structured. Wagner likewise shows the complex interplay between language, context, and identities, and at the same time documents the variability in the relationships between these constructs across children.

Though there are other similarities and contrasts across these chapters, we encourage readers to view these not as disagreements or conflicts that require resolution but as a positive sign of the multiplicity of voices engaged in identity research about young children. These differing approaches to research methods and theories highlight both the breadth of the field and the many opportunities for researchers to bring a range of diverse perspectives, theories, and methodological approaches to identity research in early childhood. The chapters in this section are examples of this diversity and hopefully also serve as an invitation to other researchers to interrogate how and through what lenses they can learn more about the literate identities of our youngest learners.

References

Albon, D., & Rosen, R. (2013). *Negotiating adult-child relationships in early childhood research.* Routledge. https://doi.org/10.4324/9780203095126

Angell, A., Alexander, J., & Hunt, J. A. (2015). 'Draw, write and tell': A literature review and methodological development on the 'draw and write' research method. *Journal of Early Childhood Research, 13*(1), 17–28. https://doi.org/10.1177/1476718x14538592

Brummelman, E., & Thomaes, S. (2017). How children construct views of themselves: A social-developmental perspective. *Child Development, 88*(6), 1763–1773. https://doi.org/10.1111/cdev.12961

Choi, J. (2021). Demystifying simultaneous triliteracy development: One child's emergent writing practices across three scripts focusing on letter recognition, directionality and name writing. *Journal of Early Childhood Literacy, 21*(4), 614–636. https://doi.org/10.1177/1468798419896064

Cimpian, A., Hammond, M. D., Mazza, G., & Corry, G. (2017). Young children's self-concepts include representations of abstract traits and the global self. *Child Development, 88*(6), 1786–1798. https://doi.org/10.1111/cdev.12925

Compton-Lilly, C. (2006). Identity, childhood culture, and literacy learning: A case study. *Journal of Early Childhood Literacy, 6*(1), 57–76. https://doi.org/10.1177/1468798406062175

Erikson, E. H. (1980). *Identity and the life cycle*. Norton.

Gee, J. P. (2002). A sociocultural perspective on early literacy development. In S. B. Neuman & D. K. Dickinson (Eds.), *Handbook of early literacy research* (Vol. 1, pp. 30–42). Guilford Press.

Genishi, C., & Dyson, A. H. (2009). *Children, language, and literacy: Diverse learners in diverse times*. Teachers College Press. https://doi.org/10.1177/1468798409355310

Gutierrez-Clellen, V. F., & Kreiter, J. (2003). Understanding child bilingual acquisition using parent and teacher reports. *Applied Psycholinguistics, 24*, 267–288. https://doi.org/10.1017/s0142716403000158

Harter, S. (2012). *The construction of the self: Developmental and sociocultural foundations* (2nd ed.). Guilford Press.

Kabuto, B. (2011). *Becoming biliterate: Identity, ideology, and learning to read and write in two languages*. Routledge.

Kendrick, M., & McKay, R. (2004). Drawing as an alternative way of understanding young children's constructions of literacy. *Journal of Early Childhood Literacy, 4*(1), 109–128. https://doi.org/10.1177/1468798404041458

Langer-Osuna, J. M., & Nasir, N. S. (2016). Rehumanizing the "other": Race, culture, and identity in education research. *Review of Research in Education, 40*, 723–743. https://doi.org/10.3102/0091732x16676468

McCarthey, S. J. & Moje, E. B. (2002). Identity matters. *Reading Research Quarterly, 37*(2), 228–238. https://doi.org/10.1598/rrq.37.2.6

Orellana, M. F., & Peer, K. (2012). Methodologies of early childhood research. In J. Larson & J. Marsh (Eds.), *Handbook of early childhood literacy* (2nd ed., pp. 633–652). Sage. https://doi.org/10.4135/9781446247518.n35

Rogers, R., & Elias, M. (2012). Storied selves: A critical discourse analysis of young children's literate identifications. *Journal of Early Childhood Literacy, 12*(3), 259–292. https://doi.org/10.1177/1468798411417370

Starmans, C. (2017). Children's theories of the self. *Child Development, 88*(6), 1774–1785. https://doi.org/10.1111/cdev.12951

Wagner, C. J. (2018). Being bilingual, being a reader: Prekindergarten dual language learners' reading identities. *Journal of Early Childhood Literacy, 18*(1), 5–37. https://doi.org/10.1177/1468798417739668

Wagner, C. J. (2020). Multilingualism and reading identities in prekindergarten: Young children connecting reading, language, and the self. *Journal of Language, Identity, & Education*. Advance online publication. https://doi.org/10.1080/15348458.2020.1810046

Wagner, C. J. (2021). Reading identities as a developmental process: Changes in Chinese-English learners from prekindergarten to kindergarten. *Bilingual Research Journal, 44*(2), 174–188. https://doi.org/10.1080/15235882.2021.1942324

Wynter-Hoyte, K., & Boutte, G. S. (2018). Expanding understandings of literacy: The double consciousness of a Black middle class child in church and school. *The Journal of Negro Education, 87*(4), 375–390. https://doi.org/10.7709/jnegroeducation.87.4.0375

1

EXPLORING, ANALYZING, INTERPRETING, AND (RE)PRESENTING POSITIVE VISIONS OF YOUNG CHILDREN'S LITERATE IDENTITIES

Lindsey Moses

Introduction

During my time as a teacher of young children, I found myself concerned with the inflexibility of curricular mandates, including approaches to assessment and instruction, that did not feel developmentally and linguistically appropriate. At the time, I initially associated this frustration with limiting my ability to make thoughtful choices about what would best support my students, but over time I realized it was more than that—it was the way our schooling context was positioning children who did not readily and successfully take up the prescribed curriculum and schooling practices built primarily for white, middle-class communities.

Now, as a researcher of young children, I find myself exploring and analyzing the ways in which educational systems, structures, curricula, and educators position young children and, in turn, the ways young children take up or resist those positions. For me, this work initially started with using critical discourse analysis (CDA) approaches to shed light on the ways these systems and experiences negatively positioned and marginalized children who were not situated directly into the curricular norms (Kress, 1996). As my research evolved, I found myself drawn to a shift in thinking. I wanted to research and write about instances of success and positive positioning of children who historically would have been (or had been) positioned negatively in the educational context.

In this chapter, I synthesize and contrast the authorial decisions and research processes across two studies focused on young children's positive literate identity negotiations. In the first yearlong study focusing on reading (Moses & Kelly, 2017), we examined how first graders, originally positioned as "struggling readers," took up various classroom literacy practices to use as tools to reposition

DOI: 10.4324/9781003271406-4

themselves as capable and competent members of the classroom community of practice. In the second yearlong study focusing on children's writing (manuscript currently under review), we analyzed how one "curricularly unruly" (Dyson & Genishi, 2013) child navigated a shift in positioning from a resistant and peripheral member to a classroom expert, leader, and innovator through agentic composing choices as he pushed back against the writing curriculum.

Theoretical Framing

The studies were grounded in various sociocultural theories in order to understand classroom experiences, community practices, and identity. Vygotsky's sociocultural theory (1980) situates human development as a socially mediated process in which the role of social interaction is essential in meaning making and development. Learning is not situated in a specific skill, milestone, or practice. To truly understand learning, one must consider the social, cultural, and historical contexts (Vygotsky, 1980). Building on these broad beliefs of learning and meaning making, I draw on three related but distinct theoretical frameworks to shape the approaches to the research of the two studies: communities of practice (Lave & Wenger, 1991; Wenger, 1998), cultural tools (Wertsch, 1998), and positioning theory (Davies & Harré, 1990).

Communities of Practice

Lave and Wenger (1991) expand on sociocultural theory by moving beyond limited definitions of learning that situate it as simply a cognitive process. They argue that situated learning is a social process that involves an individual's social, cultural, and historical context. Every community of practice has and/or develops commonly accepted practices, and members develop their identities and status as community participants based on their ability to participate in those practices. Lave and Wenger (1991) discuss these identities/statuses in relation to community membership in an evolving and fluid way that changes over time. As opposed to talking about identity and participation in binary terms, they talk about gradation (newcomer to peripheral to full): "Learning as a legitimate peripheral participation means that learning is not merely a condition for membership but is itself an evolving form of membership" (Lave & Wenger, 1991, p. 53). Legitimate peripheral participation is a core principle of situated activity because learners can move from newcomers toward full participation in the sociocultural practices of the community through mastery of knowledge and the use of cultural tools essential to their community. While this theory was originally contextualized in adult learning among practitioners such as midwives and butchers to better understand how newcomers develop professional identities and become experts, the communities of practice framework has more recently been applied in research conducted in classroom settings.

In my research, I situate the classroom as a social context in which a community of practice establishes and navigates learning and identity development through the use of cultural tools and accepted practices.

Cultural Tools

Identities as learners and members of the classroom community of practice shape and are shaped by engagement, developing mastery, and appropriation of cultural tools (Wertsch, 1998). Cultural tools contribute to cognitive development and can include technical tools such as books and computers as well as psychological tools like language and signs. Cultural tools are used in conjunction with social interaction to participate in mediated action and facilitate development. While cultural tools are often not created with the purpose of mediated action as an end goal, they are taken up and appropriated in many ways, which can have significant implications for how development occurs (Wertsch, 1998). For young children in a classroom context and community of practice, this could include taking up various literacy practices originally introduced for academic purposes as cultural tools to signal competent literate identities.

Positioning Theory

Identity is complex, ever-evolving, and socially constructed (Compton-Lilly et al., 2017; Gee, 2001; Moje et al., 2009). As Gee (2001) noted, identity is not merely how one sees themself, it also involves others recognizing that constructed identity in that particular social context. While there are many ways to approach identity research, the two studies discussed in this chapter were largely ground in identity as position. Within this framework of position, researchers frequently explore ways in which identity "thickens" or "laminates" over time as people repeatedly position themselves and/or are positioned by others in a certain way. Schooling experiences, particularly related to literacy, often position children as needing support, thriving, or somewhere in between (Holland & Leander, 2004).

For young children, identity negotiation and becoming involves claiming their places within educational contexts (Compton-Lilly et al., 2017). Positive positioning can be increasingly challenging for young children with emerging decoding and encoding skills because of the heavy emphasis placed on early literacy skills and assessments in schools (Moses & Kelly, 2017). There remains a need for more research related to how young, often marginalized children are positioned institutionally and how they take up or resist and redefine these positions through their use of cultural tools. A classroom community of practice has its own unique and evolving accepted practices, and these community practices influence children's opportunities to use cultural tools to position themselves and others. Curriculum, teachers, relationships, and communities of practice all influence the continual negotiation of identity positions, so I draw on positioning theory (Davies & Harré, 1990) to examine identity positioning in relation to the institutional structures of school.

Method

Building on the aforementioned theoretical grounding, I believe all identity research must be situated in particular social and cultural contexts and take place over a substantive amount of time. Identity claims, especially those of young children who may be in early and evolving stages of being able to discuss and reflect on identity positioning, require large amounts of data and triangulation.

The studies discussed in this chapter took place in the context of larger yearlong formative studies focused on literacy-related pedagogical goals co-constructed with the classroom teacher. As a researcher, a major goal in my work is reciprocity, so all my research is first situated in supporting teachers and children. That is why the research is formative in nature—I want to work in collaboration and learn alongside teachers and children. Because of my theoretical beliefs about teaching, learning, and research, I also purposefully select teachers whose goals extend beyond traditional literacy skills development. For example, one of the teacher's goals in Study 1 was for her students to love reading and see themselves as readers, and that same teacher had a goal in Study 2 for her students to love writing and see themselves as writers.

This collaborative, participatory, and long-term (full academic year) research also allows me to become a member of the community and helps deepen my understanding of the context and identity work. My positioning and extensive time in the classroom also influence my selection of focal participants, the development of research questions, and the ways I approach data. Using theoretical lenses of communities of practice (Lave & Wenger, 1991), cultural tools (Wertsch, 1998), and positioning theory (Davies & Harré, 1990) helps shape my research questions.

For Study 1, we were interested in examining ways monolingual and bilingual children used accepted literacy practices from the classroom community as cultural tools to resist institutional positioning as "struggling readers" and reposition themselves as confident and competent members of the literate community. (Note: While we do not believe in using the term "struggling reader," we use it in our research as an in vivo code because this was the language used to describe these children by the literacy specialist.) Based on the intersections of the previously mentioned theories and our research, the following research question guided the study: How do the literacy practices and classroom community of practice impact the identity development of Lesley and Ariana?

For Study 2, we were interested in examining a child who had been positioned by his teacher, peers, and parents as resistant to change and curricular requirements. We explored how this child found ways to push back, resist, and continually position himself as an expert, innovator, and leader. We sought to examine how he exercised agency when he resisted and appropriated classroom literacy practices to better align with his interests and multimodal composing needs. We also explored how those eventually served as cultural tools not only for composing but also for renegotiating his identity in positive ways. The following questions guided the study: (1) What agentic choices did Owen make to act on his interests and intentions for composing? (2) How did these acts influence his identity negotiations as an author and expert?

Data Collection

Yearlong formative studies that measure only academic outcomes such as scores on standardized and/or summative assessments do not require extensive qualitative data collection. However, because we believe learning is socially, culturally, and historically situated, we decided to collect rich qualitative data to examine learning and identity negotiations in context over time. In both studies, we conducted beginning, middle, and end-of-the-year interviews with the teacher and all students related to learning and identity development as readers and writers. We collected ongoing data of lesson plans for the entire year and recordings of our communication with the teacher through Voxer, a voice messaging application. This often took place multiple times a week to debrief about happenings in the classroom, ask questions, plan, and so on. We kept field notes, observational checklists, and researcher journals.

We used two video cameras to record classroom literacy instruction, small groups, and weekly teacher and researcher conferences over the academic year for both years/studies. We cataloged weekly images of all student artifacts. This included reading logs, responses, and sticky notes for Study 1 and composing drafts, illustrations, feedback, and final publications for Study 2. For both studies, we selected eight focal children with whom we tried to confer and check in with weekly. We wanted to understand the experiences of a wide range of children, so we selected children with diverse backgrounds in various areas, including academic performance, language background, social-emotional considerations, gender, socioeconomic status, and race. We gathered data on the entire class but purposefully selected the focal children to help provide a more in-depth examination of learning, development, and identity positioning over time.

The primary difference in data collection between the two studies was that we also included composition/artifact elicitation interview video recordings at the completion of each writing unit (approximately every three to six weeks) during Study 2. The video-recorded elicitation interviews included the focal children reading aloud their final published composition and discussing important elements, authorial decisions, aspects they were most proud of, aspects they found most challenging, audience considerations, and their opinion/likes/dislikes about the unit. This approach gave us significantly more insight into children's thinking and intentions beyond what we could have inferred from the compositions alone.

Data Analysis

In these studies, we used a theory-driven decision-making process for data analysis. Specifically, we used discourse analysis tools as a means to analyze and interpret literate identity negotiations among primary-aged children. We believe that initial data analysis takes place throughout the data collection period and during the transcription of video and audio recordings. We firmly believe that interaction extends beyond words that can be captured with only verbal transcriptions, so our transcriptions also captured nonverbal discourse such as gestures and facial expressions that accompanied child and adult talk.

The data analysis at the completion of both studies involved initial coding using an open coding approach to document and discover meaning related to identity negotiations and positioning (Strauss & Corbin, 1998). We first coded all classroom video recordings (whole group, small group, and conferring), then we coded all the interviews and Voxer interactions. When open coding was completed, the research team met to discuss the codes and develop a pattern coding scheme and codebook as "a way of grouping those summaries into a smaller number of sets, themes or constructs" (Miles & Huberman, 1994, p. 69) related to positioning.

In the following sections, I explain the theory and data-informed researcher decisions for data analysis for each study. I provide examples of preliminary coding and analysis, discourse analysis approaches, and finally, the reasoning behind the similarities and differences in approaches.

Study 1

We created pattern codes for data related to each documented literacy practice observed during the reading block over the course of the year. The code of literacy practice included the following subcategories: comprehension strategies, decoding strategies, literature discussions, partner coaching, language frames for participation, approximated reading, interpretive talk, and literal talk. Then, we used pattern coding to identify reoccurring practices that served as cultural tools to signal literate identities.

Open and pattern coding provided an initial level of analysis, but we wanted a deeper analysis with supporting evidence before presenting findings related to children's identity work. We selected representative videos and transcriptions from the case studies from the beginning, middle, and end of the year. The representative videos included typical classroom interactions. We wanted to analyze both the negative and positive positioning observed over the course of the year, so we began by using CDA to identify and document the ways our focal children were positioned as "struggling readers." This approach to analysis helped us identify and document in a transparent way how the focal children were positioned because of their emerging decoding status. We created templates for the analysis of the video transcriptions that included four columns: transcription, positionality, evidence (supporting analysis and evidence for positionality claims), and tools (cultural tools used in mediated action).

CDA is a powerful and important tool to expose power and critique social practices that are inequitable and dehumanizing (Kress, 1996). However, we also agree with Martin's (2004) argument that we need more research using positive discourse analysis (PDA) to better understand how positive change happens. Building on this need, we shifted our analytical lens to examine the literacy practices that mediated positive identity positioning and a redistribution of power. We used the same template and discourse analysis tools to explore what Rogers and Wetzel (2013) describe as a "positive turn" and "moments of hope, agency, and liberation" (p. 88).

Study 2

Initial open coding that involved our focal child included codes like resistance to curriculum, negotiation, passion-curriculum alignment, appropriation for agency, identity as writer, and identity as outsider. We then created pattern codes by grouping initial codes and identifying agentic acts related to writing that served as tools to position the focal child in positive ways. The broad pattern codes included the following: resistance techniques, negotiation techniques, and writing to advocate. The detailed subcodes will be discussed in more detail in the findings section.

Similar to Study 1, we wanted a deeper analysis with supporting evidence about identity that was more in-depth than coding alone could provide. We selected representative videos and transcriptions that included the focal child from the beginning, middle, and end of the year. We began with CDA to explore his positioning from the teacher, peers, and his parents as an outsider because of his resistance to the curriculum and his passion for only wanting to write and talk about Ancient Egypt. Then, like in Study 1, we used the same discourse analysis tools to shift the lens to PDA.

We created a discourse analysis template based on our findings from research question one (What agentic choices did Owen make to act on his interests and intentions for composing?) that connected to and built on our theoretical framework related to community practices, identity positioning, and cultural tools (see Figure 1.1). This template included the following five columns: transcription, Owen's agentic techniques, positionality, evidence, and community practices. We were interested in the way the focal child used his agentic techniques identified in the pattern coding and community practices as tools to resist negative positioning and persist with positively positioning himself as a leader, expert, and innovator.

Transcription	*Owen's Agentic Techniques*	*Positionality*	*Evidence*	*Community Practices*
Researcher: What does that mean?		Author	Asking for meaning and interpretation from the author	-Common practice for researchers to ask students to clarify, what it means, tell more, etc.
Owen: It's a stamp. Oh, a stamp that says Ms. Allison supports your opinion.	Writing to advocate for passion/interest Redesigning elements from the classroom	Leader Expert	Informing researcher of what it is, signaling his expertise in writing persuasively He signals his belief that she will/should support his opinion	-Students had freedom in topic and writing as long as they stayed within the genre -Allison would often provide feedback, stamps, and or smiley faces on student's work
Owen: ((whispering)) I really drew it. ((louder)) So, it's not really a stamp yet, I just drew it.	Writing to advocate for passion/interest Redesigning elements from the classroom	Leader Innovator	"yet" signals his confidence that it will become a stamp of approval that will lead to a party Creating a stamp of approval	-Allison would often provide feedback, stamps, and or smiley faces on student's work -Students frequently added images in additional to text in writing
Researcher: Oh, okay. Why did you choose to draw that?		Author	Asking for purpose from the author	-Common practice for researchers to ask students to clarify, what it means, tell more, etc.
Owen: Well, I was trying to make a joke to Ms. Allison 'cause I'm already doing the opinion on her. So- The joke is that- that um- that I'm actually doing my opinion on Ms. Allison, and she is supporting the opinion that, um, is actually doing the thing that- that she is not planning.	Writing to advocate for passion/interest	Innovator	Using humor and signaling positive response to get approval Explaining his use of humor	
Researcher: Oh my gosh. Wow, that is like really- it's funny and it's also like- kind of like a trick, right?		Innovator Author	Confirming the humor and his authorial intentions	

FIGURE 1.1 Positive Discourse Analysis Template from Study 2

Findings

In this section, I share findings from both studies with considerations for various ways of (re)presenting literate identities in writing. I use the term (re)presenting to challenge and disrupt the use of the word "representation" as a transparent documentation of reality. My work is interpretive and situated in a social context, so it is important to recognize that my research/publications are (re) presentations and can never be a truly objective factual representation of reality. I believe this distinction is particularly important when sharing research about the identity work of young children.

I share how the theory, contexts, and data influenced the methodological approaches and ways of (re)presenting and honoring children's identity work through detailed and transparent documentation of identity interpretations. While many of the aspects of these studies were similar, such as study length, a majority of the data collection methods, the use of open-to-pattern coding, and the use of CDA and PDA, there were distinct differences in the approaches to identity analysis and findings related to representations of children's identity work.

Study 1

In Study 1, we found children used accepted classroom literacy practices to construct meaning with texts. These practices, originally introduced by the teacher but taken up and appropriated by children, served as cultural tools for participation and positive identity positioning for both our monolingual and bilingual focal children. Although our focal children were initially positioned institutionally as "struggling," the teacher introduced multiple literacy practices that were inclusive and supportive for children regardless of their decoding proficiency status. The following literacy practices were strategically used by our focal children to signal competence and expertise during positive identity negotiations: language frames, comprehension strategy documentation, decoding strategies, partner reading/coaching, and discussion group practices (Moses & Kelly, 2017).

Using CDA approaches to examine beginning-of-year literacy events, we analyzed ways the children were positioned by educators and peers as readers who needed support due to their decoding challenges. During their conferring sessions and strategy instruction groups, the focal coaching and instruction in the beginning of the year for both children typically focused on a decoding skill or strategy. Initially, the classroom practices largely focused on decoding and "sounding out" and excluded the focal children from successful participation in the classroom community, positioning them as peripheral to the literate community.

For example, one focal child regularly became visibly frustrated while attempting to decode words. In one conferring session, the teacher reminded the child that she could use picture cues but that she also needed to look at and sound out the letters. After multiple unsuccessful attempts by the child, the following interaction ensued:

MERIDITH: Let's try the first sound.
LESLEY: /b/ /a/ /k/, back. (She rereads the sentence and miscues "back" again.)
MERIDITH: You said this was "back."
LESLEY: (slumps, frustrated)
MERIDITH: Come back. (reads words for her)

(Moses & Kelly, 2017)

These continued unsuccessful attempts to decode positioned her as needing prompting, more decoding strategies, and help from knowledgeable others. This was reinforced publicly when the teacher was reminding the class of the desired behavior of coaching to help a partner identify a word instead of just telling them. She told the class that Orin was a really good coach because, "instead of just telling Lesley the word, he said 'Oh, look at the picture' or 'look at the first sound.'" She went on to explain that a coach is someone who helps you, thus positioning Lesley as the one needing help in juxtaposition to Orin being the knowledgeable other and coach. She accepted this positioning when she described herself in an interview as needing to get better at reading.

As we closely examined literacy events across the year, we observed a shift in positioning as time passed. As more inclusive and a wider range of classroom literacy practices were introduced, both focal children found ways to take up and appropriate these practices to signal expertise and full membership of the literate community. The shift from a decoding focus to a comprehension and dialogue focus provided opportunities for the children to participate in mediated action and both position themselves and be positioned by others as experts. The bilingual focal child readily took up comprehension strategies and would often stop to make and share a connection with peers when she experienced challenges with oral reading. She also began using commonly accepted sentence stems that had been introduced with comprehension strategies to signal competence and successful participation in literature discussion groups. With a shift in focus to meaning making and interpretation, she began to reposition herself as a leader with regard to meaning-based discussions of literature.

When presenting these findings, we included both written reporting of the analysis from coding and discourse analysis as well as data analysis tables with transcription, positionality, supporting analysis and evidence for positionality claims, and cultural tools used in mediated action. In alignment with Smagorinsky (2008), we believe transparency and detailed descriptions with the methods, particularly data analysis, are essential to making and triangulating interpretations about identity work.

Study 2

In Study 2, we constructed codes and findings related to agentic choices Owen made to act on his interests and intentions for composing during the writing period. We found that he pushed back on the curriculum repeatedly and in multiple ways in an attempt to exercise agency in his composing. The classroom structure included genre units, author study units, and open/free units, and the children could write whatever they wanted with little requirements other than fitting into the larger theme/genre of the unit. However, Owen did not want to write in the designated genres; he just wanted to write about Ancient Egypt. We documented themes related to his identity work and curricular requirement resistance, specifically that he used resistance techniques, negotiation techniques, and writing to advocate as ways to navigate a curriculum and context that did not meet his desires and needs. Upon further analysis, we documented the following agentic behaviors: (1) resistance techniques: rejecting genre requirements, voicing dissatisfaction, and ignoring teacher instructions/requests; (2) negotiation techniques: genre bending and blending and redesigning elements from the classroom curriculum; (3) writing to advocate: writing to persuade and advocate for his composing needs and desires.

Similar to Study 1, we examined events for coding and for closer discourse analysis of representative transcripts over the course of the year. We specifically selected tools for CDA based on the previous coded agentic acts to examine ways in which these acts were used to position him or for him to position himself (see Data Analysis above for analysis template components). In the beginning of the year, we used CDA approaches to document the ways in which his teacher, peers, and parents positioned him as inflexible, an outsider, and a "curricularly unruly" child. They positioned him this way based on the following agentic techniques/behaviors: resistance, ignoring, rejecting genre requirements, and voicing dissatisfaction. However, he continually resisted this positioning and stayed persistent with his focus on composing related to his topic of interest.

The initial techniques used in the beginning of the year of resisting, voicing dissatisfaction, and ignoring the teacher requests resulted in negative positioning by others who included repeated instructions to meet requirements, children's eye rolling when he talked or wrote about Ancient Egypt, and parents telling him he had to change his interest and study something else. However, we documented an initial shift in positioning by others during the informational unit when his passion aligned with the genre. Using PDA, we documented ways Owen was able to resist and negotiate within the boundaries of the classroom community's accepted practices. For instance, when required to write a narrative/fictional story, he included characters and dialogue (the core requirements), but the characters were from Ancient Egypt and just talked to each other in facts. He was able to position himself as a full participant by working within the accepted curricular constraints while simultaneously meeting his desire of writing nonfiction by blending genres.

Owen was also positioned as an expert, innovator, and leader in the second half of the year. Figure 1.1 is an example of our data analysis template. In this example, we analyze part of a composition/artifact interview about his persuasive text attempting to convince the teacher to have an Ancient Egypt party. Here, he discusses the fake teacher stamp of approval he created.

The combination of the shift from Owen's outright refusal/resistance/ignoring to bending/blending/approximating and the teacher's shift from compliance requirements to flexible approximation requirements provided opportunities for Owen to renegotiate his identity in positive ways. When presenting these findings, we included both written reporting of the analysis from coding and discourse analysis as well as data analysis tables with transcription, Owen's agentic techniques, positionality, supporting evidence for positionality claims, and community practices.

Implications for Future Research and Practice

Both studies were grounded in sociocultural theory with a focus on identity positioning in first-grade classrooms. Findings from Study 1 indicate that there is a need for more inclusive literacy pedagogy to support positive identity negotiations. When the teacher broadened the classroom literacy practices beyond decoding to focus on meaning making and interaction, children took up those tools and used them to position themselves and be positioned by others in positive ways.

Findings from Study 2 also indicate that there is a need for more flexible curriculum and pedagogy. Unlike Study 1, where the children took up the teacher-introduced literacy practices, the focal child in Study 2 found ways to circumvent the introduced requirements by blending, bending, and using the minimal amount of accepted classroom practices necessary to avoid push back from teachers, peers, and parents. Interestingly, it was this creativity, innovation, and combination of resisting and stretching of accepted practices that eventually positioned him as an expert, innovator, and leader by his teacher and peers.

There remains a need for more research related to identity negotiations of young children, specifically related to their positioning in literacy. Pedagogical approaches and ways teachers engage or disengage with children impact possibilities for children's sense of becoming. The critical approaches of this work are important to reveal and display the power and many institutional systems that might oppress and marginalize young children. However, it is equally important to examine the instances, structures, systems, contexts, and practices that might also create opportunities for supporting and honoring young children's identity work. Identity research with young children (both CDA and PDA approaches) also requires thoughtful consideration of analytic tools and transparency around data analysis and (re)presentations of children's identities. It is only through this transparency that the field of literacy, early childhood, and identity research can evolve with a deeper understanding of children's experiences of becoming and the research processes used to report these findings.

My work in this area indicates a need for more qualitative research about young children's identity work, specifically using both positive and critical lenses for analysis. I would argue that research on identity work for young children must also span significant amounts of time. The studies described here looked at identity positioning and negotiations over the course of an academic year, so we were able to make informed interpretations because we were present for and collected data across the children's entire first-grade year. The depth of understanding would have been significantly less had we only spent a short amount of time in the classroom community of practice. Ideas for future research might include, among many others, additional studies with the following foci: examining ways decoding skills are privileged and play a role in positioning in early childhood classrooms; examining how early identity work changes or stays the same as new legislation in many states shifts to meet "science of reading" requirements that prioritize decoding and phonics instruction in the early grades; examining identity work in early childhood classrooms where all forms of meaning making in literacy are valued; and exploring ways in which children who are historically marginalized take up available cultural tools to position themselves as competent members of the classroom community of practice during literacy instruction.

Discussion Questions

1 In this chapter, I talk about my combined use of critical discourse analysis and positive discourse analysis. What are some constraints and affordances of using two contrasting approaches to analyzing data?
2 How should data collection, data analysis, and (re)presentations be approached when examining children's identity work?
3 What are the limitations of the studies described in this chapter? How can understanding these limitations shape methodological choices in research?
4 What topics or research questions might researchers address to build on the studies in this chapter?

References

Compton-Lilly, C., Papoi, K., Venegas, P., Hamman, L., & Schwabenbauer, B. (2017). Intersectional identity negotiation: The case of young immigrant children. *Journal of Literacy Research*, *49*(1), 115–140. https://doi.org/10.1177%2F1086296X16683421

Davies, B., & Harré, R. (1990). Positioning: The discursive production of selves. *Journal for the Theory of Social Behaviour*, *20*(1), 43–63. https://doi.org/10.1111/j.1468-5914.1990.tb00174.x

Dyson, A. H., & Genishi, C. (2013). Social talk and imaginative play: Curricular basics for young children's language and literacy. In D. E. Alverman, N. Unrau, & R. B. Ruddell (Eds.), *Theoretical models and processes of reading* (pp. 164–181). International Reading Association. https://doi.org/10.1598/0710.06

Gee, J. P. (2001). Identity as an analytic lens for research in education. *Review of Research in Education, 25*, 99–125.

Holland, D., & Leander, K. (2004). Ethnographic studies of positioning and subjectivity: An introduction. *Ethos, 32*, 127–139. https://doi.org/10.1525/eth.2004.32.2.127

Kress, G. (1996). Representational resources and the production of subjectivity: Questions for the theoretical development of critical discourse analysis in a multicultural society. In C. Caldas-Coulthard & M. Coulthard (Eds.), *Texts and practices: Readings in critical discourse analysis* (pp. 15–31). Routledge. https://doi.org/10.4324/9780203431382-8

Lave, J., & Wenger, E. (1991). *Situated learning: Legitimate peripheral participation*. Cambridge University Press. https://doi.org/10.1017/cbo9780511815355

Martin, J. R. (2004). Positive discourse analysis: Solidarity and change. *Revista Canaria de Estudios Ingleses, 49*, 179–200.

Miles, M. B., & Huberman, A. M. (1994). *Qualitative data analysis: An expanded sourcebook* (2nd ed.). SAGE.

Moje, E. B., Luke, A., Davies, B., & Street, B. (2009). Literacy and identity: Examining the metaphors in history and contemporary research. *Reading Research Quarterly, 44*, 415–437. https://doi.org/10.1598/RRQ.44.4.7

Moses, L., & Kelly, L. B. (2017). The development of positive literate identities among bilingual and monolingual first graders. *Journal of Literacy Research, 49*(3), 393–423. https://doi.org/10.1177/1086296X17713291

Rogers, R., & Wetzel, M. M. (2013). Studying agency in literacy teacher education: A layered approach to positive discourse analysis. *Critical Inquiry in Language Studies, 10*, 62–92. https://doi.org/10.1080/15427587.2013.753845

Smagorinsky, P. (2008). The method section as conceptual epicenter in constructing social science research reports. *Written Communication, 25*(3), 389–411. https://doi.org/10.1177/0741088308317815

Strauss, A., & Corbin, J. M. (1998). *Basics of qualitative research: Techniques and procedures for developing grounded theory* (2nd ed.). SAGE. https://doi.org/10.4135/9781452230153

Vygotsky, L. S. (1980). *Mind in society: The development of higher psychological processes*. Harvard University Press.

Wenger, E. (1998). *Communities of practice: Learning, meaning, and identity*. Cambridge University Press.

Wertsch, J. V. (1998). *Mind as action*. Oxford University Press.

2

ENHANCING STUDENTS' IDENTITIES AS READERS AND WRITERS THROUGH ASSESSMENT

Bente Rigmor Walgermo and Per Henning Uppstad

Introduction

To optimize instruction, we need to explicitly target students' identities as readers and writers. This means that we should measure those identities alongside skills. Existing formal assessments of reading and writing skills may hamper the shaping of strong reader and writer identities because of their authoritative status and intrusive character as well as the depersonalized nature of the feedback they provide. Poorly performing readers and writers will often have double negative experiences from assessment: first in the form of effortful performance without mastery and then in the form of low scores without meaningful feedback. However, teachers do receive relevant information about each student's performance from such tests. For this reason, the challenge is not how to abolish formal tests, but how to bring such tests better in line with a type of instruction that aims to support students in reaching their full potential as readers and writers. In this chapter, we make two claims about the school of tomorrow: (1) the design and use of tests and assessments must be rethought to optimally strengthen students' identities as readers and writers, and (2) assessing literate identities is pivotal in order to transform classroom instruction. After some historical background, we present a rationale for the claims made. Then, we use pilot data to demonstrate a realistic design for a third-grade literacy test where students' reader and writer identities are measured alongside their reading and writing skills. We conclude by discussing some implications for classroom instruction.

DOI: 10.4324/9781003271406-5

Why Assessment Counts in Enhancing Emergent Reader and Writer Identity

We are almost sure that none of you remember how—a few seconds into your lives—you were assessed by a nurse using the "Apgar score" to check your health. So let us jog your memories: in less than a minute, the nurse lifted you away from your mother to check your pulse, height, weight, and general condition, in a place cooler than what you had experienced until then, while you took your first breath and gave out a solid cry. The Apgar score is named for anesthesiologist Virginia Apgar, who created a standard for the examination of newborns in 1952. This standard, which has helped prevent the deaths of thousands of newborns, is still mandatory in delivery rooms worldwide. Its success is due to the combination of a high degree of usefulness and the absence of negative consequences for the child. In this sense, the Apgar score illustrates some ideals that are yet to be implemented in educational assessment of reading and writing, in particular effectiveness, an acceptable degree of intrusiveness, and the provision of information to caretakers. An additional such ideal, which is the subject of this chapter, is the absence of a negative impact on students' interest and identity.

Reader and writer identities are closely related to personality, talents, and mental abilities. Those are among the key concepts of Article 29 of the United Nations Convention on the Rights of the Child, which enshrines as a fundamental right "the development of the child's personality, talents, and mental and physical abilities to their fullest potential" (UNCRC, 1989). However, the ways in which we assess young readers' and writers' development of their potential have been influenced only to a very limited extent by the ideas that have predominated in the teaching and education field during what Alexander and Fox (2004) term the *era of engaged learning*, or the time from 1996 onward. In other words, we have not explored how assessment may strengthen or hamper students' identities as readers and writers. However, it is unlikely that a student can develop their full potential unless assessment benefits, or at least does not undermine, their reader and writer identities. Also, to help students reach their full potential it is necessary to know what they can do *now*. The test scores used to find that out will give a true picture only if the students really engage with the tasks and perform to the best of their ability, which means that they must be motivated to do so. These points call for a radical shift in classroom assessment. First, the motivational qualities of the tests used must be strengthened. Second, the assessment of motivation alongside skill is likely, in and of itself, to raise the value of motivational perspectives in instruction and to establish motivational perspectives at the center stage of teaching.

The Narrow History of Our Understanding of Human Motivation and Driving Forces

In the 20th century, instincts, needs, and reinforcement were considered the primary driving forces of human beings. These ideas came from behaviorist traditions (Hull, 1943; Tolman, 1951) via psychodynamic theories (Freud, 1964). However, in 1959 Robert White published a review entitled *Motivation Reconsidered*. There he shed light on the limitations of both the behaviorist and the psychodynamic endeavors to explain human driving forces. He claimed that on their own, drives and instincts cannot explain our motivation, which also stems from the individual's competence in dealing with the environment. He referred to this as *effectance motivation*. Unlike our drives and instincts, effectance motivation is neither inherent nor acquired through maturation but emphasizes how objects in the environment interact with the individual. From this point onward, a cognitive school of thinking gradually supplanted both the behaviorist and the psychoanalytic traditions—and it remains the mainstream framework to this day. In cognitive psychology, conscious thought was given a more prominent place than emotions and drives, resulting in an emphasis on cognition, strategies, and goals (Tønnessen, 2011). This means that some driving forces that are central to modern motivation theory were not part of its main scope. However, within this cognitive tradition, Viktor Frankl (1966, 2014) made an influential contribution to the debate about human motivation. His theories shifted the focus from individual drives and needs, as in the psychoanalytic tradition, to a more positive and constructive highlighting of humans' active search for meaning. A good illustration of this is that therapy within Frankl's framework involved the construction of meaning in the encounter between the therapist and the patient rather than focusing on the patient's past. In other words, Frankl's (2014) therapy is concerned with how we can best shape our present to make a better future. Willpower is also crucial in Frankl's theories—when we are no longer able to change a situation or condition, it is essential that we are able to change our attitudes (Frankl, 1985). Against this background, Frankl claims that hope, a factor closely related to motivation, is one of our strongest driving forces. His ideas may well apply not only to psychology in general but also to our identities as readers and writers.

An increased focus on motivation in learning situations is reflected in the historical analysis of reading research and practice carried out by Alexander and Fox (2004). The name they chose for the last of the different epochs they identified in the history of reading research (1996 and onward) is the *era of engaged learning*. In that still ongoing era, to our knowledge even more strongly since they made their analysis, studies have documented that our self-definitions and the development of reading skill are interconnected. In other words, motivation does not operate in isolation. In fact, motivation as seen today is strongly characterized by reciprocity. It drives actions, and the outcome of those actions will influence future motivation (Pintrich, 2003; Unrau & Quirk, 2014; Walgermo et al., 2018b). A recent meta-analysis of studies ranging from kindergarten through high school (Toste et al., 2020) documents the mutual reinforcement between the development of reader identity (or reader self-concept) and reading skill.

A Brief History of Driving Forces as Viewed in Reading and Writing Research

It is only recently that motivation has been thoroughly considered in reading and to a lesser degree in writing research. For reading, early attempts were made to expand the "simple view of reading," which can be represented as reading comprehension = decoding × linguistic comprehension (Gough & Tunmer, 1986), by adding motivation as a factor, which yielded reading comprehension = decoding × linguistic comprehension × motivation (Dalby et al., 1992, p. 395). However, those attempts never really took root. It could be said that while there is now an awareness of the relationship between motivation and reading development, there is no established solution for how to translate this awareness into classroom practice. However, in line with Frankl's claim about humans' search for meaning as a driving force, Finn Egil Tønnessen and one of the authors of this chapter (Tønnessen & Uppstad, 2015) offer an approach to reading skill, where reading is seen as an interpretive skill embodying the quest for meaning as a constant driving force (see also Walgermo et al., 2018b). In this approach, it is emphasized that letters, words, sentences, and texts all need to be interpreted, meaning that our understanding of them grows as we develop as readers and writers. This notion of reading and writing as interpretive skills is based on the European philosophical tradition called hermeneutics (Gadamer, 1960; Tønnessen & Uppstad, 2015). The hermeneutical method involves gaining a deeper understanding through repeated encounters with, in this case, particular letters, words, sentences, or texts. Each encounter yields a new—deeper—overarching understanding, which will then be challenged and adjusted through further encounters. In line with this, Tønnessen and Uppstad (2015) suggest that with its emphasis on interpretation, hermeneutics makes it meaningless to distinguish between decoding and linguistic comprehension. Interestingly, on this understanding of reading and writing there is more room in the theory for motivational aspects with meaning-making as humans' ultimate driving force. Both in Frankl's terms and according to a hermeneutical approach meaning is at the core of our identity in the sense that a person who has little hope of mastering mandatory challenges placed before them, and who sees no meaning in the tasks ahead, is a person whose identity is threatened. This is definitely the case for a student who struggles with reading and writing. For this reason, a shift such as that sketched above toward maintaining motivation through meaning may be necessary to ensure that children will learn enough to reach their full potential as readers and writers.

What Do Skills and Motivation Have in Common?

Unlike reading or writing skills, which are often studied as such, motivation is a potential that is most often investigated on the basis of other potentials that are seen as its components. Among such motivational components, interest and beliefs about mastery are considered especially relevant in educational settings because it is believed that they are more sensitive to environmental factors, and therefore more malleable, than other human personality features such as agreeableness, neuroticism, openness, and extraversion (Judge & Bono, 2001; Kyllonen, 2016). The supposedly malleable nature of motivational factors such as reader identities makes them particularly appealing to educators, and research shows how instructional approaches can be modified to improve students' motivation for learning (Guthrie et al., 2004; Lazowski & Hulleman, 2016; Unrau et al., 2018). It is interesting to note that, as described above, the way we conceive of motivation and drives has shifted across different epochs and theories. This includes our ideas about what motivation and drives essentially *are*. Similar to skills, motivation and drives have long been conceived of in dichotomic terms: as something you either have (are) or do not have (are not). For example, an unmotivated student is seen to lack motivation. This dichotomy has prevailed since antiquity and has strongly influenced Western thinking. However, an alternative view was available early on in Aristotelian philosophy. Based on Aristotle, Tønnessen wants to leave behind the dichotomy of *being* versus *not being* in suggesting that skills should be seen as potentials (Tønnessen & Uppstad, 2015, p. 49). One of the authors of this chapter (Walgermo, 2018) has taken these ideas one step further by applying them to motivation, claiming that both motivation and skills are potentials. Although highly theoretical in nature, this position has one immediate consequence of a very concrete nature—namely that neither motivation nor skills should be seen as static. Rather, since motivation (like skills) is a potential, it can be realized and developed.

Understanding the Malleability of Reader and Writer Identity

Researchers generally agree that motivation for reading and writing is a complex construct that consists of many interrelated components including self-concept, self-efficacy, interest, values, goals, and others (for reviews, see Conradi et al., 2014 and Troia et al., 2012). One central part of a student's motivation for learning to read and write is mediated by their developing beliefs about language, reading, writing, and self (Wagner, 2021). Students' perceptions of their own reading and writing skills form the basis for their literate identities. In young students, literate identities are commonly operationalized as reader or writer self-concept (e.g., Chapman et al., 2000; Morgan & Fuchs, 2007; Walgermo et al., 2018a). Reader and writer self-concept is part of a cluster of self-processes that have received attention in investigations of motives that drive and control our actions, our learning, our self-worth, our self-esteem, our beliefs about academic competence, and our expectations of mastery related to specific domains and tasks (Linnenbrink-Garcia et al., 2016). Interestingly, Harter (1982) organized humans' self-concepts hierarchically by domain specificity. She placed global self-concept (synonymous with our general self-esteem) at the top, as the most general level. General academic self-concept was placed in the middle, and domain-specific self-concept (of which reader or writer self-concept is an example) at the bottom as the foundational level of the hierarchy. Harter's hierarchical model is significant for practice because it makes it clear that a person's domain-specific self-concepts influence their more general academic self-concept, which in turn affects their global self-concept.

The present chapter introduces a method for assessing students' reader and writer identities (i.e., reader and writer self-concepts). Based on scores from such assessments, for educational purposes, the most interesting question here may be how to enhance students' self-concepts within the domains of reading and writing. Unrau et al. (2018) claim that our identities (self-concepts) are more oriented toward the past and characterized by relative stability—in other words, that they are more resistant to change (Unrau et al., 2018). Therefore, when aiming to strengthen student identities within the domain of reading or writing, rather than focusing directly on identities, we should work on students' expectations of mastery in relation to specific tasks within specific learning situations. In the literature, such task-oriented expectation of mastery is referred to as self-efficacy (Bandura, 1986, 2010). According to Bandura (1986), self-efficacy reflects confidence in being able to orchestrate and execute actions required for achieving intended results such as mastering a task. These expectations of mastering specific reading and writing tasks act as precursors for the development of the overall reader and writer self-concept (Bong & Skaalvik, 2003). In other words, the feelings of mastery experienced when working on specific tasks and texts will little by little shape students' reader and writer identities. This suggests that an even more fundamental level should be added to Harter's (1982) hierarchy: self-efficacy.

A Concrete Case: A New-Generation Literacy Screening Test

In Norway, a new national literacy screening test to be administered in third grade is being developed by a group of researchers in collaboration with the Norwegian Directorate for Education and Training, which is an executive agency associated with the Ministry of Education and Research. Such a test-development model is common in Norway, unlike in other countries such as the United States where test development is mainly the preserve of commercial companies. The researchers have considerable, but not complete, autonomy in their work. To add some flesh to the bones of the theoretical rationale presented in this chapter, we will briefly present and discuss the status of reader and writer self-concept as measured alongside reading in a sample of 1,249 students and spelling skills in a sample of 1,308 students at the onset of their third year of formal reading and writing instruction (mean age = 8.7 years). These data, which come from a pilot study of the new literacy screening test being developed, were collected in October 2021. The main purpose of the screening test is to help teachers identify students who need extra support in developing adequate reading and writing skills (Directorate for Education and Training, 2018). However, it also has another ambitious aim: to promote students' literacy interests and self-concept while they are being assessed. For this purpose, the tasks included in the test are designed to mirror high-quality engaging literacy instruction. For instance, the test includes a simple spelling task designed to identify the students who struggle the most with writing. However, that task is presented as a real-life situation, not as a task involving the spelling of random words. Supported by engaging pictorial support, the students are asked to help a boy their age write a wish list for his birthday. The third graders who participated in the pilot study performed two testlets, each within a timeframe of 30 minutes, across a single two-week period using their personal computers in their respective classrooms. The tasks within each testlet were related to reader and writer self-concept, interest in reading and writing, word reading, spelling, language comprehension, and reading comprehension. For more information about this test, see Walgermo et al. (2021).

The Self-Concept Tasks

The first two items in each testlet targeted the students' reader and writer self-concept. Both self-concept tasks were presented in spoken form to the students using a nonintrusive design adapted to reading and writing from Nuutila et al. (2020):

- Writer self-concept: "How good do you think you are at writing?"
- Reader self-concept: "How good do you think you are at reading?"

When measuring motivation in young children, use of pictorial support is recommended (Bandura, 2006). Here, an illustration picturing the targeted activity (students reading or writing, see Figure 2.1) was a central element in each task. The pictures were designed to elicit a more elaborate view on reading and writing, including both analog and digital activities as well as the writing of wish lists. Both pictures included boys and girls as well as children of different ethnicity. Both self-concept items were measured using a five-point Likert scale (represented by different-sized circles) ranging from 5 ("Very good") to 1 ("Not very good at all"). The design of the tasks was as follows:

A) Reader self-concept
"How good do you think you are at reading?"
(5: *Very good*) (4: *Pretty good*) (3: *Somewhere in between*) (2: *Not very good*)
(1: *Not very good at all*)

B) Writer self-concept
"How good do you think you are at writing?"
(5: *Very good*) (4: *Pretty good*) (3: *Somewhere in between*) (2: *Not very good*)
(1: *Not very good at all*)

FIGURE 2.1 Measures of reader and writer self-concept

Status of Third-Grade Reader and Writer Identities and Associations with Skill

We found that the students generally reported strong reader and writer identities (see Table 2.1). Overall 70.2 percent saw themselves as very good or pretty good readers and 64.3 percent as very good or pretty good writers. Still, many students thought of themselves as mediocre or poor readers (29.7 percent) and writers (35.7 percent). Specifically, 6.5 percent of the students reported a weak reader self-concept ("not very good" or "not very good at all") while slightly more of them, or 8.9 percent, reported a weak writer self-concept. Overall, the sample studied suggests that third graders report a stronger self-concept for reading than for writing. This difference was found to be statistically significant resulting in a very small effect size of 1.4 (Cohen, 1988), meaning the students in this sample all together reported a slightly higher self-concept for reading compared to writing.

The findings further reveal, in line with previous research, a significant but small correlation (Pearson) with actual skill level (see Table 2.2). The correlations found between self-concepts and assessed skill were ≤ .20. Even if this is a quite small correlation, it indicates that there is a minor positive association between the two.

TABLE 2.1 Descriptive Statistics Relating to Students' Self-Reported Reader and Writer Self-Concept

	Reader Self-Concept (SC)	*Writer Self-Concept (SC)*
Number of students (N)	1,249	1,308
5 Very good	34.3%	28.4%
4 Pretty good	35.9%	35.9%
3 Somewhere in between	23.3%	26.8%
2 Not very good	2.5%	4.7%
1 Not very good at all	3.9%	4.2%

TABLE 2.2 Correlation Matrix for Reader and Writer Self-Concept (SC), Reading Comprehension (RC), and Spelling in the Associated Reading Test

	Reader SC	*Writer SC*	*RC*	*Spelling*
Reader self-concept	—	.20**	.20**	.10
Writer self-concept	.20**	1	.05	.11*
Reading comprehension	.20**	.05	1	.30**
Spelling	.10	.11*	.30**	1

* p-Value is considered statistically significant at $p < .05$.

** p-Value is considered statistically significant at $p < .01$.

How Assessment Can Help Strengthen Reader and Writer Identities

As mentioned above, two main claims are made in this chapter: first, that students' identities as readers and writers should be explicitly targeted and therefore also measured alongside skills in order to optimize classroom instruction, and, second, that assessment should help foster students' identities as readers and writers even while they are being assessed. In this context, the test items presented and discussed above can also be seen as an example of a simple yet effective way of measuring young students' reader and writer identities. In the following, we will discuss some main points of relevance for classroom instruction that can be found at the intersection between the theoretical rationale and the data presented.

First, a lack of strong correlations between the levels of skill and self-concept could be a very positive result. This is because it is claimed in theory that conditions for the realization of students' potentials are not optimal if their feeling of mastery within a domain corresponds exactly to their current skill level but rather if they think of themselves as slightly more skilled readers or writers than they really are (Frankl, 1966; Bandura, 1997). This is in part because a strong self-concept makes students take on more challenging tasks and in part because when they believe they will master a task, they will persevere for longer before giving up when the task or text becomes difficult or uninteresting. However, having an unrealistically strong self-concept is not beneficial since this is often associated with overconfidence and reduced effort. For teachers, this means that part of their instructional task is to help their students develop strong yet realistic reader and writer self-concepts. While it doubtless represents a huge challenge for teachers to position the psychological needs of their students in an optimal constellation, this task may be made somewhat easier by having access to results from assessments of motivational aspects alongside skills. Since our data come from a pilot study, they provide no information at the individual level, only at a more general one. However, a full-scale real test designed in this way may provide teachers with score sheets containing information about individual students. Where such score sheets indicate that a student has a weak self-concept, this should be cause for action.

Second, in order to facilitate the right kind of action, knowledge of research-based approaches to initiate change in classrooms is needed. Over the past decades, numerous studies have aimed to identify ways of enhancing students' reader and writer self-concept. In a meta-analysis, Unrau et al. (2018) found that students' reader self-concept can indeed be modified in educational settings but that there were two main factors influencing the strength of any effect: (1) grade level/early intervention and (2) the number of Bandura's (1997) practice recommendations for enhancing self-efficacy that were explicitly addressed in a given study. According to Bandura's practice recommendations for enhancing self-efficacy—the "theory of change"—four sources are deemed central for change in our beliefs concerning task mastery: (a) experience with mastery, (b) observation of others (teacher and peers) successfully mastering a task, (c) environmental feedback, and (d) the student's psychological state. For the scope of student assessment, (a), (c), and (d) in particular are highly relevant. It should also be noted that including assessment of reader and writer identities alongside skill assessment as in the test discussed above will probably in and of itself bring a stronger focus on means to enhance weak self-concepts. As history has taught us, tests have the power to influence classroom practices. For this reason, we should have a closer look at the issue of research-based recommendations to help teachers act upon future assessment reports on reader and writer identities.

To begin with, *experience with mastery of tasks* has been described as the most important source of self-efficacy (Bandura, 1986, 1997; Deci & Ryan, 2012). This suggests that, in order for students to build positive identities as readers and writers, they need to encounter a large number of tasks where mastery is within their reach. As has been emphasized in this chapter, it is also important to consider how assessment situations contribute to students' identities as readers and writers. This does not mean that students need to experience full mastery in the assessment situations. What they need in order to feel competent is an appropriate amount of challenge at the appropriate level. One way to solve this problem is to use carefully designed adaptive digital tests, which are breaking new ground across the world and have the potential to provide students with tasks that involve both mastery and challenge—or, in other words, with tasks located in each student's zone of proximal development (Vygotsky & Cole, 1978, p. 68). This means that the choice of technology and test design may influence the shaping of reader and writer identities in assessment.

Further, the impact of negative experiences while being assessed is also important. This can be linked to Bandura's (1997) third source of self-efficacy: *environmental feedback*. While a sufficient level of challenge is important, negative experiences from encountering too many and too difficult of tasks may undermine students' motivation to engage in further reading or writing. Such negative experiences have traditionally been considered an affordable cost in the context of educational assessment. However, considering the goal of realizing all students' full potential, this cost must be deemed too high. This is because of what we now know about how the human brain takes in negative feedback. Kahneman (2011) points out that the brains of humans and other animals contain a mechanism designed to give priority to bad news, events, and feelings (e.g., feeling very poor mastery in a test situation or receiving information about a low test score). This suggests that the self is more motivated to avoid bad self-definitions than to pursue good ones. For this reason, being confronted with a demanding test situation involving feelings of poor mastery and then receiving poor scores or feedback may cause a child to avoid reading and writing and to lose interest in working on similar tasks again. What is more, the human brain processes and stores negative information more thoroughly than positive information, and bad self-definitions are established faster and more robustly than positive ones (Kahneman, 2011). This means that it is a good idea to supplement negative feedback in the form of a low test score with supportive feedback specifically related to task, strategy, or effort. In the literature, such feedback is described as a means to foster students' belief that skills can be enhanced through effort. Such a belief will lead to a mindset where students think of intelligence as malleable and thus as something it is within their own power to strengthen (e.g., Yeager & Dweck, 2012; Dweck, 2017). It is also worth mentioning that teachers' expectations of students' performance and mastery have been found to be important. Research shows that students tend to perform better when their teachers have higher expectations of them (Rosenthal & Jacobson, 1966; Gentrup et al., 2020). If we return to the Norwegian screening test being developed, these perspectives on feedback may help us decide how best to intervene when students report weak reader or writer identities.

In this chapter, it is assumed that students' reader and writer identities draw strongly upon their feeling of efficacy when performing the very specific tasks typically included in assessments of reading and writing. In other words, it is assumed that there is a close relationship between the performance of those specific tasks and students' overall self-concept. However, such an assumption is not explicitly reflected in Harter's original *hierarchy of self-concept*. In fact, the foundation of her hierarchy is domain-specific self-concept, which is more static in nature. The link between self-efficacy and self-concept is much clearer in Bandura's *theory of change*. Given that a person's sense of mastery regarding specific tasks can be considered more future oriented and can be seen as a useful source of changes in more stable self-concepts (Unrau et al., 2018), we therefore suggest combining Harter's hierarchy (1982) with Bandura's self-efficacy theory (1987), which represents the task-level expectation of mastery within a specific domain. As self-efficacy can be considered key to enhancing the individual's feeling of mastery within a domain, that in turn will, strengthen that student's more general academic self-concept and further global self-esteem. Therefore, we propose that this extended hierarchy should be referred to as the *hierarchy of change* (see Figure 2.2).

In sum, the hierarchy of change shows us that, in order to strengthen students' identities as readers and writers, we should work hands-on in every learning situation so as to strengthen students' feeling of mastery when they are engaged in their daily reading and writing tasks—and, importantly, this includes assessments. This enhancement of their task-specific self-efficacy will, in turn, have an impact on their more global self-concepts as readers and writers, which will contribute to their overall academic self-concept and then to their overall self-esteem. This may of course be easier said than done, but one crucial and specific requirement in order to make this a realistic endeavor is to reframe the making of mistakes. In fact, mistakes—especially those made during assessment—should be considered not as something reflecting a flaw in the person making them but as a

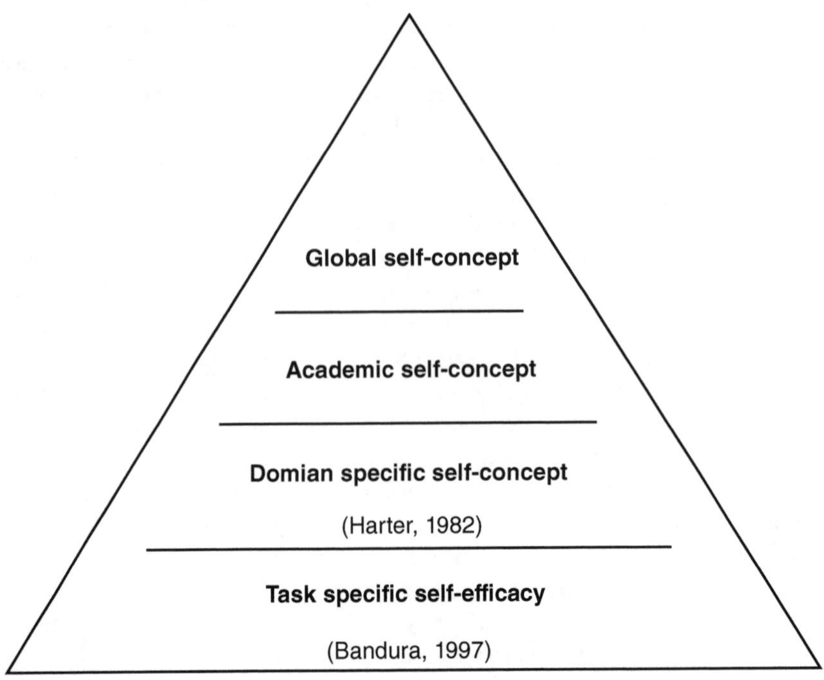

FIGURE 2.2 Hierarchy of change combining Harter (1982) and Bandura (1997)

necessary means for progress and learning. To make room for such mechanisms, we need to ensure that assessment situations are optimized for supporting reader and writer identities. A student having made a mistake during assessment should not think, "I made a mistake, so I'm a bad reader" but "I made a mistake. That can teach me how to become a better reader."

Concluding Remarks

When aiming to strengthen students' reader and writer identities or self-concepts alongside their reading and writing skill, we first and foremost need to attend to their experiences of mastery in both classroom activities and assessment situations. The theoretical rationale presented in this chapter suggests that if we want to optimize our instruction, students' reader and writer identities should be explicitly targeted and measured alongside their reading and writing skill. However, the measures and tests used should not in and of themselves undermine students' interest in reading and writing or their feeling of mastery of those skills. In fact, the opposite must be the case: if assessment is truly to be seen as an element of instruction, assessments themselves should help to strengthen students' motivation. A first step on the road toward that goal should be to avoid negative experiences during assessment. Using assessment as one of many tools to help students reach their full potential as readers and writers is an ambitious aim, but it is a realistic one. In this context, the story of the Apgar score that we opened this chapter with may serve as an illustration and a reminder of what could be a standard for the functionality of assessment in education.

It must be noted that the experimental data presented in this chapter are limited when it comes to studying design and analytic rigor. In other words, the design of the study we have discussed does not yet enable us to present a strong case for the type of assessment we argue for here. Seemingly relevant parameters, such as gender, are not reported. However, this is due to the authentic nature of the pilot study and to restrictions in the kinds of data we are allowed to report from it. Future studies should aim to use more robust experimental designs to investigate if the assessment format is capable of supporting reader and writer identities. In particular, both pre- and post-measures of self-efficacy should be included in test development so that best-practice items and formats can be identified.

Discussion Questions

1 How may your own experiences with reading and writing assessment compare to those of others, including students who did not perform well on assessments? How might your view of the needs of children be shaped by your own experiences?
2 What might a reading or writing assessment look like that is easy to manage and meaningful for students in a diverse classroom?
3 Prior to a reading screening task, the teacher tells his third-grade students: "I want you to perform this task at your very best, in order to inform me how to give you the best instruction." What are the potential motivational mechanisms in such an introduction?

References

Alexander, P. A., & Fox, E. (2004). A historical perspective on reading research and practice. In R. B. Ruddell & N. J. Unrau (Eds.), *Theoretical models and processes of reading* (5th ed., pp. 33–68). International Reading Association. https://doi.org/10.1598/0872075028.2

Bandura, A. (1997). *Self-efficacy: The exercise of control.* W. H. Freeman.

Bandura, A. (1986). *Social foundations of thought and action: A social cognitive theory.* Pearson.

Bandura, A. (2006). Guide for constructing self-efficacy scales. *Self-Efficacy Beliefs of Adolescents*, *5*(1), 307–337.

Bandura, A. (2010). Self-efficacy. *The Corsini Encyclopedia of Psychology*, 1–3.

Bong, M., & Skaalvik, E. M. (2003). Academic self-concept and self-efficacy: How different are they really? *Educational Psychology Review*, *15*(1), 1–40.

Chapman, J. W., Tunmer, W. E., & Prochnow, J. E. (2000). Early reading-related skills and performance, reading self-concept, and the development of academic self-concept: A longitudinal study. *Journal of Educational Psychology*, *92*(4), 703. https://doi.org/10.1037/0022-0663.92.4.703

Cohen, J. (1988). *Statistical power analvsis for the behavioral sciences* (2nd ed.). Erlbaum.

Conradi, K., Jang, B. G., & McKenna, M. C. (2014). Motivation terminology in reading research: A conceptual review. *Educational Psychology Review*, *26*(1), 127–164. https://doi.org/10.1007/s10648-013-9245-z

Dalby, M. A., Elbro, C., Jansen, M., & Krogh, T. (1992). *Bogen om læsning 3: Om læsehandicappede og læsehandicap*. Munksgaard Danmarks-Pædagogiske Institut.

Deci, E. L., & Ryan, R. M. (2012). Self-determination theory. In P. A. M. Van Lange, A. W. Kruglanski, & E. T. Higgins (Eds.), *Handbook of theories of social psychology* (pp. 416–436). Sage Publications Ltd. https://doi.org/10.4135/9781446249215.n21

Directorate for Education and Training [Utdanningsdirektoratet]. (2018). *Rammeverk for kartleggingsprøver på 1.–4. trinn* [Framework for screening tests at grades 1–4]. https://www.udir.no/eksamen-og-prover/prover/rammeverk-for-kartleggingsprover-pa-1.-4.-trinn/

Dweck, C. (2017). *Mindset-updated edition: Changing the way you think to fulfil your potential*. Hachette UK. https://doi.org/10.36254/978-90-8850-809-7

Frankl, V. E. (1966). Self-transcendence as a human phenomenon. *Journal of Humanistic Psychology*, *6*(2), 97–106. https://doi.org/10.1177/002216786600600201

Frankl, V. E. (1985). *Man's search for meaning*. Simon & Schuster.

Frankl, V. E. (2014). *The will to meaning: Foundations and applications of logotherapy*. Penguin.

Freud, S. (1964). *The standard edition of the complete psychological works of Sigmund Freud* (J. Strachey, Ed.). Macmillan.

Gadamer, H. G. (1960). *Wahrheit und methode. Grundzüge einer philosophishen hermeneutic*. Mohr.

Gentrup, S., Lorenz, G., Kristen, C., & Kogan, I. (2020). Self-fulfilling prophecies in the classroom: Teacher expectations, teacher feedback and student achievement. *Learning and Instruction*, *66*, 1–17. https://doi.org/10.1016/j.learninstruc.2019.101296

Gough, P. B., & Tunmer, W. E. (1986). Decoding, reading, and reading disability. *Remedial and Special Education*, 7(1), 6–10. https://doi.org/10.1177/074193258600700104

Guthrie, J. T., Wigfield, A., Barbosa, P., Perencevich, K. C., Taboada, A., Davis, M. H., Scafiddi, N. T., & Tonks, S. (2004). Increasing reading comprehension and engagement through concept-oriented reading instruction. *Journal of Educational Psychology*, *96*(3), 403. https://doi.org/10.1037/0022-0663.96.3.403

Harter, S. (1982). The perceived competence scale for children. *Child Development*, 87–97.

Hull, C. L. (1943). *Principles of behavior: An introduction to behavior theory*. Appleton-Century-Crofts.

Judge, T. A., & Bono, J. E. (2001). Relationship of core self-evaluations traits—self-esteem, generalized self-efficacy, locus of control, and emotional stability—with job satisfaction and job performance: A meta-analysis. *Journal of Applied Psychology*, *86*(1), 80. https://doi.org/10.1037/0021-9010.86.1.80

Kahneman, D. (2011). *Thinking, fast and slow*. Macmillan.

Kyllonen, P. C. (2016). Socio-emotional and self-management variables in learning and assessment. In A. A. Rupp & J. P. Leighton (Eds.), *The Wiley Handbook of cognition and assessment* (pp. 174–197). John Wiley & Sons. https://doi.org/10.1002/9781118956588.ch8

Lazowski, R. A., & Hulleman, C. S. (2016). Motivation interventions in education: A meta-analytic review. *Review of Educational Research*, *86*(2), 602–640. https://doi.org/10.3102/0034654315617832

Linnenbrink-Garcia, L., Patall, E. A., & Pekrun, R. (2016). Adaptive motivation and emotion in education: Research and principles for instructional design. *Policy Insights from the Behavioral and Brain Sciences*, *3*(2), 228–236. https://doi.org/10.1177/2372732216644450

Morgan, P. L., & Fuchs, D. (2007). Is there a bidirectional relationship between children's reading skills and reading motivation? *Exceptional Children*, *73*(2), 165–183. https://doi.org/10.1177/001440290707300203

Nuutila, K., Tapola, A., Tuominen, H., Kupiainen, S., Pásztor, A., & Niemivirta, M. (2020). Reciprocal predictions between interest, self-efficacy, and performance during a task. *Frontiers in Education*, *5*, 36. https://doi.org/10.3389/feduc.2020.00036

Pintrich, P. R. (2003). A motivational science perspective on the role of student motivation in learning and teaching contexts. *Journal of Educational Psychology*, *95*(4), 667. https://doi.org/10.1037/0022-0663.95.4.667

Rosenthal, R., & Jacobson, L. (1966). Teachers' expectancies: Determinants of pupils' IQ gains. *Psychological Reports*, *19*(1), 115–118. https://doi.org/10.2466/pr0.1966.19.1.115

Tolman, E. C. (1951). *Purposive behavior in animals and men*. University of California Press.

Tønnessen, F. E. (2011). What are skills? Some fundamental reflections. *L1-Educational Studies in Language and Literature*, 149–158. https://doi.org/10.17239/l1esll-2011.01.09

Tønnessen, F. E., & Uppstad, P. H. (2015). *Can we read letters? Reflections on fundamental issues in reading and dyslexia research*. Brill. https://doi.org/10.1007/978-94-6209-956-2_3

Toste, J. R., Didion, L., Peng, P., Filderman, M. J., & McClelland, A. M. (2020). A meta-analytic review of the relations between motivation and reading achievement for K–12 students. *Review of Educational Research*, *90*(3), 420–456. https://doi.org/10.3102/0034654320919352

Troia, G. A., Shankland, R. K., & Wolbers, K. A. (2012). Motivation research in writing: Theoretical and empirical considerations. *Reading & Writing Quarterly*, *28*(1), 5–28. https://doi.org/10.1080/10573569.2012.632729

UNICEF. (1989). *Convention on the rights of the child*. 1577 UNTS 3. https://www.ohchr.org/en/instruments-mechanisms/instruments/convention-rights-child

Unrau, N. J., Rueda, R., Son, E., Polanin, J. R., Lundeen, R. J., & Muraszewski, A. K. (2018). Can reading self-efficacy be modified. A meta-analysis of the impact of interventions on reading self-efficacy. *Review of Educational Research*, *88*(2), 167–204. https://doi.org/10.3102/0034654317743199

Unrau, N. J., & Quirk, M. (2014). Reading motivation and reading engagement: Clarifying commingled conceptions. *Reading Psychology*, *35*(3), 260–284. https://doi.org/10.1080/02702711.2012.684426

Vygotsky, L. S., & Cole, M. (1978). *Mind in society: Development of higher psychological processes*. Harvard University Press.

Wagner, C. J. (2021). Literacy and identities. In G. Noblit (Ed.), *Oxford research encyclopedia of education*. Oxford University Press. https://doi.org/10.1093/acrefore/9780190264093.013.990

Walgermo, B. R. (2018). *Motivation for reading within the first year of formal reading instruction* [Doctoral dissertation, University of Stavanger, Norway].

Walgermo, B. R., Frijters, J. C., & Solheim, O. J. (2018a). Literacy interest and reader self-concept when formal reading instruction begins. *Early Childhood Research Quarterly*, *44*, 90–100. https://doi.org/10.1016/j.ecresq.2018.03.002

Walgermo, B. R., Foldnes, N., Uppstad, P. H., & Solheim, O. J. (2018b). Developmental dynamics of early reading skill, literacy interest and readers' self-concept within the first year of formal schooling. *Reading and Writing*, *31*(6), 1379–1399. https://doi.org/10.1007/s11145-018-9843-8

Walgermo, B. R., Uppstad, P. H., Lundetræ, K., Tønnessen, F. E., & Solheim, O. J. (2021). Screening tests of reading: Time for a rethink. *Acta Didactica Norden*, *15*(1). https://doi.org/10.5617/adno.8136

White, R. W. (1959). Motivation reconsidered: The concept of competence. *Psychological Review*, *66*(5), 297. https://doi.org/10.1037/h0040934

Yeager, D. S., & Dweck, C. S. (2012). Mindsets that promote resilience: When students believe that personal characteristics can be developed. *Educational Psychologist*, *47*(4), 302–314. https://doi.org/10.1080/00461520.2012.722805

3

LANGUAGE AND MULTILINGUALISM IN YOUNG CHILDREN'S LITERATE IDENTITIES

Christopher J. Wagner

Introduction

Multilingual children are learning or exposed to two or more languages during childhood. While many patterns of language learning exist for multilingual children, all multilingual children share the experience of learning multiple languages and navigating multiple language contexts. As multilingual children learn to read and write, they construct ideas about language, their multilingualism, and who they are as readers and writers. Literate identities describe the ways that multilingual children construct the self as a reader and writer across contexts and time, and in ways that draw on their lived experiences as multilinguals (Wagner, 2018, 2021b).

An identities perspective that accounts for multilingualism frames literacy as a complex practice wherein children make and remake ideas about who they are as readers and writers within and across their languages (Kabuto, 2011; Martínez-Roldán & Malavé, 2004; Moses & Kelly, 2017). This includes ways that multilingual children navigate cultural and linguistic differences across languages, and differences in literacy practices in home, school, and other contexts where language and cultural practices differ. For some multilingual children, this includes ways they negotiate intersectional identities across dimensions of language, immigration status, race, culture, and nationality (Compton-Lilly et al., 2017).

As multilingual children enter school, particularly in the United States, reading and writing are often restrictively viewed as monolingual practices that primarily depend on the development of a narrow set of skills and strategies (Flores & García, 2017). Multilingual children are expected to navigate these monolingual literacy norms to be successful "school" readers and writers. However, these school

DOI: 10.4324/9781003271406-6

language contexts often diverge from the literacy practices that multilingual children experience in their homes and communities, which may draw across languages and include practices like translanguaging (García & Kleifgen, 2020).

Yet multilingualism does not need to be constructed as a challenge for multilingual children as they enter school. When viewed from an asset orientation, multilingualism broadens the tools, resources, and knowledge available to children as they learn to read and write (García & Kleifgen, 2020). When spaces for literacy learning across home, community, and school spaces are collectively considered, a wider range of language and literacy practices are accessible to and used by multilingual children as they are learning to read and write.

This chapter reexamines two studies on multilingual children to explore the role of multilingualism in young children's literate identities. The first study looks at children in two prekindergarten classrooms to consider how reading identities develop in ways that center multilingual practices and experiences. The second study follows children who participated in a bilingual family literacy program to explore how the languages used during literacy activities can affect children's reading identities. Together these studies provide opportunities to consider what it means to adopt a multilingual lens in the study of literate identities.

Theorizing Literate Identities for Multilingual Children

Identities and learning are interwoven phenomena. Nasir and Hand (2008) observe that participation in schooling, "extends beyond learning … to the very definition of who one is and who one is in the process of becoming" (p. 176). Moje and Luke (2009) similarly highlight the ways that "any kind of learning … of necessity involves shifting identities, whether as a requirement for the learning to occur or as a result of the learning" (p. 433). These ideas express a core assumption that underlies identity research—that learning can only be understood by considering the totality of the learner as a person.

For multilingual children, the learner as a person includes a child's multilingualism and language history. Yet the majority of identity theories do not attend to the impacts of multilingualism on identities. This includes the interrelated roles of language, race, and culture on identity construction, and the impacts of differing cultural models of literacy across school, home, and community contexts (Gee, 2011; Wagner, 2019, 2020a). This is a critical absence because as Moje and Luke (2009) observe, "subtle differences in identity theories have widely different implications for how one thinks about both how literacy matters to identity and how identity matters to literacy" (p. 416).

The two studies that are presented in this chapter both aim to consider the ways that identity theories have fallen short of explicitly considering language and multilingualism, particularly in young children. They likewise aim to consider how the conceptualization of identities and current identity theories can be broadened or reimagined to better account for language and multilingualism. Identity theories that more directly and fully attend to language, race, and culture are needed to develop more robust foundations for investigations into literate identities in multilingual children.

In these studies, I aim to sidestep theories that were developed to attend to monolingual adults to explicitly open spaces to consider how the identities of young multilingual children may differ based both on children's development and their language histories. To do this, I use sociocultural and poststructural theories to broadly conceptualize literate identities (Norton, 2013; Wagner, 2021a). These theories situate literate identities within a view of people as readers and writers who develop and apply literacy practices across varied sociocultural contexts.

From sociocultural and poststructural theories, I draw on key tenets of literate identities that are compatible with multilingualism and the development of young children. These include identities as:

- Multiple, with persons able to enact different identities across contexts;
- Learned and negotiated in social interactions with others;
- Interconnected with other identities, such as gender and race;
- Open to contradiction, as a person's multiple identities may conflict;
- Changing over time as an ongoing and fluid process; and
- Informed by the histories, practices, and norms of communities and institutions.

Some sociocultural and poststructural theories provide specific tools to conceptualize identities across sociocultural contexts in ways that are likewise compatible with multilingualism and the development of young children. I draw on two of these concepts in the studies presented in this chapter.

First, the concept of *communities of practice* (Lave & Wenger, 1991; Wenger, 1998) is used in Study 1. Communities of practice describes how persons construct identities in the social process of learning and by taking up the practices of groups of like-minded people. These identities are "long-term, living relations between persons and their place and participation in communities of practice" (Lave & Wenger, 1991, p. 53). A communities of practice perspective can be used to consider the ways that people learn and adopt literacy practices to gain acceptance as literate within various communities.

Second, the concept of *cultural models* (Gee, 2011) is used in Study 2. Cultural models are ways of being that a child learns and acts out through exposure to people with whom the child interacts regularly. As a child grows and is socialized within various language communities and contexts for literacy, they acquire cultural models of literacy or extend models that have already been acquired. Literate activities that use or span multiple languages can enable children to construct cultural models of literacy that draw on multilingual practices (Martínez-Roldán & Malavé, 2004).

Though each of these theoretical tools and the broader tenets of sociocultural and poststructural theories provide a starting point for the studies in this chapter, they are considered as only this—a starting point. These studies aimed to question, critique, extend, and raise new possibilities for how identity theories can account for language and multilingualism. Researchers of identity must not only draw on theories to inform and guide research, but must reckon with the ways that identity theories have been inequitably developed to attend to the identities of some persons and not others. This chapter takes up the ways that identity theories have not fully given space to young multilingual children.

Methods

This chapter reexamines two studies on multilingual children in prekindergarten to explore the roles of language and multilingualism in children's literate identities. I first provide information on the aims and context of each of these two studies. I then describe the data sources in these studies, which were largely similar. I then explain the analytic methods and highlight differences across the studies that align with the differing purpose of each study and the theoretical concepts used to examine literate identities in each study.

Context of Study 1

The first of the two studies sought to explore how multilingual children in prekindergarten understand and construct reading identities in relation to their multilingualism (Wagner, 2020a). This study used a multiple case study design. The design allows for the collection of in-depth data on a more limited number of children, while also allowing for analysis across children to identify patterns in identity processes and development.

The study was conducted at an elementary school in a city in the northeastern United States. Ten multilingual children from across two prekindergarten classrooms in the school participated in the study. The children were selected to include various home languages, genders, and levels of reported interest in reading. The children spoke a range of non-English languages including Spanish, Cape Verdean Creole, Haitian Creole, Portuguese, and Vietnamese.

Context of Study 2

The second of the two studies examined the ways that language contexts affect how multilingual prekindergartners construct and express reading identities (Wagner, 2020b). Language contexts were defined to include the language of books and the languages used by children and adults during literacy activities.

This study similarly used a multiple case study design to examine children's individual and collective identity experiences.

The study was conducted in a bilingual Chinese-English family literacy program held at a neighborhood elementary school in a city in the northeastern United States. The school served a population that was comprised primarily of recent Chinese immigrants. Participants were ten prekindergarten children in the program who used one or more Chinese languages (Mandarin, Cantonese, or regional Chinese languages including Fuzhouese, Hainan, and Fujian) as their primary home language.

The family literacy program was attended by the children and a parent or caregiver who spoke one or more Chinese languages. The program provided English and Chinese literacy opportunities for the participating children and family members. I led all English language activities in the program and a co-teacher led all Chinese language activities. The co-teacher was a Mandarin and English speaker who was a member of the community and a certified early childhood teacher.

Data Sources

Both studies center children as the primary source of data while also drawing on other data sources. This was done with the aim of constructing authentic portrayals of reading identities that value and have fidelity to the lived experiences of the participating children (Albon & Rosen, 2013). The use of varied and developmentally appropriate data sources ensures that multiple perspectives on the reading identities of children are considered, including the views of families, caretakers, teachers, and children's own sense-making about their reading identities.

Though some details of the data collection methods varied across these two studies, the types of data collected are described below and are representative of the data collected in both studies. The data sources in these studies included information on children across different language contexts, and whenever possible data collection was done in multiple languages to open spaces for the multilingual practices of children and their families. Descriptions of the data sources used in these studies are offered as examples of the varied ways researchers can learn about young children's literate identities.

Reading and Writing Activities

Book readings and other literacy activities, ranging from discussions of texts to oral storytelling, provide contexts for children to demonstrate literacy practices and discuss literacy in authentic contexts (Parkinson, 2001). These activities are particularly effective when children are allowed to take the lead in the literacy activity and to control the pace and direction of the activity. By asking questions during activities, children are prompted to participate in informal discussions about literacy. Changing the partner in literacy activities, such as from a researcher to a parent, teacher, or peer, can change the dynamic of the interactions and reveal new information. Researcher, parent, and peer-reading activities were used in these studies.

Observations of Children's Play

Play is often at the center of how young children learn and practice language. During imaginative and dramatic play, children frequently draw on their knowledge of texts and language to enact reading identities (Wohlwend, 2011). This can include taking on the roles and speaking patterns of characters from books and other stories, imagining and enacting new narratives, and experimenting with roles, plot structures, and other narrative devices. Observing children during play provides authentic opportunities to gather information on children's literacy-related behaviors and talk. Productive observations can focus on children's language practices and their interactions with other children, objects, or texts. A range of play events were observed across studies, including play that followed literacy activities to open spaces for children to explore and extend ideas from books with other peers.

Draw and Talk Interviews

Drawing and talking combine children's verbal and visual languages by allowing children to draw and then explain their drawings (Angell et al., 2015; Kendrick & McKay, 2004). When the topic of drawings is focused on literacy, these interviews can reveal information about a child's history with and understandings of language and literacy. Drawing allows children to add to and revise ideas, and can scaffold complex and abstract thinking. As a result, children's drawings and their explanations of them often reveal more complexity about children's identities than conversation alone. Draw and talk interviews were conducted with each of the children in the two studies. Children were asked to draw pictures of themselves reading, including any places, people, or other relevant details that connect to their reading practices.

Interviews with Children

Though activity-based interviews like the draw and talk interview are often better suited to elicit more robust responses from young children, semi-structured interviews can also provide valuable information on identities. Questions in these interviews were on reading identities and were constructed to be appropriate for the developmental and language levels of children. For example, in these studies I used open-ended questions (e.g., What do you like to read?), fill-in-the-blank statements (e.g., When I read I feel ______.), and yes/no questions (e.g., Do you read books at home?). Fill-in-the-blank and yes/no questions can reduce the language demands on children and can be effective at initiating talk with children who are shy or hesitant.

Interviews with Parents, Caretakers, and Teachers

Parents and caretakers are unique in having a long-term view of a child's literacy development and an accumulated memory of a child's literacy history. Though teachers often work with a child for only one year, they have specialized knowledge to observe children's literate practices. Parent questionnaires or interviews provide spaces to learn about family language and literacy practices, family expectations for reading, and family language goals. Teacher interviews are well-suited to learning about classroom instruction, children's language and social development, and language and reading practices in school spaces. In both studies, questionnaires or interviews were used to gather information from parents, caretakers, and teachers.

Data Analysis

The analysis of data in both studies drew on content analysis and thematic analysis (Braun & Clarke, 2006). This approach uses inductive, open coding cycles that are then developed into themes by identifying patterns and trends across codes and data excerpts. Themes are triangulated and evaluated to meet the criteria of parsimoniousness, testability, and coherence across excerpts. This inductive or "bottom-up" approach to constructing meaning from the data opens space to question the applicability of current theories and construct new conceptual understandings of identities.

In the case of Study 1, thematic analysis was used to construct themes that described the specific identity processes of multilingual children. In the case of Study 2, thematic analysis followed a deductive coding process that built on findings from Study 1. In Study 2, two deductive coding processes were used: one coding process to identify the language contexts by coding for the languages used in texts and interactions, and a second deductive coding process to identify children's expressions of reading identities. The latter were directly drawn from the findings of Study 1. Thematic analysis was then used to explore children's expression of reading identities within and across language contexts.

By utilizing the findings from Study 1 to inform the analysis of data in Study 2, these studies show how researchers can successively build on prior findings to answer increasingly complex questions about identity and language processes. When a specific aim of research is to question whether current theories and conceptualizations of identity adequately account for diverse populations, both developing and applying new ways of conceptualizing identities are important to moving forward understandings of identities in diverse populations.

Findings

From a Monolingual to a Multilingual Lens on Literate Identities

Findings from Study 1 draw attention to the ways that multilingual children engage in identity processes that are uniquely responsive to their multilingualism. These findings push back on a monolingual lens on literate identities, which has led to an overlooking of the more expansive set of language practices, skills, and dispositions that shape the literate identities of multilingual children. In Study 1, I drew from the concept of communities of practice to identify three constructs that characterize ways that multilingual children incorporated their multilingualism into their reading identities: language awareness, language preferences, and metalinguistic awareness. Here I briefly discuss each and show how these constructs can lead toward a multilingual lens on literate identities.

Language Awareness

Language awareness is a consciousness that multiple languages exist and can be used for reading. Many children become aware of languages incrementally as they move toward a broader understanding of languages and how they are used in reading and writing, and become better able to differentiate between languages. Often this begins with an awareness of the languages the different people in a child's life use in specific communities of practice. One child, Stanley, explained how when his family talks at home, "my mommy say Creole and my sister say Creole and my grandma say Creole and my nana say Creole … my mommy talk to my my mommy talk to my grandma and my nana."

This awareness of the different languages people use often extends to reading and writing. For example, Jackie could identify the languages used in various books. She differentiated between English and Vietnamese books she had at her home, describing how "I got two book … I got an English book, Vietnamese book." Another child, Caleb, connected his own multilingualism to the writing in a bilingual book. During a reading, he pointed to an English-Spanish bilingual book and said, "I speak like this one a little Spanish and English." Each of these children began to see communities of practice and literacy artifacts that reflected the languages they used, which allowed them to begin to conceptualize literacy as a multilingual activity.

Language Preferences

Language preferences are a desire to read or write in a language or to learn to do so. Preferences can reflect affective, personal, or practical desires to become literate in or use a language. Some multilingual children like Yara express clear language preferences. Yara vocalized a preference to read in Spanish over English, explaining, "I like Spanish more better." When I asked if she liked reading books in English, she replied, "No ... I like in Spanish." Yara often put this preference into action. During book readings, Yara made repeated efforts to shift the language of reading from English to Spanish. Yara would interrupt an English reading to ask "Can I read it?" and then begin talking in Spanish. When presented with a bilingual English-Spanish book, she suggested that we read in Spanish and, if needed, offered, "I can help you with Spanish."

For other multilingual children, language preferences are not limited to a single language. Some children like Caleb resisted sharing a preference for a single language and instead vocalized a preference to read in multiple languages. Caleb self-described that he could read in English and that he wanted to learn to read in Spanish. When presented with bilingual books, he explained that he preferred the way the Spanish and English were included together. Caleb's preference for bilingual books and reading were likely influenced by his family community of practice and his mother, who he identified as a good reader and about whom he repeatedly reported, "My mom speak English and Spanish."

Metalinguistic Awareness

Metalinguistic awareness is a consciousness of the connections between languages. For young children, metalinguistic awareness often includes a growing awareness of how to apply cross-linguistic knowledge and skills to reading and writing, and an increasing ability to make choices about which language to use and how translanguaging practices can connect their languages. This often appears when children make visible connections across languages. For example, when Caleb heard the word "crocodile" during a read aloud, he connected it to the cognate "cocodrilo" and wanted to share this discovery.

Though young children are still developing awareness and agency in their language choices, some are able to make active choices about their language practice. For example, Elizabeth showed a particular attention to the languages she used in literacy tasks. Elizabeth switched between English and Spanish as she worked on literacy activities with different partners. When working on a letter activity, she started on her own in English. When Adrián, a Spanish-dominant child, joined her, she switched to naming letters in Spanish. Elizabeth applied information about her context to make conscious decisions about her languaging practices that responded to a change in her local community of practice.

At other times, children's movements across languages showed their still-developing ability to make language decisions. Raina occasionally switched languages during reading events, and she sometimes described these as unintentional. While talking in English about a book, Raina switched to Cape Verdean Creole. After a moment she paused and, appearing confused, explained, "Sorry. I kind of my brain I talk Creole sometimes and English sometimes." Though Raina could not always explain why she self-corrected, in these moments she expressed a growing awareness of her translanguaging practices, the monolingual English orientation of the community of practice she was reading within, and the cognitive processes involved in thinking about and managing her languages.

By surfacing the roles of language awareness, language preference, and metalinguistic awareness in these children's literate identities, I show in Study 1 how these constructs can shape the literate identities of multilingual children. Just as a monolingual lens on literacy has normalized literate practices that overlook the unique languaging practices of multilingual children, the normalization of a monolingual lens on literate identities has made it easier to overlook the ways that language and literate identities are interconnected. Looking for and considering multilingual aspects of literate identities is a critical part of moving from a monolingual to a multilingual lens on literate identities.

Language Contexts Matter

Findings from Study 2 show how multilingual children are responsive to changes in language contexts, and how differing language contexts inform how multilingual children develop and express reading identities. That differences were observed in children's reading identities across language contexts shows how multilingual children are in the process of learning various cultural models of reading and that multilingual children consider the language contexts of reading events when they make decisions about which of these cultural models to draw on and enact. Like the findings from Study 1, these findings challenge researchers to question how monolingual framings of literate identities can obscure factors that are important to how multilingual children construct literate identities.

Monolingual Reading Contexts

Monolingual reading contexts featured the use of only English or Chinese in books and talk. For many of the children, aspects of their reading identities were connected to cultural models of reading tied to a language. For example, for some children monolingual Chinese contexts for reading functioned as a space that centered family members and grandparents, regional Chinese languages, and the use of culturally valued texts. In one instance of this, a family described how a child's grandfather helped him to read and memorize Tang poems. These monolingual Chinese contexts were often described by families as vital spaces for family literacies and histories.

These monolingual Chinese spaces for reading showed children ways of doing reading that were distinct from school practices. In many cases grandparents provided reading contexts that were distinct even from those provided by parents, often centering regional Chinese languages and cultural practices that many parents reported not learning or having forgotten from their own childhood, such as the reading and memorizing of Tang poems mentioned above. Because these interactions provide access to ways of reading that are not included in school spaces, monolingual Chinese contexts were an important resource for these multilingual children to construct reading identities that connected to the cultural and linguistic identities of their families and that drew from cultural models of reading that differ from those they were exposed to in school.

For children with emerging English language proficiency, monolingual English contexts for reading presented vastly different opportunities to be a reader. Many of the children showed limited comprehension of books when readings were conducted only in English. Though these children actively engaged with illustrations during these readings, their talk did not always reflect an engagement with the story's narrative and often included retellings of recent experiences from their own lives. In these cases, children may have been looking for meaningful ways to interact with texts and made attempts to draw connections to their own knowledge. This represented a way for children to "be a reader" in contexts when comprehension of the text was not always possible.

Multilingual Reading Contexts

Multilingual reading contexts featured both Chinese and English language talk with Chinese or English language books. When more than one language was used, opportunities to learn about language and its role in reading were made visible to children. Children's and adults' varied ways of moving across languages provided children with ways to understand how they can operate as a multilingual when reading, and how their multilingualism can be used to enact reading strategies that support comprehension and engagement with texts. This provided spaces for children to view multilingualism as part of reading and being a reader, and provided an explicit context for children to see cultural models that included their own multilingualism as part of who they are as a reader.

Cross-linguistic or translanguaging exchanges were one way that parents supported children's reading and modeled how multilingualism could be incorporated into children's reading identities. In this exchange, a mother moves across English and Cantonese to help her child identify the syntactic patterns in an English version of the book *No, David!* by David Shannon:

MOTHER: Okay, we'll read. Just read no:: ((points to the page)) N-O okay? ((points to the page)) No, David!

CHILD: No, David.

MOTHER: What is this thing? ((points at the page))

CHILD: Bear cook=

MOTHER: Cookies! ((laughs)) ((points to a different part of page)) Sugar. Flour. 呢度做咩? [What is he doing here?] No=

CHILD: =David

MOTHER: David, No係咪啊? [Right?] 寫住No, David, no. [It is written: No, David, no.] 係咪啊? [Right?] No, David, no. And then 呢度寫咩。[And then what is written here?]
CHILD: No, David, No
MOTHER: No, No, No. 三个No. [Three No's.] No, No, No.
CHILD: Three No.
MOTHER: Three No.

The mother's movement across languages was central to how she explained the language structure of this English text. Her Cantonese functioned as a tool for explicit English language instruction, allowing her to explain the repetitive syntactic structure of the text, and at the same time model a reading strategy. Unlike English-only contexts, this interaction modeled how multilingualism can be used as a tool by readers to construct meaning from a monolingual text. These practices show children how multilingualism can be used to constructively support reading, providing a cultural model that shows how children can connect their identities as readers and multilinguals.

Opening spaces for multilingualism likewise opened choices for children to either reject or enact their multilingualism as part of their identity as a reader. In one instance, a child rejected his mother's attempt to read a Chinese book with him by asking her to tell the teacher that he was not Chinese:

CHILD: Why did you get this book?
MOTHER: 依個係老師比㗎。唔係我攞嘅。老師話要睇中文。[This book was given to me by the teacher. I didn't choose to take this book. The teacher says we need to read in Chinese.]
CHILD: Read it.
MOTHER: 狼婆婆 [Grandma Wolf.]
CHILD: Then just say I'm not Chinese. Did you say I'm- say that I'm not Chinese, okay?
MOTHER: ((laughs)) You are Chinese.

Though the child could speak Mandarin, his insistence that his mother "say I'm not Chinese" is an apparent attempt to claim a monolingual, English identity as a reader, and to have the teacher view him as an English reader. These kinds of responses to the use of specific languages during reading events show the ways that children actively adopt or reject labels as users or non-users of certain languages as a reader, and how specific cultural models of language and multilingualism are foregrounded as parts of their reading identities in these contexts.

By looking at how children developed ways of being readers across language contexts, I show in Study 2 the complex interplay between language and identities. Reading across monolingual and multilingual language contexts supported children's sense-making of texts, and provided explicit spaces for children to examine, experiment with, and construct reading identities that spanned their languages. Without contexts that provided various cultural models of reading, children did not have opportunities to engage as multilinguals with written texts, and therefore to construct reading identities as multilinguals. These findings from Study 2 highlight the particular need to look beyond classrooms and to understand the roles of home and community language practices in multilingual children's literate identities.

Implications

The two studies presented in this chapter speak to the interrelationship between children's multilingualism and literate identities and the ways that multilingual children construct literate identities that are grounded in their experiences with language. For researchers and teachers to understand multilingual children's literate identities, there must be a collective shift from a monolingual to a multilingual lens that accounts for the contexts and language practices that comprise multilingual children's literacy experiences. That such a lens remains underdeveloped in the current literature on literate identities points to a need to more fully explore, understand, and value the ways that multilingualism informs and shapes the identity processes of young multilingual children.

The findings from these studies show how multilingual children learn to act and think like a reader through the observation and apprenticeship of others across communities of practice (Wenger, 1998). The language practices and cultural models that children are exposed to matter, and affect how multilingual children take up and make sense of the interactions they have around language and literacy (Gee, 2011). The observed differences in how multilingual children construct literate identities across contexts provide continued evidence that the various site-specific demands on literate identities, including the language of instruction and the presence or absence of multilingualism, are important factors in the development of literate identities for multilingual children.

Together, the two studies shared in this chapter highlight both the promise and need for more research on the interrelationships between early literacy, multilingualism, and identities. This includes a need for data that span contexts and time so that the development of literate identities can be better understood. There is likewise a need for research that considers curriculum and program structures, including how the presence and kind of multilingual instruction may mediate or enable the construction of literate identities in early childhood classrooms. Attention to questions of practice like these can help teachers and researchers to consider how literate identities can be leveraged to support the literacy and language development of multilingual children, and can inform continued theorization about literate identities that more fully account for language and multilingualism.

These questions draw attention to the ways multilingual children learn, use, and connect language systems as they learn to read. At the same time, they highlight complexity and variation in how multilingualism shapes literate identities that require a nuanced understanding of the processes and mechanisms involved in identity development at an early age. Developing such an understanding requires continued efforts to open spaces for multilingual children in current research and theories of identity, and the specific roles of multilingualism, language, and culture in how literate identities develop and inform young children's domain-specific learning.

Discussion Questions

1. How might some theories overlook the literacy or identity practices of young children, multilingual children, or other groups?
2. How can identity research be designed to create space for the development of new theories or the refinement of current theories?
3. How do many approaches to literate identities reflect a monolingual lens, and what does it mean to take a multilingual lens to literate identities?

References

Albon, D., & Rosen, R. (2013). *Negotiating adult-child relationships in early childhood research.* Routledge. https://doi.org/10.4324/9780203095126

Angell, A., Alexander, J., & Hunt, J. A. (2015). 'Draw, write and tell': A literature review and methodological development on the 'draw and write' research method. *Journal of Early Childhood Research, 13*(1), 17–28. https://doi.org/10.1177/1476718x14538592

Braun, V., & Clarke, V. (2006). Using thematic analysis in psychology. *Qualitative Research in Psychology, 3*(2), 77–101. https://doi.org/10.1191/1478088706qp063oa

Compton-Lilly, C., Papoi, K., Venegas, P., Hamman, L., & Schwabenbauer, B. (2017). Intersectional identity negotiation: The case of young immigrant children. *Journal of Literacy Research, 49*(1), 115–140. https://doi.org/10.1177/1086296x16683421

Flores, N., & García, O. (2017). A critical review of bilingual education in the United States: From basements and pride to boutiques and profits. *Annual Review of Applied Linguistics, 37*, 14–29. https://doi.org/10.1017/s0267190517000162

García, O., & Kleifgen, J. A. (2020). Translanguaging and literacies. *Reading Research Quarterly, 55*(4), 553–571. https://doi.org/10.1002/rrq.286

Gee, J. P. (2011). *Social linguistics and literacies: Ideology in discourses* (4th ed.). Routledge.

Kabuto, B. (2011). *Becoming biliterate: Identity, ideology, and learning to read and write in two languages.* Routledge.

Kendrick, M., & McKay, R. (2004). Drawing as an alternative way of understanding young children's constructions of literacy. *Journal of Early Childhood Literacy, 4*(1), 109–128. https://doi.org/10.1177/1468798404041458

Lave, J., & Wenger, E. (1991). *Situated learning: Legitimate peripheral participation.* Cambridge University Press. https://doi.org/10.1017/cbo9780511815355

Martínez-Roldán, C. M., & Malavé, G. (2004). Language ideologies mediating literacy and identity in bilingual contexts. *Journal of Early Childhood Literacy, 4*(2), 155–180. https://doi.org/10.1177/1468798404044514

Moje, E. B., & Luke, A. (2009). Literacy and identity: Examining the metaphors in history and contemporary research. *Reading Research Quarterly, 44*(4), 415–437. https://doi.org/10.1598/rrq.44.4.7

Moses, L., & Kelly, L. B. (2017). The development of positive literate identities among emerging bilingual and monolingual first graders. *Journal of Literacy Research, 18*(3), 307–337. https://doi.org/10.1177/1086296x17713291

Nasir, N. I. S., & Hand, V. (2008). From the court to the classroom: Opportunities for engagement, learning, and identity in basketball and classroom mathematics. *Journal of the Learning Sciences, 17*(2), 143–179. https://doi.org/10.1080/10508400801986108

Norton, B. (2013). *Identity and language learning: Extending the conversation* (2nd ed.). Multilingual Matters.

Parkinson, D. D. (2001). Securing trustworthy data from an interview situation with young children: Six integrated interview strategies. *Child Study Journal, 31*(3), 137–155.

Wagner, C. J. (2018). Being bilingual, being a reader: Prekindergarten dual language learners' reading identities. *Journal of Early Childhood Literacy, 18*(1), 5–37. https://doi.org/10.1177/1468798417739668

Wagner, C. J. (2019). Connections between reading identities and social status in early childhood. *TESOL Quarterly, 53*(4), 1060–1082. https://doi.org/10.1002/tesq.529

Wagner, C. J. (2020a). Multilingualism and reading identities in prekindergarten: Young children connecting reading, language, and the self. *Journal of Language, Identity, & Education*. Advance online publication. https://doi.org/10.1080/15348458.2020.1810046

Wagner, C. J. (2020b). Reading identities across language contexts: The role of language of text and talk for multilingual learners. *Journal of Early Childhood Literacy*. Advance online publication. https://doi.org/10.1177/1468798420981758

Wagner, C. J. (2021a). Literacy and identities. In G. Noblit (Ed.), *Oxford research encyclopedia of education*. Oxford University Press.

Wagner, C. J. (2021b). Reading identities as a developmental process: Changes in Chinese-English learners from prekindergarten to kindergarten. *Bilingual Research Journal, 44*(2), 174–188. https://doi.org/10.1080/15235882.2021.1942324

Wenger, E. (1998). *Communities of practice: Learning, meaning, and identity*. Cambridge University Press.

Wohlwend, K. E. (2011). Mapping modes in children's play and design: An action-oriented approach to critical multimodal analysis. In R. Rogers (Ed.), *An introduction to critical discourse analysis in education* (2nd ed., pp. 242–266). Routledge.

SECTION II

Literate Identities in Middle Childhood

Introduction to Literate Identities in Middle Childhood

Christine M. Leighton

Introduction

As children enter middle childhood, described in this volume as children aged 9–13 and grades 4–8, complex developmental factors inform their views of themselves as readers and writers. First, children at this age demonstrate a desire for more independence from adults and more agency, highlighting the need for choice in what they read, how they read, and with whom they read. Additionally, in the context of US schools, state standards and curricula put increasing importance on children at this age learning about complex topics and concepts through independent reading and taking stances on topics using evidence to support their thinking orally and in writing. Children begin to give more weight to the opinions of their peers, which has implications in the classroom for grouping practices and how social practices in the classroom inform students' literate identities. As children try to determine where they "fit" socially and academically, there can be a tendency to sort and label one another into different categories. In the United States and other countries with neoliberal education systems, there is an increased emphasis on standardized test scores, typically starting in third grade, which can result in classroom practices that sort and categorize children based on their scores and reify labels (e.g., good reader, poor reader) as they continue on in their schooling.

These and other myriad factors that inform children's literate identities at this age demonstrate just how dynamic and fluid this concept is, yet reliance on external measures of achievement can lead children, teachers, parents, and others to hold static views of what it means to be a reader and writer. These fixed views may become more established as children move from upper elementary into middle school and can be detrimental to their growth as readers and writers.

DOI: 10.4324/9781003271406-8

For example, children who are positioned and labeled as "struggling" readers or writers may avoid engaging in literacy tasks (Enriquez, 2011; Hall, 2010), contributing to long-term literacy difficulties (Eklund et al., 2013). Yet, directly attending to children's literate identities informed by their social, cultural, and linguistic backgrounds can help support them in "rejecting deficit narratives about themselves and claiming more productive reading [and writing] identities" (Skerrett, 2020, p. 332).

Theorizing Identities in Middle Childhood

Theories informing researchers' understanding of literate identities in middle childhood must address the complexities of these developmental factors. In educational contexts, for example, standardized testing and skill-based curricula tend to privilege the cognitive dimensions of reading—that is, an individual's efforts to use decoding and comprehension skills and strategies to read and make sense of text. Yet, helping children "rewrite" fixed and negative reading identities often attached to test scores requires extending beyond cognitive processes and outcomes. This has led literacy researchers to ground their work in other theories such as sociocultural, poststructural, critical, and integrative perspectives (see Wagner, 2021) to attend to social and cultural contexts and their associated power dynamics. Questions of power and agency are important for all readers, but particularly for students, and often students of color, who have been historically marginalized in schools by labels assigned to them by external measures of success and deficit narratives (Muhammad & Mosley, 2021; Tatum & Muhammad, 2012). Thus, putting literate identities into conversation with children's other identities, including racial identities, often requires integrating other frameworks (e.g., culturally sustaining pedagogy [see Paris and Alim, 2014], critical race theory in education [see Ladson-Billings & Tate, 1995]) that explicitly attend to questions of power and counter deficit narratives with asset-based and holistic perspectives of learners.

Moreover, children at this age have also established longer literate histories that extend beyond the oral language experiences common in early childhood to encompass more robust reading and writing practices that inform their views of themselves as readers and writers. In the classroom context, "teachers and students engage with each other based on these histories and their understandings of who a person is as a reader and what it means to hold a particular reading identity" (Hall, 2016, p. 79). Hall reminds us that even when a student adopts a different view of their literate identity, others in the classroom may not recognize this shift and interact with that student in ways that align with previously assigned labels. As such, researchers often ground their work in theories such as communities of practice (Wenger, 1998) and positioning theory (Davies & Harré, 1990) to explore these lived, literate histories and illuminate how these are negotiated with and recognized by peers and teachers.

Research Methods in Middle Childhood and Early Adolescence

Grounding literate identity research in theories that explore social and cultural contexts and practices and interrogate the associated power relations requires methods that unearth these complex dynamics. Test scores alone will not illustrate students' enactment, construction, and negotiation of literate identities, leading researchers to collect multiple data sources such as interviews, classroom observations, and student work that illuminate the contexts and experiences of literacy learning. Likewise, just as children's identities have come to be established over time, if the goal is to explore how their literate identities develop, research is strengthened when data collection takes place over an extended period of time.

Because of the robust literate histories of children in middle childhood, research is strengthened when children at this age are given the chance to express their own views about who they are as readers and writers. Using data sources such as interviews and/or written reflections is a way to explore children's own views of their literate histories and identities and center their voices in the process.

Similarly, the ways others (e.g., teachers, peers, other adults) interact with children are informed by their perceptions of the children's literate identities. In the classroom context, using methods such as teacher interviews and observations allows researchers to explore the teacher's role in the process. Approaches such as practitioner inquiry (see Cochran-Smith & Lytle, 2009), and formative design (see Reinking & Bradley, 2008) create further opportunities for findings to directly inform teachers' instruction and understanding of students' literate identities. These methods can create space for teachers to reflect on their beliefs about what it means to be a reader and writer and how those views inform their instruction and interactions with their students.

Additionally, just as teachers are not neutral outsiders in these interactions, neither are the researchers as their own multiple identities (e.g., literate, racial, linguistic) inform their views and interpretations of children. Thus, the researcher is often called on to consider their own positionality and make their multiple identities explicit in reports of their research, which productively disrupts previously held boundaries of what it means to be an "objective" outsider. Likewise, researchers are called on to view research sites as what Fecho and Meacham (2007) call "transactional spaces" and consider how both the researcher and the participants are mutually informed by the research. In doing so, researchers make a commitment to researching *with* a community and ensuring that the participants are seen as knowers and doers in their own right (Haddix, 2020).

Chapters in This Section

The three chapters in this section explore the literate identities of children in middle childhood, specifically children in grades 4–8, while Section III focuses on older youth. Across the chapters, the authors demonstrate how researchers can build on various theories and methodologies to capture the complexities of literacy and identity development.

In Chapter 4, Francois joins culturally relevant pedagogy and sociocultural theory to explore students' reading identities. The study took place at Grant Street, a secondary urban school serving students in grades 6–12, recognized as a school community that promoted a "culture of reading" and emphasized humanizing school literacy practices. Analysis of middle school student interviews indicated the importance of both school context and text selection in affirming students' reading identities, particularly during independent reading. Francois leaves the reader to consider how the participatory and inclusive literacy practices at Grant Street inform our understanding of literacy and identity as evolving, performative, and social.

Sociocultural theory, culturally responsive pedagogy, and asset-based perspectives urge researchers, teachers, and administrators to adopt holistic views of students and their literate identities. Likewise, using student interviews as a data source centers students' voices and offers them agency in how they tell their stories and express who they are as readers. Overall, Francois's perspectives, methods, and findings offer a powerful counter-narrative to the all-too-pervasive deficit views of minoritized students and the overreliance on rote and remedial learning.

In Chapter 5, Giunco, Leighton, and O'Brien examine how a fifth-grade teacher engaged in practitioner inquiry with her literacy coach to implement literacy instruction centering students' literate identities and shift away from teacher-centered methods. The resulting unit integrated student choice, shared reading, and balanced cognitive and sociocultural dimensions of literacy. Analysis of lessons, student journals, partner discussion field notes, and student interviews suggested that instruction encouraged students to "try on" differing ways of being a reader and exert agency, despite the complexities of distributing power between students and the teacher.

Giunco and colleagues' exploration of literate identities was guided by sociocultural theory and questions of power as conceptualized by Freire (1970/2000). Their chapter offers insight into how teacher researchers can use theory to directly inform instructional decisions to make space for students to construct, enact, and negotiate their multiple literate identities. Giunco and colleagues conclude by discussing how critical dimensions of reading identity (e.g., race, power, oppression) could be more explicitly explored in the next phase of their collaboration. In doing so, they encourage other researchers to consider the same questions in their work.

In Chapter 6, Hall draws on models of reading identities and sociocultural perspectives to explore the interactions and power dynamics that emerged in a classroom where students were positioned as different types of readers. Drawing on a year-long case study in an eighth-grade classroom, this chapter shifted from previous research that focused on students who held negative views of themselves as readers to instead explore a student who considered herself to be an excellent reader and was positioned so by her teacher and her peers. Through analysis of classroom observations, questionnaires, and teacher and student interviews, and using direct quotes from students, findings illustrated how reading identities were reified in the classroom by teachers and peers alike, and at times further marginalized those who were identified as "struggling" readers.

Hall suggests that moving away from autonomous models of identity to ideological models that account for the social and cultural practices of a community may help create more expansive views of reading identities and a more nuanced understanding of what it means to be a reader. She concludes by asking researchers to consider ways to disrupt damaging power dynamics and practices and make space for more equitable experiences around reading for all students.

Across chapters, these authors emphasize the importance of looking beyond discrete skills when exploring literate identities to include sociocultural dimensions of literacy development and instruction. Moreover, each chapter demonstrates the potential for research to be mutually transformative for the researcher and participants at the sites where they conducted their work. In the chapters by Francois and Giunco and colleagues, the teachers were also the researchers, and their work was informed by what their students were telling and showing them about their literate identities. By using a formative design, Hall was deeply immersed in the classroom by taking field notes multiple times a week, observing 60 times, and interviewing students and teachers several times during the year. The three chapters offer insight into the ways others can conduct community-engaged research. Moreover, these three chapters also demonstrate how the authors attempted to center the students' voices and what they were saying about themselves as readers and writers.

Each of these chapters concludes with thoughtful questions about where the field might go next. While the chapters discuss the dynamic power relations in the field, they also suggest a need for engaging even more deeply with critical perspectives. We hope readers walk away with ideas for how they can extend and build on this work to engage more deeply and explicitly with ideas of power, race, and oppression.

References

Davies, B., & Harré, R. (1990). Positioning: The discursive production of selves. *Journal for the Theory of Social Behavior, 20*(1), 43–63. https://doi.org/10.1111/j.1468-5914.1990.tb00174.x

Eklund, K. M., Torppa, M., & Lyytinen, H. (2013). Predicting reading disability: Early cognitive risk and protective factors. *Dyslexia, 19*, 1–10. https://doi.org/10.1002/dys.1447

Enriquez, G. (2011). Embodying exclusion: The daily melancholia and performative politics of struggling early adolescent readers. *English Teaching: Practice and Critique, 10*(3), 90–112.

Fecho, B. & Meacham, S. (2007). Learning to play and playing to learn: Research sites as transactional spaces. In C. Lewis, P. Enciso, & E. B. Moje (Eds.), *Reframing socio-cultural research on literacy: Identity, agency and power* (pp. 163–187). Lawrence Erlbaum Associates. https://doi.org/10.4324/9781003064428-10

Freire, P. (2000). *Pedagogy of the oppressed* (30th anniversary ed.). Continuum. (Original work published in 1970).

Haddix, M. (2020). This is us: Discourses of community within and beyond literacy research. *Literacy Research: Theory, Method, and Practice, 69*(1), 26–44. https://doi.org/10.1177/2381336920937460

Hall, L. A. (2010). The negative consequences of becoming a good reader: Identity theory as a lens for understanding struggling readers, teachers, and reading instruction. *Teachers College Record, 112*(7), 1792–1829. https://doi.org/10.1177/016146811011200708

Hall, L. A. (2016). "I don't really have anything good to say": Examining how one teacher worked to shape middle school students' talk about texts. *Research in the Teaching of English, 51*(1), 60–83.

Ladson-Billings, G., & Tate, W. F. (1995). Toward a critical race theory of education. *Teachers College Record, 97*(1), 47–68. https://doi.org/10.1177/016146819509700104

Muhammad, G. E., & Mosley, L. T. (2021). Why we need identity and equity learning in literacy practices: Moving research, practice, and policy forward. *Language Arts, 98*(4), 189–196.

Paris, D., & Alim, S. H. (2014). What are we seeking to sustain through culturally sustaining Pedagogy? A loving critique forward. *Harvard Educational Review, 84*(1), 85–100. https://psycnet.apa.org/doi/10.17763/haer.84.1.982l873k2ht16m77

Skerrett, A. (2020). Social and cultural differences in reading development: Instructional processes, learning gains, and challenges. In E. B. Moje, P. P. Afflerback, P. Enciso, & N. K. Lesaux (Eds.), *Handbook of reading research* (Vol. 5, pp. 328–344). Routledge. https://doi.org/10.4324/9781315676302-17

Tatum, A. W., & Muhammad, G. E. (2012). African American males and literacy development in contexts that are characteristically urban. *Urban Education, 47*(2), 434–463. https://doi.org/10.1177/0042085911429471

Wagner, C. J. (2021). Literacy and identities. In G. Noblit (Ed.), *Oxford research encyclopedia of education*. Oxford University Press. https://doi.org/10.1093/acrefore/9780190264093.013.990

Wenger, E. (1998). *Communities of practice: Learning, meaning, and identity*. Cambridge University Press.

4

A SOCIOCULTURAL APPROACH TO SCHOOL LITERACY

Navigating Identity Through Culturally Relevant Pedagogy

Chantal Francois

Introduction

Since the mid-1990s, researchers, educators, and policymakers have responded to an "adolescent literacy crisis" characterized by what they saw as catastrophic reading achievement by proposing solutions for advancing middle- and high-school students' literacy development (Jacobs, 2008). But scholars observe that researchers' and policymakers' preoccupation with "functional" literacy skills (Faggella-Luby et al., 2009) has been equally catastrophic, ultimately reproducing the very social inequities reform efforts claimed to dismantle (Au, 2016; Darling-Hammond, 2007). Coinciding with external accountability measures like high-stakes standardized tests, researchers argue that curricular reforms harm minoritized students—Black, Latinx, and indigenous youth, often in urban areas and often living in poverty—most acutely. Studies indicate that such curriculum ignores minoritized students' identities, assets, and resources, in turn privileging a narrow, Eurocentric conceptualization of literacy that privileges rote and remedial learning while deemphasizing critical thinking (Lewis & del Valle, 2009; Diamond, 2012). Consequently, deficit narratives depict minoritized students as "struggling," "demotivated," or even "nonreaders" (Lenters, 2006). But Alvermann (2001) contends that *schools* make struggling readers, ultimately solidifying minoritized students' role in our nation's social order as compliant, unimaginative, and impotent.

From the mid-1970s, scholars have offered alternate visions for school pedagogy that affirm students' cultural and individual identities. Ladson-Billings's (1995) seminal contribution called for educators to embrace culturally relevant pedagogy. Building on cultural anthropologists' research, she advocated for educator stances that simultaneously advanced student achievement, affirmed students' cultural

DOI: 10.4324/9781003271406-9

identities, and fostered critique on social inequities. Ladson-Billings joins other voices (see Aronson & Laughter, 2016 for a review) who advocate for similar orientations. In literacy, Bishop (1990) expands on one dimension of culturally relevant pedagogy, diverse texts as "mirrors" into students' experiences and "windows" to invite them to explore unfamiliar circumstances. This work understands students' literacy learning as identity-validating, rigorous, relational, and transformative.

While these contributions move closer to centering students' identities in schools, researchers call for more studies documenting how youth perceive and interact with relevant pedagogy (Sleeter, 2012). This call matters especially in urban areas, where, as Welsh and Swain (2020) report, deficit-fueled accountability era rhetoric negates that "considerable assets exist within 'urban' communities that scholars have yet to fully discuss or empirically document" (p. 99). Moreover, some call for more research that includes students' voices to uncover class- and school-level factors shaping their literacy experiences and identities (Intrator & Kunzman, 2009). Responding to these calls, I wanted to understand how students perceived their literacy experiences at one urban middle and high school. Data analysis from 23 student interviews revealed an inclusive school literacy, one where participating in independent reading and its associated routines affirmed students' personal identities and fostered their identities as agentic and confident readers. These findings hold important implications for school-level practices to advance diverse urban middle school students' literacy development.

Theoretical Framework

Sociocultural and Asset-Based Perspectives

Sociocultural theories, proposing that reading develops through interaction and environment, frame this study (Vygotsky, 1978). The sociocultural perspective of literacy posits that readers constantly move across texts, their lives, and the world (Galda & Beach, 2001). Sociocultural perspectives explain that contexts send messages about what kind of reading members value, reading's purposes, and even what counts as reading (Heath, 1983). Sociocultural perspectives focus attention on how contexts shape readers' experiences rather than focusing on individual traits alone (Galda & Beach, 2001). The sociocultural perspective suggests agency in the reading process, as readers produce traditional and nontraditional literacy experiences, even when traditional literacy tasks may not account for their agency.

Scholars who study diverse student populations have placed sociocultural perspectives in conversation with culturally responsive teaching (Gay, 2010), culturally relevant pedagogies (Ladson-Billings, 1995), culturally sustaining pedagogies (Paris & Alim, 2014), multicultural education (Banks & Banks, 2019), and funds of knowledge (Moll et al., 1992). These asset-based approaches to learning refine sociocultural perspectives, compelling educators and researchers to consider youths' and families' cultural strengths, diverse learning styles, and personal histories that have rendered dynamic young people who continually navigate historical and spatial contexts (Gutiérrez & Stone, 2000).

Both sociocultural contributions and asset-based theories inform how I define identity and its relationship to literacy in this study. First, identity includes how youth see themselves and how others view them (Boston & Baxley, 2007). Further, literacy and identity are socially situated, involving the everyday experiences and stories in which we participate, the places we are, and the people with whom we interact (Gee, 1996; Lave & Wenger, 1991; Moje et al., 2009). Moreover, literacy and identity continually evolve, challenging the notion that "to be literate" is a finite object that one can accomplish (del Valle & Lewis, 2008). Finally, youth perform their literacies and identities broadly—for example, as students, as youth, as male and female, as gay and straight, as Black and of Asian descent, as car lovers, and as social media creators. Thus, reading is a moment when young people negotiate who they are, both individual and group-based, both familiar and possible (McCallister, 2004; McCarthey & Moje, 2002)—these are reading identities.

Literature Review

Independent Reading as a Culturally Relevant Pedagogy

Skerrett's (2020) review of sociocultural literacy research establishes independent reading as one instructional approach that can affirm students' identities and their sociocultural resources while growing their reading prowess. Nancie Atwell, a middle school teacher and pioneer of independent reading, described independent reading simply as *frequent, voluminous reading* (Atwell, 2007). During this time, students choose titles they want to read from a classroom or school library and read, typically every day for 20 minutes or more. Associated routines include individual teacher conferences, book recommendations, goal setting, and reflecting on reading habits (Atwell, 2007; Francois, 2013b).

Sociocultural researchers regard prior knowledge as a meaningful element of independent reading. Researchers have widely established that prior knowledge contributes to readers' understanding of texts (Schwanenflugel & Knapp, 2015), facilitating their comprehension as they move between their personal knowledge and the knowledge presented in the texts they encounter. Thus, sociocultural theorists understand that students can develop their literacy through frequent exposure to texts from which they can draw upon their "vast funds of knowledge, including cultural and linguistic resources, as well as prior experiences, and textual information to construct and build new knowledge and, in essence, learn from texts" (Hattan and Lupo, 2020, p. 284).

Sociocultural theorists and some independent reading advocates focus on acknowledging and incorporating students' lived knowledge in the classroom to support their confidence and agency with reading. These are the texts that "mirror" students' schemas, or familiar knowledge frameworks, and are within proximity of what students know and who they are (Vygotsky, 1978). Meanwhile, as students often read voluminously in classrooms that emphasize independent reading, they can gain unfamiliar and needed knowledge about worlds that are "windows" to their experiences (Bishop, 1990).

Independent Reading Transforming Learning, Identity, and Classrooms

Indeed, researchers of literacy among diverse readers have explored independent reading's role as a project of identity development and literacy growth. Independent reading hinges on compelling titles, which, for adolescents, often include middle-grade and young adult fiction. These books highlight relevant youth issues and offer a textual space to interrogate personal experiences, surrounding communities, and society (Boston & Baxley, 2007; Francois, 2013a; Frankel et al., 2018; Ivey & Johnston, 2013). Also, these texts can affirm students' all-encompassing identities and enable youth readers to explore their possible selves (Bishop, 1990; Markus & Nurius, 1986). Independent reading of middle-grade and young adult literature may be even more important as a schoolwide practice for youth of color as a practice to cultivate their reading identities through the years.

Finally, Ladson-Billings' (1995) beliefs about culturally relevant pedagogy resonate with independent reading as she envisioned transformed classrooms as learning communities. Independent reading assumes mutual participation, because all students, and often the teacher, are "just plain reading" (Ivey & Broaddus, 2001, p. 350) alongside one another. Successful independent reading necessitates that teachers are familiar with titles that will appeal to students and are knowledgeable about their students' strengths and interests (Atwell, 2007; Francois, 2013b). Thus, students and teachers engage in a community of practice (Lave & Wenger, 1991) where learning occurs, not through the *teaching* of reading but through the *practice* of reading with others who are similarly engaged (Francois, 2013b). Independent reading assumes that youth become more engaged and develop their literacy by reading books they want to read (Francois, 2013a; Ivey & Johnston, 2013; Skerrett, 2020). As Atwell observes, "literacy blooms wherever students have access to books they want to read, permission to choose their own, and time to get lost in them" (2015, 9:26).

Methodology

School Context and Positionality

My research (Francois, 2013a, 2013b, 2015, 2021a, 2021b) has documented literacy instruction and learning at Grant Street Secondary School, a small urban public school serving mostly Latinx students in 6th to 12th grades. I was once a teacher and literacy coach at Grant Street and wanted to understand what many saw as "a culture of reading." My research found that professional routines—including frequent teacher collaboration, systems to know students and families, and monitoring individual student progress—sustained a schoolwide vision for relevant, relational, and rigorous literacy pedagogy (Francois, 2021a). This literacy pedagogy, supported by a principal who prioritized advancing students' reading in his vision (Francois, 2021b), informed numerous instructional elements including independent reading, access to diverse texts, class discussions about social inequalities, and performance-based assessments. This research situates students' reading identities in the school culture and prompted me to revisit the data for this chapter to examine their identities in the context of independent reading at Grant Street.

Participants

I created a purposeful interview participant sample informed by students' achievement, classroom observations, teacher recommendations, and school-based literacy tasks. I was an 11th-grade teacher when I collected data for this study. The sample represents diverse ethnicities, genders, grade levels, achievement levels, and special education statuses. Table 4.1 lists participants' demographic information.

Data Collection and Procedures

Moje et al. (2009) suggest that "identities are not only represented but also constructed in and through the stories people tell about themselves and their experiences" (p. 427). Interviews invited students to tell their stories. The semi-structured interview protocol asked students about their lives and their interests. The protocol also asked students about their learning and reading experiences at Grant Street, including questions about notable routines, favorite titles, reading strengths and challenges, and their reading growth during their time at Grant Street. I interviewed each student once for 20 to 45 minutes. Each interview was recorded, transcribed, and served as my data source.

Data Analysis

I extracted excerpts associated with reading identity from the transcripts. I developed topic codes informed by patterns in students' responses, my research questions, and my prior research (e.g., talk, recommendations, independent reading, growth, choice). As I conducted my analysis, I realized that students were actually talking about their identity when they discussed their participation in reading-related school activities, even when those interview questions did not explicitly ask about identity. This discovery in my analysis corroborated the idea of identity

TABLE 4.1 Demographic Information for Student Interview Sample (N = 23)

Grade	*Name*	*Gender*	*Race/Ethnicity*	*Ec. Dis.*	*Spring GMRT Score*
6th	Luis	Male	Latino	Yes	NA
6th	Melinda	Male	Black	Yes	Below
6th	Tommy	Male	Latino	Yes	Above
7th	Denise	Female	Black	Yes	Below
7th	Deondre	Male	Black	No	NA
7th	Leo	Male	Latino	No	Above
7th	Sharon	Female	Latino	Yes	Above
7th	Tanesha	Female	Black	Yes	Above
8th	Asia	Female	Black	Yes	NA
8th	Monaya	Female	Black	Yes	NA
8th	Wesley	Male	Asian	Yes	NA
8th	Zara	Female	Black	Yes	NA
9th	Amanda	Female	Black	Yes	At
9th	Lubna	Female	Asian	Yes	Above
9th	Martin	Male	Latino	Yes	Below
10th	Clarence	Male	Black	Yes	NA
10th	Jason	Male	White	No	Above
10th	Latressa	Female	Black	No	Above
10th	Stephen	Male	Black	Yes	Above
11th	Brianna	Female	Black	Yes	At
11th	Mario	Male	Black	Yes	Above
11th	Tiffany	Female	Latino	Yes	At
12th	Yronelis	Female	Latino	Yes	NA

Note: I used results from the Gates-MacGinitie Reading Test as one indicator of students' reading achievement. Scores indicate if students scored below, at, or above grade level in comprehension on a Spring posttest. NA means no test score data was available for the student.

development through social activity (Lave & Wenger, 1991). It also led me to develop two themes, *talk during independent reading*—that would reveal much about the school's context—and *favorite books*—the artifacts that reflected both who they were and their relationships with texts. For each theme, I developed analytic codes and wrote memos that generated hypotheses and assertions about literacy and identity within and across transcripts (Erickson, 1986). This process also allowed me to capture the themes on literacy and identity that converged with other students' responses, that diverged from them, or that illuminated new ways to understand the themes.

Findings

Youth Voices: Context and Reader Identity

Data analysis reveals a humanizing approach to school literacy where participating in independent reading and its associated routines affirmed students' personal identities and fostered their identities as readers. Here, I center students' voices to highlight Grant Street's most identity-affirming practice, independent reading.

Though I feature mostly middle school students' responses, I include high school students' responses whose words helped to extend the themes or whose stories reflected on their Grant Street middle school experiences.

Grant Street, a "Reading School"

Seventy-two percent of the students I interviewed attributed their reading engagement and improvement to independent reading at Grant Street. Each sixth through tenth grader participated in independent reading every day for 30 minutes during their English classes and weekly for 50 minutes in the 11th and 12th grades. Observations, interview data, and documents revealed shared routines and expectations. For example, between 15 and 25 percent of students' final grades in these classes reflected independent reading, including expectations for reading progress at school and home, reading growth, and their willingness to experiment with new genres, evidenced through reading logs, conferences, and written reflections. Teachers expected students to read between 25 and 45 different books each year. During independent reading, teachers read and conferred with students.

Students recognized Grant Street as a "reading school." For example, Tanesha, a seventh-grade student, said,

> [There's] always pictures of books coming out now and Jack [the principal] is always pushing you to read, read, and read, my Humanities teacher is pushing me to read, and read, and read. So reading is a big thing at this school.

Similarly, sixth grader Melinda recalled the book displays at her new student orientations at Grant Street, confirming her hunch that "all they want me to do is read." She continued that teachers' expectations for her reading volume improved her attitude toward reading in school. Clarence, now a tenth grader, illuminated that beyond hearing expectations from teachers, peers, too, modeled and defined what it meant to read at Grant Street. Clarence recalled that before he came to Grant Street, he rarely read books. But when he first attended the school in seventh grade, he observed,

> Cause seeing everybody else reading was like, I wanted to be a part of that, and I'd be like an outcast, so it pushed me to find the right book... It's like you watch everybody else read. You stand out there and you see they're all doing the right thing ... and you figure that out, and you want to do the right thing.

Clarence articulated that his peers were important agents in the school's reading culture; their participation influenced his identification and involvement with reading at Grant Street.

Teachers Recommend and Read Books Kids Want to Read

Seventy-five percent of the sample reported that their conversations with teachers about reading habits and interests—along with teachers' vast knowledge of appealing books—scaffolded reading expectations and connected students to reading. Asia, an eighth grader, described how Theresa, her English teacher, recommended books to her:

> My teacher … picked out books for me that she thinks I'm interested in. She looked at my reading record, and she asked me what type of genres I'm into, and she recommended books she's already read, that are good for me. She checks my reading record every day to see how my progress is going.

Students also trusted that teachers knew countless captivating titles. Brianna, an 11th grader who had attended Grant Street since middle school observed, "you know the good thing about the librarian, she's read every book inside the library, so anything you [want], she says, 'like this'?" Students also recognized teachers' enthusiasm for reading the same books during independent reading. Sharon, a seventh grader, described independent reading with Keena, her teacher, and other students:

> One of the things Keena does is sometimes when we read a book and talk about it she ends up liking it. She reads the book with us to help us understand. She reads with us and then, while she's reading … we have conferences with her about it, like, 'oh yeah, we like this part!'

Students' responses illustrate the interplay between context and identity; students saw their teachers reading, recommending, and enjoying appealing books. In turn, teachers' reading identities and practices influenced how students perceived their experiences with reading at Grant Street.

The Principal's Book Club

Close to 50 percent of participants said the principal's book club enhanced their reading. Jack, the principal, identified between four and eight books throughout the year that would appeal to Grant Street students, sometimes including an author visit. For instance, young adult author Alan Lawrence Sitomer, who wrote *The Hoopster* (2006) and *Hip Hop High School* (2007), visited Grant Street during the Spring. Jack publicized Sitomer's visit with fliers that featured the books' covers and blurbs; he also introduced the titles during school assemblies or classroom visits. Jack bought copies for each Humanities and English teacher's classroom library to distribute to students. For other book clubs, Jack included poetry, realistic fiction, historical fiction, contemporary novels, informational texts, graphic novels, and memoirs; sometimes, students recommended his picks. Then, students could volunteer to read the title and attend a book club meeting over lunch.

During the year, I observed five book club meetings where between 10 and 25 students sat around the conference table in Jack's office discussing authors' messages, character development, and implications for students' lives and society. Students appreciated that, like their teachers and the librarian, Jack read middle-grade and young adult titles. They believed they could trust his recommendations. And they appreciated visiting his office to check out books from his library. Students saw that participating in Jack's book club was a rare opportunity to participate in cross-grade interactions about a common text. Wesley, an eighth grader, commented that the principal's book club encouraged him to read because it facilitated "critical reading;" students went "deep down into the characters, what they're trying to say." Leo, a seventh grader, added, "you go and everyone else read the book and gives different input. I look at the chapter in a way I never thought of it, like a surprise."

Summary

Data reveal the school-level factors that sustained a participatory literacy through which Grant Street students and staff co-constructed their reading identities. For example, teachers set clear and ambitious expectations to read voluminously. Teachers scaffolded those expectations by offering ample time, texts, and choice. Students also appreciated teachers' commitments to knowing students' reading habits and interests. Further, students regarded teachers as knowing, reading, and enjoying the books students wanted to read. They talked with teachers often about those books and their reading lives. Even the school's principal participated in students' reading, inviting them to read and talk about books that mattered to them and solidifying schoolwide intentions to support meaningful reading. Finally, students modeled what it meant to read at Grant Street, in turn apprenticing new students. Structural and social features ultimately supported students' agency to explore their personal identities through the books they read.

Youth Voices: Texts and Reader Identity

Students reported that the availability of thousands of enticing texts at school helped them to enjoy reading and to grow in their reading. Here, students discuss the books they enjoyed in relation to their views of themselves as readers at Grant Street.

Connecting to Characters

Every student I interviewed enjoyed books that enabled them to connect characters' experiences (or memoir authors' experiences) to their lives. For example, ninth grader Lubna, a student of Bengali descent, was drawn to books featuring Asian characters or issues about immigration that mirrored her family's experience. Lubna's reading record included *The Kitchen God's Wife* by Amy Tan (2006), *A Fine Balance* by Rohinton Mistry (1997), and Khaled Hosseini's *A Thousand Splendid Suns* (2007) and *The Kite Runner* (2013). She stated that these books "make you feel, I'm not the only one with these problems, so I could relate to that." Similarly, seventh grader Denise had recently read Reymundo Sanchez's *My Bloody Life: The Making of a Latin King* (2000), whose memoir chronicles his involvement in the Latin Kings gang in the 1980s. She selected the book because,

> I realize the stuff he was going through in his life, ever since from being a child all the way up to, like, his age... I see people going through things like ... that every day and, like, they take certain steps because they think they have to because the ... people they hang around push them to it. So there's a lot of peer pressure in that book and I realize that I'm around that stuff like every day. So, and that's what made it really stick out for me.

Lubna's and Yronelis's book choices illuminate the purposes of Grant Street's reading program in that it allowed students to choose the texts that they wanted to read, ones that would enable them to understand how their identities fit in the broader scheme of the world.

Seeking Out the Unfamiliar

While most students appreciated books whose stories were connected to their lives, a small but notable group of students—35 percent—remarked that they wanted to read books depicting lives entirely different from theirs. These books helped them to visualize and understand unfamiliar worlds. Leo in the seventh grade stated that he was drawn to Walter Dean Myers's novels about young black soldiers in the War in Iraq and the Vietnam War, including *Fallen Angels* (2008) and *Sunrise Over Fallujah* (2009), during independent reading because

> My grandfather was in World War II as a marine. I would ask him questions about the War and he wouldn't answer them. I would read these books and—I do this all the time—I put my grandfather's name in the place of the main character, and try to imagine what it was like there, and what he might have been feeling.

Additionally, many students who stated that they enjoyed reading about other worlds during independent reading tended to appreciate action and fantasy books because, as seventh grader Deondre remarked, "You read about something you can dream about. You know it can't happen, but it's still good to dream about it."

Though students selected action and fantasy books for escape, some saw themselves as part of these stories. Mario, an avid graphic novel reader, described that Spiderman was just like him because, beyond being a superhero, Spiderman was also trying to deal with the everyday joys and struggles of being a teenager: "You got school, social life, and your image, the image you want to uphold. It's the exact same thing for teenagers. That's why I love Spiderman." While, for some students, independent reading allowed students to find themselves, this time also allowed students to lose themselves in unfamiliar worlds, thus describing reading as an act of complex identity making.

Empathizing with the Character

Beyond enjoying books with different worlds or ones with familiar circumstances, 43 percent of the student sample enjoyed books where they could empathize with the character. Seventh grader Deondre discussed that he liked books that "make you understand … the character. Like the character's not just some person in the book, he's not just a made-up character. I consider characters in a book real people." Similarly, Monaya, an eighth grader, reminisced about a moment during independent reading when she didn't want to close her book.

> I read the book and I somehow morphed into Dylan [the main character in *Theories of Relativity* by Barbara Haworth-Attard (2005)] and it became like I could feel all his emotions. Once you are in the book you can't get out and it is like you can't help but feel exactly how the character feels or you can't help but think, if I was there, I would have said something different.

Like Monaya and Deondre, students elaborated on reading instances when they moved beyond their worlds and into the worlds of others. Martin did more than simply relate to Dave Pelzer's autobiography about the child abuse he endured in *A Child Called It* (1995). He reflected that while reading the book, he continually asked himself, "How would I feel if I was in that type of situation? When I get deeply in the book, that's the way I feel, and I start crying at times." Seventh grader Leo simply articulated, "characters affect who I am in the real world."

Summary

Not one student preferred a single book genre during independent reading at Grant Street. Denise, who discussed reading books that depicted gang life, also enjoyed reading young adult romance novels. And Leo, who enjoyed reading books about war to help him visualize his grandfather's role as a marine, also liked reading books about teen characters' school lives. Independent reading at Grant Street gave its students the space to explore who they were, to enter unknown worlds, to empathize with the character, and to "try on" the identities of others, all ultimately shaping their reading identities.

Discussion

This study examined how middle-grade students perceived their reading experiences at one urban secondary school. Analysis reveals a participatory, inclusive form of school literacy that revolved around independent reading. Students describe how independent reading and its related routines affirmed their personal and reading identities. These findings resonate with three major understandings of literacy and identity in sociocultural and asset-based reading research discussed below: literacy and identity as ever-evolving, performative, and socially situated. These findings also hold important research and practice implications for moving beyond a single classroom's efforts and providing possibilities for reimagining school literacy.

Findings illuminate how a school can nurture students' literacy and identity's ever-evolving natures in which students engage with multiple and fluid ways to see themselves as they read. For example, participants asserted that there wasn't one book genre eternally suitable for them. In books that reflected students' experiences, characters' stories validated their realities. In the texts that differed from their lives, students were still able to identify with the unfamiliar and learn something new about the world. In books whose characters enabled them to empathize, students stated they came to understand more about humanity. In this study, students' experiences underscore an evolving view of reading, less as an outcome to be achieved but more as a vehicle through which readers can negotiate who they are. Diverse learners often face a dual problem of fixed traits, either by having to receive static labels such as "struggling reader" (Northrop & Kelly, 2019) or by having to endure monolithic assessments of group attributes to determine their interests (Gutiérrez & Rogoff, 2003). Like Grant Street staff, teachers can challenge pernicious tendencies to impose oversimplistic labels by coming to know students' interests and reading habits intimately enough to recommend titles that can appeal to each dynamic identity.

Findings also offer insight into how a school can attend to literacy and identity's performative nature. While most students navigate predetermined schedules throughout the school day, Grant Street's independent reading was a rare time when students could exert some agency over how they participated in an academic task. Indeed, participants revealed numerous agentic processes engaged with Grant Street's independent reading: beyond choosing titles, students connected and empathized with characters, imagined and escaped to other worlds, and modeled reading expectations for their peers. Findings resonate with Gee's (2001) assertion that the texts we read allow us to scaffold and articulate our experiences in the world, and they allow us to gain perspectives on new experiences. Schools can offer reading activities like those at Grant Street, ones through which students choose texts to author their reading lives, to grow as readers, and to share in that process with others.

Finally, findings show how a school can support literacy and identity's social nature. Bartlett (2007) suggests that although reading appears private, people connect to one another and articulate their selves through reading. Such connection aligns with a community of practice (Lave & Wenger, 1991), where students see themselves—and see others who are like them—as part of a given activity, thus encouraging them to engage in that activity. Lave and Wenger assert that participating in a community of practice is in part about becoming oneself, becoming part of others in the community, and in defining the kind of person one wants to become. Even older Grant Street students, reflecting on their middle school experiences, explained that they increasingly saw themselves as readers because of the repeated practices and messages staff and peers modeled and communicated about reading at Grant Street. Thus, this study holds important implications for literacy leadership, calling for school administrators and teacher leaders to make time for, nurture relationships around, and develop coherent routines for humanizing, participatory school literacy.

Conclusion

In a time when researchers document disjuncture between students' lives and their school lives, Grant Street students' voices highlight how school adults embraced a culturally relevant stance toward literacy, foregrounding their identities to encourage their in-school literacy. Further, students explained that their powerful engagement with reading was the result of a socially interactive environment that allowed them the time to engage with books meaningfully, opportunities to see school adults passionately engaged with reading young adult books, and the benefit of receiving thoughtful book recommendations from teachers. This study holds implications for understanding reading as a social activity to nurture students' reading enjoyment and reading growth. By doing so, schools can support students to construct more holistic, fluid views of readers.

Discussion Questions

1. How do this study's findings contribute to your overall understanding of sociocultural and culturally relevant literacy in the middle grades?
2. How do this study's findings about literate identities inform your research (i.e., study design, incorporating students' voices, analyzing data)?
3. How do this study's findings about literature identities inform your teaching (i.e., your stance toward literacy, interactions with students, curriculum, teaching practices)?

References

Alvermann, D. E. (2001). Reading adolescents' reading identities: Looking back to see ahead. *Journal of Adolescent and Adult Literacy, 44*, 676–690. https://www.jstor.org/stable/40018739

Aronson, B., & Laughter, J. (2016). The theory and practice of culturally relevant education: A synthesis of research across content areas. *Review of Educational Research, 86*(1), 163–206. https://doi.org/10.3102/0034654315582066

Atwell, N. (2007). *The reading zone*. Scholastic.

Atwell, N. (2015). *Keynote speech: Clinton global initiative*. [Video]. Vimeo. https://vimeo.com/142631700

Au, W. (2016). Meritocracy 2.0: High-stakes, standardized testing as a racial project of neoliberal multiculturalism. *Educational Policy, 30*(1), 39–62. https://doi.org/10.1177/0895904815614916

Banks, J. A., & Banks, C. A. M. (2019). *Multicultural education: Issues and perspectives*. John Wiley & Sons.

Bartlett, L. (2007). To seem and to feel: Situated identities and literacy practices. *Teachers College Record, 109*(1), 51–69. https://doi.org/10.5752/P.2358-3428.2013v17n32p73

Bishop, R. S. (1990). Mirrors, windows, and sliding glass doors. *Perspectives: Choosing and Using Books in the Classroom, 6*(3), 1–2. https://scenicregional.org/wp-content/uploads/2017/08/Mirrors-Windows-and-Sliding-Glass-Doors.pdf

Boston, G. H., & Baxley, T. (2007). Living the literature. *Urban Education, 42*(6), 560–581. https://doi.org/10.1177/0042085907305186

Darling-Hammond, L. (2007). Race, inequality and educational accountability: The irony of 'No Child Left Behind'. *Race Ethnicity and Education, 10*(3), 245–260. https://doi.org/10.1080/13613320701503207

del Valle, A., & Lewis, C. (2008). Literacy and identity: Implications for research and practice. In L. Christenbury, R. Bomer, & P. Smagorinsky (Eds.), *Handbook of adolescent literacy research*. The Guilford Press.

Diamond, J. B. (2012). Accountability policy, school organization, and classroom practice: Partial recoupling and educational opportunity. *Education and Urban Society, 44*(2), 151–182. https://doi.org/10.1177/0013124511431569

Erickson, F. (1986). Qualitative methods on research in teaching. In M. C. Werlin (Ed.), *Handbook on research in teaching* (pp. 119–161). MacMillan Publishing Company.

Faggella-Luby, M. N., Ware, S. M., & Capozzoli, A. (2009). Adolescent literacy—Reviewing adolescent literacy reports: Key components and critical questions. *Journal of Literacy Research, 41*(4), 453–475. https://doi.org/10.1080/10862960903340199

Francois, C. (2013a). Reading is about relating: Urban youths give voice to the possibilities for school literacy. *Journal of Adolescent & Adult Literacy, 57*(2), 141–149. https://doi.org/10.1002/JAAL.218

Francois, C. (2013b). Reading in the crawl space: A study of an urban school's literacy-focused community of practice. *Teachers College Record, 115*(5), 1–35. http://www.tcrecord.org/Content.asp?ContentId=16966

Francois, C. (2015). An urban school shapes young adolescents' motivation to read. *Voices from the Middle, 23*(1), 68–72. https://library-ncte-org.proxy-tu.researchport.umd.edu/journals/VM/issues/v23-1/27486

Francois, C. (2021a). Expectations, relevance, and relationships: Striving toward ideals for adolescent literacy instruction in an urban secondary school. *Reading & Writing Quarterly*, 1–20. https://doi.org/10.1080/10573569.2021.1878403

Francois, C. (2021b). Urban literacy leadership: Examining one principal's vision and practice. *Education and Urban Society*. https://doi.org/10.1177/00131245211062537

Frankel, K. K., Fields, S. S., Kimball-Veeder, J., & Murphy, C. R. (2018). Positioning adolescents in literacy teaching and learning. *Journal of Literacy Research, 50*(4), 446–477. https://doi.org/10.1177/1086296X18802441

Galda, L., & Beach, R. (2001). Theory into practice: Response to literature as a cultural activity. *Reading Research Quarterly, 36*(1), 64–73. https://doi.org/10.1598/RRQ.36.1.4

Gay, G. (2010). *Culturally responsive teaching: Theory, research, and practice*. Teachers College Press.

Gee, J. P. (1996). *Social linguistics and literacies: Ideology in discourse*. Falmer.

Gee, J. P. (2001). Reading as situated language: A sociocognitive perspective. *Journal of Adolescent & Adult Literacy, 44*(8), 714. https://www.jstor.org/stable/40018744

Gutiérrez, K. D., & Rogoff, B. (2003). Cultural ways of learning: Individual traits or repertoires of practice. *Educational Researcher, 32*(5), 19–25. https://doi.org/10.3102/0013189X032005019

Gutiérrez, K. D., & Stone, L. D. (2000). Synchronic and diachronic dimensions of social practice: An emerging methodology for cultural-historical perspectives on literacy learning. In C. D. Lee (Ed.), *Vygotskian perspectives on literacy research: Constructing meaning through collaborative inquiry* (pp. 150–164). Cambridge University Press.

Hattan, C., & Lupo, S. M. (2020). Rethinking the role of knowledge in the literacy classroom. *Reading Research Quarterly, 55*, S283–S298. https://doi.org/10.1002/rrq.350

Haworth-Attard, B. (2005). *Theories of relativity*. Henry Holt and Co.

Heath, S. B. (1983). *Ways with words: Language, life and work in communities and classrooms*. Cambridge Core. https://doi.org/10.1017/CBO9780511841057

Hosseini, K. (2007). *A thousand splendid suns*. Riverhead Books.

Hosseini, K. (2013). *The kite runner*. Riverhead Books.

Intrator, S. M., & Kunzman, R. (2009). Who are adolescents today? Youth voices and what they tell us. In L. Christenbury, R. Bomer, & P. Smagorinsky (Eds.), *Handbook of adolescent literacy research* (pp. 29–45). Guilford Press.

Ivey, G., & Broaddus, K. (2001). "Just plain reading": A survey of what makes students want to read in middle school classrooms. *Reading Research Quarterly, 36*(4), 350–377. https://doi.org/10.1598/RRQ.36.4.2

Ivey, G., & Johnston, P. H. (2013). Engagement with young adult literature: Outcomes and processes. *Reading Research Quarterly, 48*(3), 255–275. https://doi.org/10.1002/rrq.46

Jacobs, V. A. (2008). Adolescent literacy: Putting the crisis in context. *Harvard Educational Review, 78*(1), 7–39. https://doi.org/10.17763/haer.78.1.c577751kq7803857

Ladson-Billings, G. (1995). Toward a theory of culturally relevant pedagogy. *American Educational Research Journal, 32*(3), 465–491. https://doi.org/10.3102/00028312032003465

Lave, J., & Wenger, E. (1991). *Situated learning*. Cambridge University Press.

Lenters, K. (2006). Resistance, struggle, and the adolescent reader. *Journal of Adolescent & Adult Literacy, 50*(2), 136–146. https://doi.org/10.1598/JAAL.50.2.6

Lewis, C. & del Valle, A. (2009). Literacy and identity: Implications for research and practice. In L. Christenbury, R. Bomer, & P. Smagorinsky (Eds.), *Handbook of adolescent literacy research* (pp. 307–322). Guilford Press.

Markus, H., & Nurius, P. (1986). Possible selves. *American Psychologist, 41*(9), 954–969. https://doi.org/10.1037/0003-066X.41.9.954

McCallister, C. (2004). Schooling the possible self. *Curriculum Inquiry*, *34*(4), 425–461. https://doi.org/10.1111/j.1467-873X.2004.00305.x

McCarthey, S. J., & Moje, E. B. (2002). Conversations: Identity matters. *Reading Research Quarterly*, *37*(2), 228–238. https://doi.org/10.1598/RRQ.37.2.6

Mistry, R. (1997). *A fine balance*. Vintage.

Moje, E. B., Luke, A., Davies, B., & Street, B. (2009). Literacy and identity: Examining the metaphors in history and contemporary research. *Reading Research Quarterly*, *44*(4), 415–437. https://www.jstor.org/stable/25655467

Moll, L. C., Amanti, C., Neff, D., & Gonzalez, N. (1992). Funds of knowledge for teaching: Using a qualitative approach to connect homes and classrooms. *Theory into Practice*, *31*(2), 132–141. https://doi.org/10.1080/00405849209543534

Myers, W. D. (2008). *Fallen angels*. Scholastic Press.

Myers, W. D. (2009). *Sunrise over Fallujah*. Scholastic Press.

Northrop, L., & Kelly, S. (2019). Who gets to read what? Tracking, instructional practices, and text complexity for middle school struggling readers. *Reading Research Quarterly*, *54*(3), 339–361. https://doi.org/10.1002/rrq.237

Paris, D., & Alim, H. S. (2014). What are we seeking to sustain through culturally sustaining pedagogy? A loving critique forward. *Harvard Educational Review*, *84*(1), 85–100. https://doi.org/10.17763/haer.84.1.9821873k2ht16m77

Pelzer, M. (1995). *A child called it*. Health Communications Inc.

Sanchez, R. (2000). *My bloody life: The making of a Latin king*. Chicago Review Press.

Schwanenflugel, P. J., & Knapp, N. F. (2015). *The psychology of reading: Theory and applications*. Guilford Publications.

Sitomer, A. (2006). *The hoopster*. Hyperion.

Sitomer, A. (2007). *Hip-hop high school*. Hyperion.

Skerrett, A. (2020). Social and cultural differences in reading development: Instructional processes, learning gains, and challenges. In E. B. Moje, P. Afflerbach, P. Enciso, & N. Lesaux (Eds.), *Handbook of reading research* (1st ed., Vol. 5, pp. 328–344). Routledge.

Sleeter, C. E. (2012). Confronting the marginalization of culturally responsive pedagogy. *Urban Education*, *47*(3), 562–584. https://doi.org/10.1177/0042085911431472

Tan, A. (2006). *The kitchen god's wife*. G. P. Putnam's Sons.

Vygotsky, L. S. (1978). *Mind in society: Development of higher psychological processes*. Harvard University Press.

Welsh, R. O., & Swain, W. A. (2020). (Re)defining urban education: A conceptual review and empirical exploration of the definition of urban education. *Educational Researcher*, *49*(2), 90–100. https://doi.org/10.3102/0013189X20902822

5

DESIGNING LITERACY INSTRUCTION TO SUPPORT READING IDENTITY NEGOTIATIONS

The Case of One Fifth-Grade Classroom

Kierstin Giunco, Christine M. Leighton, and Lisa M. O'Brien

Introduction

Kierstin (first author) wanted to do something different in her fifth-grade English Language Arts (ELA) class. She observed low student engagement during reading instruction and wondered if students were not seeing themselves in her curriculum. To resolve this, she intentionally designed instruction around her students, their purposes for reading, and how they built meaning of texts together and with her. She wanted to center students' reading identities and, in doing so, shift the power dynamics of the class from being teacher-centered to being student-centered. Guided by practitioner inquiry (Cochran-Smith & Lytle, 2009), Kierstin collaborated with her literacy coach, Christine (second author), to better understand balancing the sociocultural and cognitive dimensions of reading mandated by curricular standards.

We grounded our shift to student-centered curricula and instruction in the assumption that reading is not a neutral act because readers are not neutral. McCarthey and Moje (2002) remind us that readers bring varying backgrounds and experiences within a larger sociopolitical context to their interactions with text, which in turn "influences how they interact, respond, and learn in classrooms" (p. 228). Moreover, they assert engaging in literate practices can inform and change how readers view themselves. Given all that influences readers as they experience instruction in a sociocultural context (i.e., classroom), meaningful reading instruction is not simply teaching a neutral set of reading skills and strategies. It also attends to students' reading identities (Moje & Luke, 2009; Wagner, 2020) as negotiated among members within a sociocultural context (Gee, 2015).

DOI: 10.4324/9781003271406-10

We define reading identities as the situational and dynamic self-concepts (McCarthey & Moje, 2002; Moje & Luke, 2009) readers construct and negotiate across multiple, social, and fluid contexts (Gee, 2015). These constructions and negotiations occur in contexts where power relations are continually at play, and in classrooms students' efforts to exert agency in their learning can be supported or constrained by their teacher and peers (Moje & Lewis, 2007). To make space for students' evolving sense of who they were as readers, Kierstin sought to shift from a teacher-to-student unidirectional instructional flow to partnering with her students to "become jointly responsible for a process in which all grow" (Freire, 1970/2000, p. 80). Through approaches such as the students and teacher jointly defining their reading purposes, Kierstin sought to encourage students to assume control in their identity construction and negotiation as they engaged in literacy practices.

In this chapter, we discuss how Kierstin, in collaboration with Christine, conceptualized reading identity and how sociocultural theory and questions of power informed that understanding. We then describe key instructional approaches that effectively support sociocultural dimensions of literacy learning while also balancing power between teacher and students. Next, we explain how Kierstin put these theories into practice. Finally, we present findings for three purposefully selected students showing how they enacted and negotiated their reading identities with their teacher and peers while experiencing literacy instruction.

Understanding Reading Identities

Consistent with sociocultural theory, we view reading identities as a social construct involving interplay between a reader's self-concept (e.g., view of reading competence), their experiences (e.g., cultural, historical), and ways of enacting literacy practices in a social context through their interactions with and recognition by others (Gee, 2015). In other words, individual students bring to reading events varying funds of knowledge, purposes, self-concepts, and ways of enacting literacy practices that depend on their experiences in and out of school. As students enact literacy practices at school, they forge new identities that are negotiated and constructed with others in the classroom community (Skerrett, 2012, 2020). Because reading identity construction, enactment, and negotiation happen in classrooms shaped by power relations, we turned to critical sociocultural theory (Moje & Lewis, 2007) as this theoretical perspective accounts for how power and agency shape reading identity development.

Moje and Lewis (2007) suggest critical sociocultural perspectives may be the only way to explore "how children's opportunities to learn are both supported and constrained by the role of power in everyday interactions of students and teachers and by the systems and structures that shape the institution of schooling" (p. 16). Therefore, we must also consider the role agency and power play in students' negotiation and enactment of their reading identities if we are to provide teachers with actionable guidance. Moje and Lewis define agency as the "strategic making and remaking of selves, identities, activities, relationships, cultural tools and resources, and histories as embedded within relations of power" (p. 18) demonstrating just how intertwined these constructs are.

Classroom teachers play a major role in maintaining or disrupting power dynamics in the classroom. Teachers can adopt what Freire (1970/2000) calls the banking concept of education where teachers are *the* experts, do *the* instructing, and students are passive recipients of *their* knowledge. Alternatively, teachers can adopt a problem-posing concept of education where students and teachers partner to learn together. In the former approach, students' voice and agency are limited as teachers hold all power in instructional decisions. In the latter, space is created for learners to bring who they are, their reading purposes, and their ways of identity negotiation into instruction. In this context, students are empowered to exert agency and intentionally influence the flow of instruction. We argue this mutual and humanizing approach to education is critical in nurturing students' reading identities. So, how do teachers create such an instructional context?

Instructional Approaches That Support Reading Identities

Attending to reading identities during instruction is complex. As Hall (2016) explains, doing so means "teachers need to be able to provide instruction and experiences that respond to a diverse range of readers and navigate a range of social histories and identities" (p. 57). Teachers also need to support the multiple ways students express their reading identities and exercise agency, including how they strategically negotiate classroom practices (Frankel, 2016). To do so requires that teachers mediate the constant push and pull of choice and constraints in classrooms (Skerrett, 2020).

As we considered Kierstin's classroom context and this evidence, we focused on implementing more opportunities for student choice and collaboration to better make connections and empower students to construct and negotiate their multiple identities as they engaged in literacy practices. At the same time, we were mindful of school mandates, such as small-group reading instruction, and the importance of integrating reading, writing, listening, and speaking. We identified three key approaches that, when effectively joined, we believed would meet these various goals: providing student reading choice, using shared reading, and balancing cognitive and sociocultural aspects of reading (see Skerrett, 2020). Below we briefly describe each.

Scholars argue that students need access to texts that are relevant to their lives and identities (Husband & Kang, 2020; Johnson, 2018; Muhammad & Haddix, 2016; Skerrett, 2020). This is particularly true for students of color, who often experience a troubling mismatch between their identities, their teachers' identities, and classroom texts (Gay, 2013; Husband & Kang, 2020; Muhammad & Haddix, 2016). Thus, there is a need to provide a wide variety of texts aligned to students' diverse and multiple identities and promote agency by allowing students to determine which texts they find interesting and relevant (Ivey & Johnston, 2017). Offering text selection choice fosters students' understanding of themselves (Ivey & Johnston, 2017), including how they understand themselves as readers (Skerrett, 2020).

Teachers also need to consider how students collaboratively construct meaning with others. In particular, building understanding through shared reading nurtures students' reading identities (Skerrett, 2020). Yet, collaboration is situated within classroom power structures that influence how students work together to make sense of texts. Social barriers, for instance, students' perceptions of their own and others' academic abilities, can marginalize students and limit their access to academic conversations with peers (Johnson, 2018). Additionally, students and teachers may have different ideas of what it means to be a "good reader," which may create conflict and tension during instruction (Frankel, 2016). Creating space for students' agency and the varied ways they enact their reading identities permits teachers to mediate some of these challenges.

Lastly, instruction is enriched when cognitive and sociocultural practices are used in complementary ways. Connecting students' cultural, linguistic, and racial identities to literacy instruction has been shown to increase engagement (Ivey & Johnston, 2017) and reading skills (see Skerrett, 2020 for a review). For example, Levine (2014) found that students' interpretive reading skills grew when taught to strategically use everyday affective responses to move from a literal to an interpretive analysis of text. By blending cognitive and sociocultural approaches, teachers can nurture students' dynamic reading identities while also building reading skills and strategies.

Planning the Literacy Instruction

Focal instruction occurred daily during a 75-minute ELA block in a fifth-grade classroom within an urban Catholic PreK-6 school, serving 213 students (138 Black, 63 Multiracial, 7 White, 1 Asian, 4 unknown; 21.5% Hispanic, and 2% English learners). The class comprised 19 students whose ages ranged from 10.5 to 11.5 years and represented the overall school demographics.

Kierstin, a second-year elementary teacher in her first year teaching fifth grade, took an inquiry stance toward her teaching (Cochran-Smith & Lytle, 2009). She collaboratively engaged in practitioner inquiry with Christine, an associate professor of education and former elementary education teacher. Kierstin's positionality as a White woman teaching all students of color led her to question teacher-directed instruction and Eurocentric texts and shift to student-centered instruction to support and nurture students' multiple identities. With this aim, Kierstin and Christine designed fifth-grade ELA instruction that integrated student choice and shared reading, and balanced cognitive with sociocultural dimensions. The literacy block instruction (LBI) included whole-group lessons (approx. 20 minutes) followed by work time where students worked independently, in partners, or in teacher-facilitated small groups (TFSG).

Choice in Text Selection

We decided to honor students' multiple identities by ensuring access to and choice among a wide range of representative texts. We selected 65 representative texts with protagonists representative of class demographics and content we hoped connected to students' lived experiences, including stories about moving, friendship, and entrepreneurship (Giunco et al., 2020). Students browsed all books listing their favorites, and Kierstin then matched students to their preferred texts. In this way, Kierstin offered her students power and agency as they decided which texts were relevant to their lives, which in turn became "their" text for instruction. Doing so moved beyond a narrow focus on reading levels as *the* determining factor when matching students with texts and created space for attention to reading identities. Students read and annotated their self-selected texts independently for approximately 30 minutes of LBI noting questions, connections, or reactions.

Shared Reading

Students also engaged in shared reading with a partner. Kierstin asked students to identify peers they considered good learning partners and then paired students by partner and text preferences so partners read the same text. Again, choice was incorporated to make space for student agency and balance power. Partners worked together through partner journals and discussions. These opportunities provided space for students to negotiate reading purposes and co-construct understanding with one another with minimal teacher facilitation.

Partner Journals

Adapted from a teacher-student dialogue-journal framework (Feger, 2006), students wrote to their partner every other day about their texts during independent work. Students were asked to write a minimum of one sentence responding to a partner's question, four sentences responding to their reading, and one question for their partner.

Partner Discussions

Four times during the unit, students met with their partner to discuss their texts. In preparation for these discussions, students reviewed their annotations and composed one to three questions, comments, or reactions that they wanted to discuss.

Balancing Cognitive and Sociocultural Dimensions

To support cognitive factors, Kierstin also "wove in" reading skills and strategies instruction, such as modeling active reading by making personal text connections during the teacher-led portion of LBI. These same goals were then emphasized during partner work; for instance, asking students to make personal connections during partner discussions. While partner work was used to nurture agency and balance power relations as students negotiated their reading purposes (e.g., reading for enjoyment, to make connections), it is important to note that Kierstin also influenced the cognitive focus of that work by setting task parameters.

Analyzing the Literacy Instruction

Following Kierstin's inquiry stance toward her practice, we used "data of practice to investigate [her] questions critically and collaboratively" (Cochran-Smith & Lytle, 2009, p. 121). As such, we continually collected and analyzed data to help us understand students' reading identity construction, enactment, and negotiation. Below, we describe data collection and analyses.

Parents of 14 out of 19 students consented to their children's participation. We focused on three participants (student names are pseudonyms) purposefully selected to represent various aspects of student identity in the classroom, such as reading achievement, race, and gender. Reading achievement ranged (low [Yonas], low average [Briana], average [Landon]) based on schoolwide assessment scores [Measure of Academic Progress (NWEA, 2011)]. All participants identified as Black or multiracial. Two were male; one was female. All were fluent English speakers; Yonas also spoke Amharic at home.

To capture their experiences, we collected three data sources. We video-recorded 11 LBI across six weeks. Ten were transcribed; we discarded one due to audio distortion. Participants' partner discussions were audio-recorded, and Kierstin listened to recordings, taking detailed field notes. We collected participants' journal entries (5 for Yonas and Briana, 4 for Landon). Christine interviewed participants at the unit's end using an adapted interview protocol (Toppel, 2015) including questions about topics students' enjoyed reading/writing about, their perceived literacy strengths and weaknesses, and their preferred way to work with others (i.e., small groups, partners, whole class). All interviews were transcribed.

To understand the contextual and dynamic ways readers enacted and constructed identities, all authors analyzed data with collaborative coding (Smagorinsky, 2008) and content analysis (Patton, 2002). Working collaboratively allowed us to benefit from our varied expertise (i.e., classroom teacher, professors of education). Furthermore, because the third author was not involved in the classroom, she provided an outsider's perspective, allowing checks for potential bias and addressing rival theories or alternative explanations. Coding occurred in three iterative phases.

In Phase One, we developed our codebook. First, we independently reviewed one LBI transcript for observations about students' reading identities. Due to differences we observed in students' construction and negotiation, we segmented transcripts by context within each LBI (i.e., teacher-led lessons, independent work, and TFSG). We created a coding scheme for student purpose, student negotiation, and teacher negotiation to capture various sociocultural and cognitive reading dimensions and to explore power relations in the classroom. See Table 5.1 for example codes.

In Phase Two, we collaboratively applied these codes to all LBI transcripts. Because partner field notes and discussions held little direct teacher involvement,

TABLE 5.1 Example of Codes

Types of Purpose	**Student Views Reading as About...**
Accomplishment	Celebrating planned/unplanned success with reading tasks
Active (Connections)	Making connections with the text
Active (Critical)	Evaluating and making a judgment beyond the text
Active (Interpretative)	Determining implied meaning of a text
Active (Literal)	Determining explicitly stated meaning of a text
Enjoyment	Aligning to preference and interest
External Expectations	Meeting the teacher's and/or peers' agendas
Learning In and Out of School	Applying lesson learned from the text to own life
Social	Building an understanding of the text together
Type of Student Negotiation	**Student Negotiates Their Literacy Learning By...**
Autonomous	Setting and following own agenda
Contribute	Recognizing and following teacher agenda as presented
Displace	Positioning a peer's agenda as inferior
Help-Seeking	Relying on expert and seeking approval
Social Partnership (Peer to Peer)	Building understanding with peers and recognizing their contributions as valuable
Social Partnership (Student to Teacher)	Building understanding with teacher and recognizing her contributions as valuable
Strategic Agent	Recognizing and following teacher's agenda but in own way
Type of Teacher Negotiation	**The Teacher Responds By...**
Acknowledge	Neutrally affirming contribution
Acknowledge-Constrain	Acknowledging contribution but following with restriction
Constrain	Restricting the student's agenda/contribution
Recognize as valuable	Allowing student's contribution to direct the conversation

Note: If the student's contribution is related to behavior or procedure, and not directly related to reading (NDR), it was coded NDR.

they did not lend themselves to coding for teacher negotiation. Therefore, we coded these for student purpose and negotiation.

In Phase Three, we conducted case study analysis (Yin, 2018) for a nuanced exploration of how readers constructed and negotiated reading identities in various contexts and spaces. Specifically, we calculated the frequency of reading purposes and student and teacher negotiation styles. To triangulate findings and simultaneously center students' voices, we created narrative profiles (Seidman, 2019) from each student's interview using their own words. Doing so also provided us greater insight into how students viewed their reading purposes and negotiation styles.

Reflecting on Literacy Instruction Analysis

Because we found each student had their own ways of "being" a reader, below we provide what we learned about individual cases (i.e., students' reading purposes and negotiation styles [teacher and student] during classroom-based tasks). Each case concludes with a narrative profile to emphasize each student's reading identity portrayal in their words.

Briana

Literacy Block Instruction

Briana was an active participant in LBI who often read to meet Kierstin's expectations and demonstrate accomplishment, particularly when working independently. For example, she frequently clarified directions and then expressed pride when experiencing success such as calling out "Ms. G!" to share her progress on a spelling game. Presumably, her desire to meet expectations seemed linked with her desire to be seen as successful by the teacher. In fact, during independent work, her enthusiasm to share her progress sometimes led her to distract other students or miss directions, and she was more frequently redirected behaviorally or constrained by Kierstin.

During LBI, Briana's negotiation styles varied. In addition to contributing to Kierstin's agenda during teacher-led instruction and independent work, she negotiated through help-seeking like asking Kierstin about a word's pronunciation or definition. During independent work and TFSG, Briana also negotiated for autonomy and strategic agency in her learning, and Kierstin's responses to Briana varied. For example, in one exchange, Briana expressed concern about finishing a book in time. Kierstin recognized this and reassured Briana that she would not be rushed to finish. Other times, Kierstin constrained Briana, such as when Briana did not want to mark down her thoughts while reading on sticky notes, but Kierstin asked her to do it anyway. Overall, during LBI, there appeared to be a back-and-forth in power relations between Briana and Kierstin.

Partner Discussions and Journals

In partner discussions, Briana read for social purposes by making personal connections and asking questions that required her partner to share an opinion. During these instances, she negotiated through social partnership; however, at times Briana negotiated by contributing. For example, when Briana shared a quote and said, "I'm done" rather than trying to co-construct with her partner, she focused on contributing her ideas as the task required then moved on to her partner's turn. Similarly, once Briana and her partner determined they were finished, they would engage in conversations irrelevant to their texts.

During partner journals, Briana demonstrated that she also read for accomplishment and enjoyment. She celebrated finishing different texts: "I am so glad that we finished the book!!! When we get new books we always finish our book so I think we should keep up the good work." In addition, she enacted all types of active reading, including critical interpretations such as "I really think that his boss should give a raise." Briana negotiated these reading purposes by partnering with her peer. That said, other times, Briana negotiated through contributing as she met expectations but did not deeply engage with her partner to build understanding. For example, Briana followed directions to write about their text by summarizing a plot point, but her entry did not prompt for collaborative meaning making.

Overall, these spaces appeared to be a place of "equal partnership" between Briana and her partner; yet, there were moments where she seemed to "go through the motions" to meet Kierstin's agenda and expectations. Kierstin held power by setting activity parameters; in turn, Briana met them but at times did so with little enthusiasm.

Interview

The following narrative profile provides Briana's perspective on herself as a reader.

> I take my time when I read to make sure I actually understand what I'm reading and not just trying to keep up with the other person. I think I'm good at the writing part and the reading part, cause– well we have to do journals. Because when [my partner] writes, I can take off some of her ideas, whatever she wrote and think what she's thinking of and put it to what I think of. I like whole groups because sometimes you don't just want to hear one friend's idea, you want to hear multiple. Like with [my partner] it is fun reading with her, but I feel like if you have two more people it's like, you can hear their part and what they have to say.

Her statements about reading for enjoyment, making connections, and social purposes aligned with the reading purposes we observed during instruction. In addition, she described journals as a context where she was able to build meaning with her partner, matching the times we observed her negotiating through social partnership. However, she said that sometimes she wished partner work would be expanded to include others as she valued hearing multiple perspectives. This may explain, in part, her shift away from social partnership we observed during partner activities, as she was ready to collaborate with more peers.

Landon

Literacy Block Instruction

Landon frequently participated during LBI and seemed to hold competing desires and purposes. Often, Landon engaged in behaviors not directly related to reading, such as asking if he could move his seat, moving around the classroom to get something, and at times, bickering with classmates. He frequently asked Kierstin for reminders and sometimes expressed annoyance with a task. Yet, he still frequently engaged with Kierstin, seeking her help to ensure he met her expectations. This push and pull is exemplified in the following exchange:

KG: Have you been doing your sticky notes, Landon?
LANDON: This is my first one.
KG: Okay.
LANDON: How many do we need again?
KG: I'm hoping the whole thing [notepad] is gone by the time you're done with the book.
LANDON: What?!
KG: Lots of thoughts, Landon. Lots of thoughts.

Kierstin checked to see if Landon was on task. He confirmed he met her expectations and clarified how many sticky notes were needed. When she responded, he expressed dismay at her expectations; in a good-natured tone of voice, she explained she expected him to have lots of thoughts while reading. We see him negotiating with Kierstin by seeking her help on the task but then attempting to exert autonomy (i.e., saying "what?!" suggested he did not want to do it). Like Briana, Kierstin constrained Landon most during independent work, often to keep him on task, and we see vacillation over whose agenda is maintained.

Partner Discussions and Journals

During partner discussions, Landon demonstrated his purpose was active reading to interpret the plot and make predictions. Additionally, power relations between his partner and the teacher occurred in interesting ways. This is exemplified during a partner discussion wherein Landon acted as a strategic agent.

While discussing a book Landon commented that he did not write a question but thereafter posed one for his partner to consider. In this way, he still met the teacher's agenda of asking a question but did so on his terms. Other times, Landon and his partner argued and in one discussion, they displaced each other. They disagreed about the main characters' friendship to the point that they called into question each other's ability to interpret the text correctly.

Landon continued to negotiate for agency and autonomy during partner journals. Kierstin directed students to use journals as a space for partners to engage with each other's ideas; yet, Landon often wrote his as an independent entry. There was limited indication that he read his partner's entry as he did not respond to any of his partner's questions. He demonstrated he read actively as he wrote about text interpretations, made personal connections, and included his thoughts and opinions, but he defined using the journal as a personal diary rather than a dialogue journal. As Kierstin minimally directed this activity, he had the power to direct the activity content.

Interview

Landon's narrative profile offers insight into his ways of being a reader.

> I'm a really good reader. Any reading I'm good at. I can spell really big words. I'll try to look up words or try to find like the hardest words to spell. Anywhere I can find them I will try to study them. I like to spell cause I could help them one day if they don't know how to spell stuff. I could one day maybe like give [Kierstin] spelling words for a test. I enjoy talking about basketball books or chapter books. I like [whole] group because I like to hear people's opinions on what we're talking about.

In several ways, Landon's narrative profile aligned with our observation and analysis, particularly his active participation during LBI and his agentic efforts (e.g., stating he can help his peers, wanting to give the words for the spelling test). He demonstrated his sense of pride in his abilities and accomplishments, and he expressed interest in socially engaging with his peer's opinions related to the text. In this way, his narrative profile allowed us to see additional aspects of Landon's reading identity that were not always as apparent during instruction.

Yonas

Literacy Block Instruction

Yonas tended to read actively and meet expectations during LBI, particularly during teacher-led instruction. However, during independent time, he also argued with peers (e.g., disagreeing about whose turn it was to write in the journals) or walked around the classroom. As such, he engaged in tasks not directly related to reading more during independent work. Yonas showed different patterns when collaborating in TFSG, such as making more personal connections. Consider this conversation as Kierstin works in a small group with Yonas and Mark while reading about Mahatma Gandhi:

KG: And Yonas, do any of your sticky notes tell us something at least about what he's doing in India?
YONAS: Yeah … he talked in the book how … like when you're in India it's like you just feel the connection to your ancestors… I want to see my notes.
MARK: He says such specific things.
YONAS: I can't find it. He, I think he had a speech.
KG: Okay
YONAS: …It shows power of words, like Martin Luther King.
KG: Oh! I love that!

During this exchange, Yonas demonstrated his purpose to read actively, and his negotiation shifted from solely contributing to Kierstin's agenda by answering her question to a social partnership as he explained his connection to Martin Luther King, Jr. Kierstin recognized his connection as valuable and Yonas's partner also joined in when he commented on the author's specificity in their text. In this way, all three held joint responsibility for understanding the text.

Partner Discussion and Journals

In both formats, Yonas worked in a group of three. In partner discussions, Yonas read for social purposes. Frequently, he asked his partners questions and elaborated on their answers. For example, during one discussion, Yonas and his partners discussed Gandhi's sacrifices, particularly going to jail and risking his life. By working together, they deepened their understanding of Gandhi's life, with Yonas' concluding: "If he was sentenced to jail and death, he at least had respect on his name to die. If you had the guts to die for something you love, then you really know what is happening."

In Yonas's partner journals, he initially built understanding through social partnership but shifted after a few entries. In his first two entries, he demonstrated his desire to engage his peers in active reading by asking: "Who do you think [Gandhi] got inspired by?" After asking this question twice and receiving no response from his peers, in remaining entries, he negotiated by contributing to Kierstin's agenda; he met task requirements but stopped engaging his partners in discussion. In this situation, Yonas's purposes and agency appear to be constrained by his peers.

Interview

The following narrative profile presents Yonas's views of himself as a reader.

> I was talking about in my journal how like some people get inspired. [My character] gets inspired by his dad and I get inspired by multiple people. I like stories that have a lesson. I can go really fast with reading and writing. I like reading with one person, like a school teacher. I [also] like a small group because if you do it with a partner, that partner is one person that you discuss with. If you discuss with the whole class, there's a lot of people. A group is small and you can just share your thoughts and they can share their thoughts.

In Yonas' narrative profile, he described reading actively to interpret and make connections to the text by discussing sources of inspiration. He described his preference to work with the teacher and in a small group, aligning with what we saw during TFSG and partner discussions. Yonas often demonstrated a desire to partner with others, yet we also observed tension with his teacher and peers during independent work over completing task objectives.

Discussion

Using practitioner inquiry, we explored how students enacted and negotiated their reading identities during literacy instruction by examining their reading purposes, teacher negotiation styles, and student negotiation styles. Our findings suggest that teachers can balance sociocultural dimensions with cognitive dimensions of reading development. For example, teachers can use representative texts and shared reading to create a context where multiple reading identities are nurtured rather than narrowly focusing on reading skills with leveled text. When they do, it provides students opportunities to "try on" differing ways of being a reader and exert agency. As we consider how Kierstin did this, we also recognized that this process is nuanced and complex in that teachers must weave together myriad factors, including individual (e.g., interest, lived experience, growing need for agency) and contextual (e.g., curricular mandates, power dynamics, social). To provide teachers guidance in making space for students to have a prominent role in shaping their reading identities, we share lessons learned from our observations in one fifth-grade classroom.

First, when teachers create differing spaces for students to enact literacy practices and choose what they read, why they are reading, and with whom they read, students have opportunities to "try out" various aspects of their developing literate identities. We observed a shift in students' reading purposes and negotiation styles depending on how students engaged in literacy practices in a sociocultural context (e.g., through teacher-led discussions, in partner discussions, in partner journals). As we looked across these spaces, we gained a fuller picture of students' reading purposes and negotiation styles. For example, during teacher-led instruction, Yonas focused mainly on following Kierstin's expectations by contributing to her agenda; however, during TFSG he shifted to partnering with her and his partner as they co-constructed meaning of the text.

Second, when teachers distribute power between students and themselves, students take this up in productive and complex ways. We observed that in certain spaces (e.g., independent work, partner journals) students more often attempted to negotiate literacy practices through strategic agency and autonomy. Concurrently, Kierstin varied her negotiation style, suggesting this shifting power dynamic was not free of tension. During independent work, Kierstin frequently constrained students, particularly when she determined they were not on task or not engaged with the reading as she designated. Yet, during partner journals and discussions, Kierstin seemed to "let go" of her agenda by allowing students to steer the direction of their learning. While Kierstin fostered mutual partnership in these spaces, students, at times, played out their own power relations as they either engaged with their partner's ideas or constrained them. Our observations of three students show some of the ways students and teachers are often "mired" in power relations (Moje & Lewis, 2007, p. 17) that are difficult to disrupt.

Finally, we recognize that although these three students benefited from Kierstin's instruction in many ways, there were some missed opportunities for broader considerations of race, power, and oppression and for students to engage in "true reflection and action upon reality" (Freire, 1970/2000, p. 84). This is important because identity development is influenced by individual, local (e.g., classroom, peer-group), and distal contexts [e.g., sociopolitical, historical (Muhammad & Haddix, 2016)]. For example, while we attempted to support students' identities through their immediate circumstances (e.g., protagonists that were relevant to their lives), we did not contextualize this conversation within wider sociopolitical events occurring at the time (e.g., Black Lives Matter movement). This lesson raised several questions for us: What would happen if students were included in explicit discussions around their literate identities within local and distal contexts? How would students' literate identities be nurtured if Kierstin more intentionally made space for students to reflect and act on their realities while reading about topics of importance to them and their community? These questions informed the next phase of their work together as Kierstin continued working with the students in sixth grade.

Findings suggest that teachers can create instructional contexts that simultaneously distribute power and make space for students' reading identities. Teachers and practitioner researchers can draw from Kierstin's and her students' experiences as they work toward understanding and implementing practices that center students' literate identities.

Discussion Questions

1 How were Kierstin and Christine successful at adapting curricula to create space for students to construct and negotiate reading identities? What else might they try?
2 How did Kierstin and Christine take up a critical sociocultural perspective? What next steps are important for implementing critical pedagogy?
3 How can we draw from reading identity theories to help teacher-researchers understand and foster students' reading identities?

References

Cochran-Smith, M., & Lytle, S. L. (2009). *Inquiry as stance: Practitioner research for the next generation*. Teachers College Press.

Feger, M. (2006). I want to read: How culturally relevant texts increase student engagement in reading. *Multicultural Education, 13*, 18–19.

Frankel, K. (2016). The intersection of reading and identity in high school literacy intervention classes. *Research in Teaching of English, 51*(1), 37–59.

Freire, P. (2000). *Pedagogy of the oppressed* (30th anniversary ed.). Continuum. (Original work published in 1970).

Gay, G. (2013). Teaching to and through cultural diversity. *Curriculum Inquiry, 43*(1), 48–70. https://doi.org/10.1111/curi.12002

Gee, J. P. (2015). *Social linguistics and literacies: Ideology in discourses* (5th ed.). Routledge.

Giunco, K., Leighton, C. M., & Balthazar, K. (2020). Enhancing reading engagement through the use of representative texts and grade-level "literacy partners". *Massachusetts Research Association Primer, 48*(2), 24–38.

Hall, L. A. (2016). The role of identity in reading comprehension development. *Reading & Writing Quarterly, 32*(1), 56–80. https://doi.org/10.1080/10573569.2013.861332

Husband, T., & Kang, G. (2020). Identifying promising literacy practices for Black males in P-12 classrooms: An integrative review. *Journal of Language and Literacy Education, 16*(1), 1–34.

Ivey, G., & Johnston, P. (2017). Emerging adolescence in engaged reading communities. *Language Arts, 94*(3), 159–169.

Johnson, A. M. (2018). Scholastic liberation: Schools' impact on African American academic achievement. *Language Arts Journal of Michigan, 34*(1), 32–37. https://doi.org/10.9707/2168-149X.2198

Levine, S. (2014). Making interpretation visible with an affect-based strategy. *Reading Research Quarterly, 49*(3), 283–303. https://doi.org/10.1002/rrq.71

McCarthey, S. J., & Moje, E. B. (2002). Conversations: Identity matters. *Reading Research Quarterly, 37*(2), 228–238. https://doi.org/10.1598/RRQ.37.2.6

Moje, E. B., & Lewis, C. (2007). Examining opportunities to learn literacy: The role of critical sociocultural literacy research. In C. Lewis, P. Enciso, & E. B. Moje (Eds.), *Reframing sociocultural research on literacy: Identity, agency and power* (pp. 15–48). Lawrence Erlbaum Associates. https://doi.org/10.4324/9781003064428-3

Moje, E. B., & Luke, A. (2009). Literacy and identity: Examining the metaphors in history and contemporary research. *Reading Research Quarterly, 44*(4), 415–437. https://doi.org/10.1598/RRQ.44.4.7

Muhammad, G. E., & Haddix, M. (2016). Centering Black girls' literacies: A review of literature on the multiple ways of knowing of Black girls. *English Education, 48*(4), 299–336.

Northwest Evaluation Association. (2011). *Technical Manual for Measure of Academic Progress & Measure of Academic Progress for Primary Grades.* https://www.richland2.org/RichlandDistrict/media/Richland-District/AdvancED/Standard%205/5.1/5-1-NWEA-Technical-Manual-for-MAP-and-MPG.pdf

Patton, M. Q. (2002). *Qualitative research & evaluation methods* (3rd ed.). SAGE.

Seidman, I. (2019). *Interviewing as qualitative research* (5th ed.). Teachers College Press.

Skerrett, A. (2012). "We hatched in this class": Repositioning of identity in and beyond a reading classroom. *The High School Journal, 95*(3), 62–75. https://doi.org/10.1353/hsj.2012.0008

Skerrett, A. (2020). Social and cultural differences in reading development: Instructional processes, learning gains, and challenges. In E. B. Moje, P. P. Afflerback, P. Enciso, & N. K. Lesaux (Eds.), *Handbook of reading research* (Vol. 5, pp. 328–344). Routledge. https://doi.org/10.4324/9781315676302-17

Smagorinsky, P. (2008). The method section as conceptual epicenter in constructing social science research reports. *Written Communication, 25*(3), 389–411. https://doi.org/10.1177%2F0741088308317815

Toppel, K. (2015). Enhancing core reading programs with culturally responsive practices. *The Reading Teacher, 68*(7), 552–559. https://doi.org/10.1002/trtr.1348

Wagner, C. J. (2020). Seeing and nurturing young children's reading identities. *Journal of Language and Literacy Education, 16*(1), 1–14.

Yin, R. K. (2018). *Case study research and applications: Design and methods* (6th ed.). SAGE.

6

"THEY WILL SHUT YOU OUT IF THEY THINK YOU CAN'T READ"

Navigating Diverse Models of Identity in an Eighth-Grade Classroom

Leigh A. Hall

Introduction

> I'm very good at reading... I'm one of the best readers in here. And most people, they know I can read very well and so that's why you see so many people asking me for help all the time and I help them because I can... I think when you're one of the best readers you should help others who have a hard time

Christina (all names are pseudonyms) was an eighth-grade student in Ms. Winters' English class. Her statement is a reminder that how students self-identify as readers, and how they are identified by their peers and teachers, shapes the experiences they have with reading in school (Hall, 2016). Students' identities as readers are formed at an early age (Wagner, 2019). Through their experiences with reading, students formulate their understandings about what it means to be a particular type of reader (i.e., good/bad) and then categorize themselves based on which profile they believe they fit. Their identities are then reinforced over time through their experiences with reading in school.

A number of factors can contribute to how students identify as readers as well as how others identify them. How teachers talk about reading can send messages about what it means to be a particular type of reader as well as the kind of reader a teacher believes a student is. Students who experience a more autonomous, skill-based approach will often judge how successful they are based on how quickly and easily they can learn and apply skills and strategies (Moses & Qiao, 2018). However, classrooms that privilege meaning-making, see reading as a social activity, and view skill development as a process can help students develop a more

DOI: 10.4324/9781003271406-11

positive experience with reading early on and create a dynamic, and more fluid, view of themselves as readers (Nkomo, 2018).

Instruction though is not the only factor that shapes students' reading identities. Students experience reading among their peers inside the social world of their classroom. Through social interactions (i.e., who gets to speak about texts; whose questions are valued), students position each other as particular types of readers (Skerrett, 2012). Once these positions are established, they are likely to take root and remain in place as students progress through the grades.

Although research on reading identities with adolescents is limited, it has primarily focused on understanding students who self-identify as poor readers (Enriquez, 2011; Hall 2016). Students who see themselves as poor readers may embody their identity and behave in ways they believe align with it (Enriquez, 2011). They may struggle to get their teachers and peers to find value in what they have to say (Glenn et al., 2016). This can result in them reading very little, failing to complete assignments, and limiting their participation around texts. These students are aware of their decisions, and the consequences of their actions, but often believe they have nothing to offer and do not want to expose their perceived weaknesses to their peers.

Less research has focused on students with positive reading identities and how those identities play out not just when they read but when they interact with other students around texts and instruction. Students with positive reading identities are more likely to attempt challenging texts, apply reading instruction, and participate in text-based discussions (Hall, 2012a). They believe that their contributions are seen as valuable and could help others improve as readers, which could result in them participating more frequently (Learned et al., 2017). However, their view as providing valuable contributions may lead some of them to engage in actions that marginalize students with a more negative reading identity (Hall, 2012a).

Understanding not just how reading identities are communicated but how they are enacted by students who are seen as being among the best readers is critical. Students like Christina are positioned in ways, by both teachers and students, that give them privileges and power that students who are identified as poor or struggling readers do not possess. Looking at how students like Christina enact their reading identity, and how they use it to frame their interactions with others, can provide important information about the social dynamics of middle school classrooms and how to structure interactions and experiences with texts so that they support the positive development of reading identities for all students.

In this chapter, I drew on a year-long case study, conducted in a middle school classroom, to examine:

1. How does a teacher understand models of reading identities and assign them to students?
2. How does a student, who is identified as an excellent reader, enact her reading identities in social contexts?

Theoretical Framework

Drawing on sociocultural perspectives, reading identities can be understood as how students define themselves in relation to institutional norms regarding what it means to be a particular kind of reader (i.e., good, average, or poor). These norms create what Wortham (2006; p. 30) has referred to as "models of identity." Models of identity are explicit accounts, typically communicated through language, that state the characteristics associated with a given identity. Models of identity provide a framework for what it means to be a certain type of reader within a given context and serve as a way to create and reinforce the reading identities students place on themselves and each other.

In classrooms, models of identity for reading are often centered on the skills and strategies that students do/do not possess (O'Brien et al., 2009). Reading identities are then grounded in an autonomous model (Street, 1984) where reading is viewed as a neutral, skill-based practice without any social or cultural influences. As a result, how adolescents are identified as readers in school is often connected to how well they do/do not enact the skills that align with teachers' expectations of what they should know and be able to do at a given age (Coombs, 2012). Over time, as the models are reinforced and reenacted, a habitus begins to form where students' past histories and experiences with reading inform their current ones and patterns around what it means to be a particular type of reader continue to be reinforced (Bourdieu & Wacquant, 1992).

As a result, power structures form and become more recognizable over time. Through classroom interactions, students send messages about who is/is not considered knowledgeable about what is read and discussed in class (Wodak, 2011). Students who have obtained a good reader identity become more likely to control interactions around texts and are viewed as the ones who engage with texts in "correct" ways (White & Lowenthal, 2011). Students who have a history of being seen as a poor reader are more likely to be viewed as not having anything of value to contribute and may be silenced and shut out by their peers (Hall, 2016). Therefore, taking a closer look at how these interactions and power structures play out in classrooms, particularly as it relates to a student who possesses a positive reading identity, can help educators design instruction that works to undo them and, ideally, limit or even prevent their formation.

Methods

This study took place in Ms. Winters' eighth-grade English class at Hazelwood Middle School and focused on designing instruction that supported and/or maintained positive reading identity development for all students. Ms. Winters was in her ninth year as an English teacher at Hazelwood Middle School. She had a master's degree in reading, was licensed as a reading specialist, was certified to teach English for grades 6–12, and was chair of the English Department.

While Ms. Winters was new to the concept of reading identities, she was interested in how reading identities intersected with instruction and what she could do to better understand and be responsive to them.

Twenty students were in the class that this study was situated in. Fifteen students were White, four were African-American, and one was Hispanic. Seventy percent of the students scored below grade level on the end-of-year reading exam in the seventh grade.

I identified five focal students in order to understand how their reading identities were enacted and shaped by instruction and classroom interactions. Table 6.1 provides demographic information on each student including how they identified as readers at the start of the study. In this chapter, I focus on how the student who self-identified as an excellent reader, Christina, interacted with others in relation to her understanding of what it meant to be identified as a particular type of reader.

Study Design and Data Sources

The study with Ms. Winters was a formative design (Reinking & Bradley, 2007) that focused on understanding how instruction could be created that supported and/or maintained positive reading identity development. I took field notes two to three times per week for 50 minutes each and completed 60 observations. I documented all instructional tasks and reading instruction that took place as well as how each focal student engaged with instruction and assignments. All students completed a questionnaire in September, January, and May to understand how they identified themselves as readers over time and what they were/were not doing as it related to classroom reading practices.

Ms. Winters, and each focal student, were privately interviewed four times (September/November/January/May). During the interviews with Ms. Winters, I discussed her approach to understanding and being responsive to reading identities and her interpretations of what was happening with each focal student. For the focal students, I focused on understanding what I had observed, their approaches to reading in and out of school, how they identified themselves as readers, and how and why those identities did or did not shift over time. Through observations, questionnaires, and interviews, I was able to understand how and

TABLE 6.1 Focal Student Demographics

Name	*Reading Level*	*Identity*	*Ethnicity*	*Native Language*
Antony	3.4	Poor	African-American	English
Sylvia	6.1	Poor	Hispanic	Otomi
Dana	6.4	Good	Caucasian	English
Christina	9.4	Good	Caucasian	English
Nolan	9.9	Poor	Caucasian	English

why students held particular reading identities, how their identities did/did not evolve over time, and how they used their identities to frame both what they did in the classroom and their interactions with others.

Data Analysis

For data analysis, I followed the recommendations of Saldaña (2016). For each research question, I engaged in an iterative, inductive approach where I sought to identify patterns within the data without imposing a set of codes upon it. My first step was to review transcripts, field notes, and questionnaires to learn how Ms. Winters understood models of reading identities. I looked for evidence where she explicitly communicated, either to me or to students, what it meant to be a particular type of reader. Next, I considered how Christina understood the available models of identity and identified places where she explicitly communicated not just what made someone a particular type of reader but also who she placed into the existing categories. I then looked for how she enacted her understanding of what it meant to be an excellent reader alongside what it meant to work with students she considered to be poor readers.

Once I had established pattern codes for each of the above areas, I collapsed patterns that were related and grouped them together under themes (e.g., types of reader, reader characteristics, use of power). Once themes had been established, I developed assertions. I then grouped themes and patterns under the appropriate claim.

Findings

Understanding and Assigning Models of Identity

When I started working with Ms. Winters', her definition of the models of identity students could have been constructed through an autonomous model of reading (Street, 1984). For example, in explaining her model of identity for a good reader Mrs. Winters told me:

> By 8th-grade, students should have a fair amount of reading skills under their belt. I expect that they will need continued instruction because reading can still be hard and many of them have not acquired the skills of a good reader...So I look at who my struggling readers are, and I learn what skills they need help with, and I try to provide that on a regular basis.

Ms. Winters was also aware of students' histories with reading in school through conversations with previous teachers and reviewing report cards and test scores. She used this information, particularly at the beginning of the year, to inform her understanding about students as readers. For example, in discussing Christina,

Ms. Winters explained to me, "Christina is an outstanding reader! Her grades are strong, and she has a history of being a leader. I expect that to continue this year."

However, in discussing Antony, who had a history of being a poor reader, Ms. Winters said:

> Antony has always had difficulties in school, particularly with reading. You can look at his history and see that his grades are always very low, and so are his test scores. He tests below grade-level in reading every year...I hope I can help him turn it around this year, but I'm realistic about where he is starting.

At the start of the school year, Ms. Winters was able to go through her roster and provide an explanation of which students she identified as being excellent, average, or poor readers. Once students had been assigned a reading identity, it appeared to stick. Students who had acquired a positive one did not need to continue to demonstrate the characteristics that aligned with it. Students who were assigned a positive reading identity but did not engage with or limited their involvement with classroom reading practices, were still seen as strong readers but were labeled as being "lazy" or "unmotivated" when it came to reading in school.

For example, Nolan was able to read texts on a high school and college level and was considered by Ms. Winters to be an exceptional reader. At the start of the school year, he was reading George Orwell's 2021 for the second time and was able to discuss it at length. In describing Nolan as a reader, Ms. Winters' said:

> Nolan is absolutely one of the best and most brilliant students I have ever had...He is an amazing reader - like off the charts amazing - and he asks the most challenging questions about what we read in here...He's quiet though, pretty reserved, I'd say a little shy, and he doesn't participate a whole lot...when he chooses to talk I think a lot of what he says might go over the other kids' heads.

During the eight months I spent in Ms. Winters' class, I rarely saw Nolan contribute to classroom discussions or participate in small groups unless he was specifically asked. He also developed a pattern of turning in assignments that were partially completed at best—if he turned them in at all. However, his low grades and lack of participation did not change his status as an exceptional and brilliant reader. Instead, Ms. Winters' believed that he was likely "bored" and that she needed to do more to challenge and motivate him.

Compare this against Antony. Antony was also in Ms. Winters' class but tested on a third-grade reading level and had spent his school career being identified as a poor/struggling reader. Antony did not openly demonstrate that he had acquired, or was interested in acquiring, the reading skills and strategies that were appropriate for his grade. He rarely submitted assignments and was not passing most of his classes.

However, like Nolan, Antony had a thriving independent reading practice. He regularly visited the public library with his family and loved to read nonfiction. He could engage in conversations about what he was reading if you asked him, and he could tell you what he was hoping to read in the future. However, when I spoke to Ms. Winters about him in November she said:

> Antony has a lot of difficulties with reading...He almost didn't pass the seventh grade, and he had to go to summer school to get here...He rarely participates, doesn't turn his work in, and I don't see him really doing what he needs to do so that he can get better at reading. I have a lot of concerns about him.

While Antony may have enjoyed reading outside of school, his reading abilities were not on par with Nolan's. However, in order to shift out of being identified as a poor reader, Antony needed to engage in actions that aligned with Ms. Winters' model of identity of a good one. Regardless of what Antony thought of himself as a reader, and regardless of if he held the same model of identity as Ms. Winters, he could not make such a shift until he aligned with the good reader model as it was defined by her.

Enacting Models of Identity: The Privileges and Influence of a "Good" Reader

Students in Ms. Winters' class, who had a history of being identified as good readers, had more control over who they worked with and how they participated in discussions and assignments that were text-based. Other students regularly sought them out to work with and viewed what they had to say as being valuable and helpful in their learning. During my time in Ms. Winters' classroom, Christina emerged as being considered one of the best readers and someone who was highly sought after for assistance and insight into reading-based assignments. During the year, I documented 12 out of 20 students making a total of 62 statements about Christina's reading abilities that positioned her as being a strong reader who could help others better understand texts. For example, one student said to me, "Christina always helps me when I get stuck on a word or something. She always knows what it means."

Students' perceptions of Christina as someone who was an excellent reader resulted in her being in high demand when doing small group work. Ms. Winters typically had students work in groups one to two times a week. On average, students were able to select their own groups 65 percent of the time. When allowed to form their own groups, students explicitly wanted Christina to join their group and would call out to her. For example, one day I observed a student yelling across the room, "Christina will you let me work with you? Please! Let me join your group."

I spoke to students about what motivated them to seek out Christina. Collectively, students explained that when given the opportunity to form their own groups, the reading abilities of the other students in it were important. Patrick explained:

> I'm a good reader, but I need to put myself in a group with other good readers. I think my group will do fine no matter what, because the good readers will get it done, but your group members are important, they can help you learn and stuff and make sure it all gets done…I just want good readers in my group because I know I can count on them.

When I talked to Christina about how she decided who to work with, she explained that she paid attention to the type of reader each student was:

> I'm picky about who I will let join my group, and that's because I care about my grade. The type of reader is important. You have to think about how good of a reader each person is because if you get a bad one, watch out! Like they are not good. They will probably not read or do any of the work.

Students who were not identified as good readers often found themselves on the sidelines when groups were being formed. They were not invited to groups and were often only let into a group as a last resort. These students were aware of their status and, while they agreed that they did have reading difficulties, they believed they had something of importance that could be offered to their group. When I asked Antony his thoughts on how student selected their groups he explained:

> …some people are very popular because they are smart and everyone wants to work with them, and they don't want me because they think that I'm not smart and can't read…Reading is hard for me, but I think I ask good questions that people don't always think of, and I pay attention.

While Ms. Winters liked to give students choice in who they worked with, she noted, "they largely just work with the same people each time. I think it's important that they work with a range of people and learn how to do that well." In assigning groups, Ms. Winters told me that she tried to create mixed-ability groups based on students' reading abilities. However, she viewed the students who were in the position of being the good reader as the leader of each group. She said:

> When I think about students who are really strong readers, I really see them as having a strong leadership potential. Students know that they [the good readers] are good at reading and will show up to the group prepared to do the work. They also know that it's these students who can help them

> better understand something...And obviously many of them [the good readers] are fine taking that role on because reading comes so easily for them, and they can really be a resource and a model for other students.

When I spoke with Christina about her perceptions of being assigned to a group, she told me that she preferred to create "a team of very good readers" but understood that sometimes she would have to work with people she would not normally select and that she was expected to take a leadership role. However, she did not see the approach as successful because, according to her, students who were poor readers, "...don't pay attention or really do anything in the group but they do get the good grade that the rest of us worked for...I try to help them. I tell them what to do, but they ignore me."

Antony however had a different take on working in assigned groups where a student was positioned as being the good reader and thus the leader. He noted that often these students "don't listen to what anyone else has to say." He explained that it was often the leader who tried to enforce their ideas and interpretations of a reading onto the group as being the correct ones. Finally, Antony noted that the student positioned as the leader did not appear interested in his questions. He said:

> I kinda give up on these groups because whoever's in charge doesn't listen...And I can ask a question and it'll get ignored or someone will say, "We've already answered that" and I can't get anyone to talk to me about it...And if I offer an idea I'm told I'm wrong and sometimes I know I'm not...They don't listen to me.

Antony's experiences highlight a critical tension in creating a culture where certain students are positioned as the leader and a more knowledgeable other. Students placed in leadership positions will have their own interpretation of what their role entails and may believe that their ideas, questions, and interpretations carry more weight. They will likely not view students like Antony as equals who can play an important role in discussions about texts.

When Good Readers Dominate: Understanding Power Dynamics

During my time in Ms. Winters' classroom, I witnessed how Christina was able to use her status as an excellent reader to dominate discussions and shut down students who were considered to be poor readers. Christina repeatedly talked over students she considered to be poor readers, told them that their ideas were "wrong," and excluded them from group activities as much as possible. For example, during a whole class discussion about Sharon Draper's *Forged by Fire* (1998), Ms. Winters asked students to summarize what the first chapter was about.

When Sylvia was called on, she stated, "Chapter 1 is about Gerald when he was very little, and he was playing with fire, and he caught the house on fire."

Christina began to talk over Sylvia saying:

> That isn't right. Gerald's mom caught him playing with a lighter and punished him. She was very mean, and she tried to teach Gerald not to play with fire, but he didn't listen. His mom left him alone so she could go out and get drugs and while she was gone, he started a fire, but it was an accident. He almost died.
>
> Sylvia looked over at Christina, "What I said is right."

Christina replied, "Uh, not really. Maybe like a little right, but mostly it wasn't."

When I talked to Christina about these types of interactions, she appeared to be more than aware of them. She nodded her head and explained:

> Some of the kids in this class they are not the best at reading, and what they have to say is wrong. They should listen to what I say because I can help them…I can help them know more about a book or sometimes it might even help them get better at reading just a tiny bit…and we shouldn't be listening to an answer that's wrong because that can just confuse people anyways.

"Do you think," I asked, "that it should be up to Ms. Winters to decide what to do if an answer is wrong or incomplete?"

> I guess, but it drives me crazy! Like, why should we have to sit around and listen to wrong answers and stuff when there are people who have the right ones and can tell everyone?

While Christina may have tried to talk over or shut down ideas she deemed as wrong, she did not view her actions as inappropriate. Instead, she saw herself as a knowledgeable member of the classroom community who could help her peers—a task she appeared to take very seriously. When I spoke to Ms. Winters about Christina and how she engaged in discussions she seemed unaware that Christina shut down other students. Instead, she told me that she thought Christina often tried to "help out others, especially when someone is confused about something we've read."

Antony and Sylvia were both aware of how they were shut down by Christina. In an interview with Antony, he brought up how Christina often refused to let him speak or outright ignored him:

> I know she thinks I can't read and that she is always right, but she needs to let others talk. She does that to everyone she thinks isn't a good reader…

> like we should only listen to her or other people she thinks are good at reading, and that's just not right...I don't care if someone gets an answer right...I want to learn and talking helps me learn. Listening to other people helps me learn.

Students who self-identified as good readers also seemed aware of Christina's behavior. In speaking with these students, both in interviews and during class, they collectively said that Christina was "trying to help." Even students who identified her as "bossy" and "sometimes rude" noted that Christina was trying to help students get better at reading. Dana said:

> I think it's rude when she does that. Like she is always interrupting if she doesn't agree with you, and I think people do get tired of that...but I know that she is trying to help. Like she knows the answer, and she is trying to make sure everyone understands it. She is the best reader in here.

The reflections and statements made about Christina's behavior show that not everyone found her actions to be acceptable. However, they also framed her actions as being grounded in good intentions. By comparison, no student ever spoke out on behalf of those who were interrupted or shut down by Christina suggesting that, at the very least, her behaviors were tolerated and normalized.

Discussion

Students' Understandings of What It Means to Be a Reader

Students' understandings of what it means to be a reader are formed early on and then reinforced over time. They construct their reading identities based on multiple factors including (a) the language teachers use around what it means to be a particular type of reader, (b) their interpretations of how well they align with their understanding of a given identity, and (c) comparisons they make about their abilities in relation to their peers. Students may not always have an accurate interpretation of the models of identity available to them or how well they align with them. Regardless, their interpretations inform how they self-identify as readers and influence how they engage with classroom reading practices (Hall, 2012b).

Understanding when and how reading identities are formed gives teachers the ability to set students up for success from the earliest grades. If we want students to have more expansive models to draw on, then reading identities need to be communicated in a way that is aligned with an ideological approach (Street, 1984). Within an ideological model, reading skills and strategies are still taught, used, and valued. However, because instruction and experiences with texts are grounded in the social and cultural norms of the classroom community, it allows for a more flexible and responsive model around reading identities. An ideological model provides a more flexible approach toward developing reading identities by giving students input into what it means to be a reader and what they need to do to become the kind of reader they wish to be. Having more expansive, context-centered models can help students see broader and more nuanced purposes for and ways of reading while also showing them that reading is a lifelong process.

Privileges and Power

Reading identities can serve as a way for teachers and students to position each other and create structures that suggest how students can and should participate in classroom reading practices. Students who are viewed as advanced readers are often seen as being more knowledgeable and having something of value to offer their peers. Like Christina, they may find themselves placed into leadership positions where they are expected to assist students who are considered to be poor readers. As a result, students who are identified as poor readers may find themselves on the margins where they are viewed through a deficit lens and seen primarily as someone who needs assistance from a more knowledgeable other.

By the time students enter middle school, they will have formed a habitus around what it means to be identified as a particular type of reader within their class (Bourdieu & Wacquant, 1992). Undoing these mindsets, and the power structures that reside within them, is critical to provide more equitable opportunities for students who have long been positioned as poor readers. How to do this is complex as students who have negative reading identities may not be comfortable, or see it as their place, to critique existing power structures. When they do, they may run up against students who do not see their ideas as valid and believe they have nothing to contribute.

While limited research has been done on helping adolescents reconstruct their identities (Hall, 2016), future research will want to consider what it means for teachers to understand and disrupt the power dynamics and cultural practices around reading. Researchers will want to focus on helping teachers shift the cultural dynamics around reading so that students with more negative positions have space to fully participate. Additionally, work that centers on how to help students establish and maintain positive reading identities early on, even in the face of having difficulties with texts, is critical to ensure that students engage with texts throughout their academic careers. Rather than focus on what it means to be a particular type of reader, researchers should help teachers and students create models for what it means to be a reader within a particular context and the norms that can support a positive experience within that context.

Discussion Questions

1 How can classroom reading practices be constructed so that students with positive reading identities make space for students whose models differ from their own?

2 How can we better prepare teachers to understand the concept of reading identities and design instruction so that it takes into account the variations in the models students possess?

3 Reading identities are constructed at an early age and reinforced over time. How might future research examine the power structures that are enacted based on models of identity and the consequences that emerge from them? How can researchers help undo damaging power structures in ways that allow for more equitable experiences for students with varying reading and models of identity?

References

Bourdieu, P., & Wacquant, L. J. D. (1992). *An invitation to reflexive sociology*. University of Chicago Press.

Coombs, D. (2012). Using Ricoeur's mimetic process to examine the identities of struggling adolescent readers. *English Teaching: Practice and Critique, 11*(1), 82–103.

Draper, S. (1998). *Forged by fire*. Atheneum Books for Young Readers.

Enriquez, G. (2011). Embodying exclusion: The daily melancholia and performative politics of struggling early adolescent readers. *English Teaching: Practice and Critique, 10*(3), 90–112.

Glenn, W., Ginsberg, R., & King-Watkins, D. (2016). Resisting and persisting: Identity stability among adolescent readers labeled as struggling. *Journal of Adolescent Research, 33*(3), 306–331. https://doi.org/10.1177/0743558416684953

Hall, L. A. (2016). "I don't really have anything good to say": Examining how one teacher worked to shape middle school students' talk about texts. *Research in the Teaching of English, 51*(1), 60–83.

Hall, L. A. (2012a). Moving out of silence: Helping struggling readers find their voices in text-based discussions. *Reading and Writing Quarterly, 28*(4), 307–332. https://doi.org/10.1080/10573569.2012.702037

Hall, L. A. (2012b). The role of reading identities and reading abilities in students' discussions about texts and comprehension strategies. *Journal of Literacy Research, 44*(3), 239–272. https://doi.org/10.1177/1086296x12445370

Learned, J. E., Morgan, M. J., & Lui, A. M. (2017). "Everyone's voices are to be heard": A comparison of struggling and proficient readers' perspectives in one urban high school. *Education and Urban Society, 51*(2), 195–221. https://doi.org/10.1177/0013124517715065

Moses, L., & Qiao, X. (2018). Literate identity development in first grade: A cross-case analysis of students with strong and emerging decoding skills. *Journal of Language & Literacy Education, 14*(2), 1–31.

Nkomo, S. A. (2018). Grade 3 learners' imagined identities as readers revealed through their drawings. *Reading & Writing - Journal of the Reading Association of South Africa, 9*(1), 1–9. https://doi.org/10.4102/rw.v9i1.163

O'Brien, D., Stewart, R., & Beach, R. (2009). Proficient reading in school: Traditional paradigms and new textual landscapes. In L. Christenbury, R. Bomer, & P. Smagorinsky (Eds.), *Handbook of adolescent literacy research* (pp.80–97). Guilford Press.

Orwell, G. (2021). *Nineteen eighty-four*. Penguin Classics.

Reinking, D., & Bradley, B. A. (2007). *On formative and design experiments*. Teachers College Press.

Saldaña, J. (2016). *The coding manual for qualitative researchers*. Sage Publishers.

Skerrett, A. (2012). "We hatched in this class": Repositioning of identity in and beyond a reading classroom. *High School Journal, 95*(3), 62–75. https://doi.org/10.1353/hsj.2012.0008

Street, B. V. (1984). *Literacy in theory and practice*. Cambridge University Press.

Wagner, C. J. (2019). Connections between reading identities and social status in early childhood. *TESOL Quarterly, 53*(4), 1060–1082. https://doi.org/10.1002/tesq.529

White, J. W., & Lowenthal, P. R. (2011). Minority college students and tacit "codes of power": Developing academic discourse and identities. *Review of Higher Education, 34*(2), 283–318. https://doi.org/10.1353/rhe.2010.0028

Wodak, R. (2011). Language, power, and identity. *Language Teaching, 45*(2), 215–233. https://doi.org/10.1017/s0261444811000048

Wortham, S. (2006). *Learning identity: The joint emergence of social identification and academic learning*. Cambridge University Press.

SECTION III

Literate Identities in Adolescence

Introduction to Literate Identities in Adolescence

Katherine K. Frankel

Introduction

The topic of this third section is literate identities in adolescence, which we distinguish from the previous section's focus on middle childhood by focusing predominantly on youth in high school. In the United States, high school typically means grades 9–12 and corresponds approximately to ages 14–18. However, alongside these parameters, we also acknowledge that the term "adolescence" is slippery. Sometimes, adolescence refers to the second decade of a child's life (approximately ages 10–20). Other times, particularly in US educational contexts, adolescence refers to the middle and high school years (grades 6–12, or approximately ages 11–18). The distinction between the two is significant. The former foregrounds a young person's individual development, including individual-context relations, for example, concerning puberty and moderating factors such as gender, racial, and ethnic identification (Lerner et al., 2023). The latter attends to the contexts in and through which young people live, learn, and develop, individually and collectively, through social interaction with others (Engeström, 2015; Leont'ev, 1978; Vygotsky, 1978). In the United States, sixth grade typically marks a shift to multiple teachers across separate content-area classes, such as English language arts, history, math, and science. This may be why much of the theory and research labeled "adolescent literacy" focuses on young people in secondary (i.e., middle and high school) contexts (Moje et al., 2008).

The chapters in this section reflect the slipperiness of the term "adolescence." Taken together, they explore literate identities as they are theorized, taken up, and enacted by young people in diverse educational contexts, including a public high school in the northeastern United States, a secondary classroom on Dutch Sint Maarten, and an out-of-school STEAM/digital literacy workshop

DOI: 10.4324/9781003271406-13

also in the United States. As the chapter authors show, literate identities are complex for youth as they move within and across the varied and sometimes-contradictory contexts of their academic, personal, professional, and increasingly digital and global lives. While literate identities are always complex and dynamic, for older youth navigating a multitude of expectations and responsibilities across diverse contexts (e.g., increased independence alongside school requirements, employment/job demands, familial monetary and childcare obligations, peer networks and social relationships on and offline, and college/career planning), these complexities and related tensions influence and are influenced by their literate identities.

Theorizing Identities in Adolescence

Recent theorizing of literate identities in adolescence increasingly requires attention to the complexities of the contexts in and through which young people engage in literacy and how they understand and navigate those contexts. This is evident across the theoretical spectrum, from socio-cognitive studies of motivation and engagement among older readers, where attention to contextual factors (e.g., curriculum) is built into the study design (e.g., Guthrie et al., 2013), to sociocultural studies of adolescent literacy and identity, where young people's situated literacy practices are conceptualized as hybrid, metadiscursive, and spatial (Lewis & Del Valle, 2008).

Much of the scholarship on literate identities in adolescence, including the three chapters in this section, conceptualizes both literacy and identity as part of social practices that foreground context and power (Street, 1984). Some of the scholarship from a sociocultural perspective also draws on positioning theory (Davies & Harré, 1990; Harré & van Langenhove, 1999) to analyze the ways in which individuals position themselves and are positioned by others through literacy practices (Frankel, 2017; Frankel et al., 2018; McVee et al., 2011); critical theories (Crenshaw, 1989; Ladson-Billings & Tate, 1995) to call attention to power, equity, and justice in literacy teaching and learning (Paris & Alim, 2017; Lewis et al., 2007); and theories of multiliteracies and multimodality (New London Group, 1996; Kress, 2010) to expand definitions of what it means to engage in literacy across modes (e.g., speech, image, and sound) and for diverse purposes.

When selecting theories of literacy and identity, researchers should consider combining theories to support robust conceptual frameworks that attend to the complexities of young people's literate identities across space and time. These complexities include, for example, what adolescents think about the literacy practices in which they engage across contexts and how broader institutional structures, policies, and practices may shape their experiences and perspectives. Robust, multidimensional frameworks like the ones theorized in the chapters in this section are important to (a) name and interrogate deficit-focused understandings of adolescents' literacies and related approaches to secondary literacy teaching and learning (Alvermann, 2001; Frankel & Brooks, 2018; Learned et al., Chapter 7) and (b) design humanizing literacy learning opportunities for adolescents that speak back to skills-focused perspectives (Gutiérrez et al., 2009; Lewis Ellison, Chapter 9; Muhammad, 2018; Skerrett, Chapter 8).

Research Methods in Adolescence

Studying literate identities in adolescence requires methods that are detailed and comprehensive enough to understand the complexity of the contexts in and through which youth's identities are embodied, enacted, and understood across space and time. The three chapters included in this section, like much of the scholarship on literate identities in adolescence, ask questions about literate identities that tend to utilize qualitative methods as a way to gather rich and nuanced information about youth's lived experiences and perspectives. Some of these methodological approaches, like ethnography (Heath & Street, 2008) or case study (Dyson & Genishi, 2005), typically involve researchers engaging in participant observation, collecting observational data (e.g., field notes, artifacts, audio/video recordings), and conducting interviews with young people, among other data collection techniques. Other approaches involve practitioner research (Cochran-Smith & Lytle, 2009) and social design research (Gutiérrez, 2016) where educators and researchers may work alongside or in partnership with youth to create different kinds of opportunities for literacy and learning. In many of these cases, qualitative data collection includes attention to (a) what young people say about themselves as readers and writers and what others say about them (e.g., in interviews or focus groups or through literacy artifacts such as journals), (b) how young people are positioned by themselves and others through social interactions and how they, in turn, position others (e.g., during participant observation or in audio/video recordings), and (c) how they are positioned by (and, in turn, position) the larger structures and the institutional policies and practices unique to particular social contexts (e.g., within a school community or society more broadly). An advantage of identity research with adolescents as compared to younger children is that they often are able to draw on their relatively longer histories and experiences with literacy, to reflect extensively and in depth on their multiple identities over time and across contexts within and beyond school, and to engage actively as research partners.

When crafting a methodological approach, researchers should consider selecting methods that are nuanced enough to support a comprehensive understanding of the complexities of young people's literate identities as they move across contexts and as their identities develop over time. A diversity of data sources is important to (a) guard against the essentialization of young people's literate identities as simplistic or static (Lewis & Del Valle, 2008; Moje & Luke, 2009) and (b) attend to the social, cultural, historical, and political factors—including those tied to race, class, gender, and language, among others—that are intertwined with their literate identities (Baker-Bell, 2020; Muhammad, 2018).

Chapters in this Section

This section includes three chapters on literate identities among older youth. (See Section II for chapters focused on literate identities in middle childhood, grades 4–8, and Section IV for chapters that consider literate identities longitudinally as well as cross-sectionally across childhood and adolescence.) All of the authors of these chapters draw on critical and sociocultural theoretical frameworks and nuanced methodological approaches to understand adolescents' literate identities in diverse contexts.

In Chapter 7, Learned, Dacus, and Burgess examine literate identities across two research studies in one public, racially and ethnically diverse high school context. They show how tracking and high-stakes testing constrained understandings of readers and reading by failing to recognize the dynamic nature of reading and by labeling students as deficient. They argue for the need to disrupt inequitable school systems that position youth readers and impact their literate identities in negative and problematic ways.

Learned and her colleagues ground both of their studies in sociocultural perspectives on literacy, which means they conceptualize literacy as dynamic social practices that are contextualized and purposeful. For these authors, contexts for literacy are constructed through social interactions and the circulation of texts. Moreover, contexts—and related literacy practices—are marked by issues of power, which contribute to how individuals are positioned by themselves and others. Over several years and two studies, the authors used qualitative methods—including observations, interviews with 11th graders and their teachers, and the collection of artifacts—to document the ways that students and teachers navigated and resisted the realities of literacy-related tracking and testing at their school. Ultimately, they show how attention to school structures like tracking and testing, and their consequences, have important implications for young people's literate identities (e.g., their understanding of reading and positioning as readers) and content-area learning.

In Chapter 8, Skerrett focuses on young people's transnational literate identities and composing practices in a secondary classroom on the island of Dutch Sint Maarten. She demonstrates how two focal students enacted transnational identities and literacies through the creation and presentation of multimodal compositions. As the teacher of the focal class, Skerrett also provides insights into what it looks like to create a literacy unit that centers students' transnational identities and experiences. Moreover, she details how she came to view classroom interactions from a de/colonial perspective to explore how students' diverse transnational identities can be celebrated as well as marginalized through social interactions.

Like Learned and colleagues, Skerrett grounds her study in sociocultural perspectives. She also draws on theories of multiliteracies and multimodality to expand print-centric conceptualizations of writing to a reorientation toward multimodal composing. Finally, she draws on positioning theory to understand the complex and dynamic nature of transnational literate identities as they are negotiated during social interactions. The Literate Lives Unit that is the focus of this chapter is part of a long-term qualitative inquiry into the literacy lives of transnational youth with ties to the Caribbean. Skerrett used qualitative methodologies—including audio and video recordings and transcripts of classroom activities, field notes, teaching and learning artifacts (e.g., students' multimodal compositions), and interviews—to trace the ways that two focal students, Annemarie and Jekke, used the practice of multimodal composing and their interactions with each other and other members of the classroom to foreground and strengthen their transnational identities. In her analysis, Skerrett also calls attention to the ways that transnational identities were hierarchically ordered (i.e., students' ties to the United States were privileged over other transnational affiliations) and calls for more explicit attention to decolonizing literacy education in research and practice.

Finally, in Chapter 9, Lewis Ellison, Robinson, and Qiu bring together ideas related to intersectionality; science, technology, engineering, arts, and mathematics (STEAM); and multimodal digital design to propose and theorize the concept of literate intersectional identities (Lewis Ellison et al., 2020). They illuminate the concept through the case of one adolescent Latina who participated in a STEAM workshop and show how she enacted literate intersectional identities through the creation of a mobile app to support and advocate for her Puerto Rican community in the wake of Hurricane Maria.

Like the other authors in this section, this study is grounded in sociocultural theories of literacy and identity, particularly Vasudevan et al.'s (2010) use of the term "literate identities," which posits that identities are inseparable from social contexts that can enable or constrain them. They also draw on intersectionality and multimodality to further theorize the concept of literate intersectional identities. The focal case discussed in this chapter is part of a larger qualitative study of girls who participated in the researcher-developed, culturally affirming *Dig-A-Girls* STEAM/digital literacy workshop designed to support and foster agency and positive self-representation. The authors used qualitative methods—audio/video-recorded observations, surveys, interviews, photographs, and artifacts (e.g., journal entries, digital apps)—to understand how the digital design process of one participant, Suzanna, interacted with her literate intersectional identities. They found that her multiple identities were nurtured through the intersectional practices of STEAM learning and multimodal digital design. They urge teachers and researchers to look for intersections as a way to make visible the relationship between power and young people's multiple identities.

Each of these chapters emphasizes that sociocultural context, power, and agency all matter when it comes to theorizing and studying literate identities in adolescence (Lewis et al., 2007). For example, Learned and her colleagues explore and critique how existing, formal school contexts and related structures can constrain literate identities (i.e., through tracking and high-stakes testing) while simultaneously documenting how young people and their teachers navigate and resist these constraints. Taking a different approach, the other two chapters in this section describe innovative learning spaces like Skerrett's Literate Lives Unit and Lewis Ellison et al.'s *Dig-A-Girls* STEAM workshop. In these contexts, researchers, teachers, and young people themselves had opportunities to imagine and design new possibilities for the exploration of literate identities. In addition to expanding conceptualizations of literate identities to encompass young people's multiple and intersecting identities (e.g., transnational, racial, ethnic, gendered, linguistic, cultural, and familial), these authors also expand definitions of literacy to encompass multimodal and disciplinary literacies (Frankel et al., 2016). These complementary theoretical and methodological approaches to conceptualizing and analyzing literate identities in adolescence are important and point to key considerations (e.g., the salience of multimodality, multiple identities, and agency) for researchers and practitioners seeking to design and study contexts for literacy learning that support, foster, and extend adolescents' complex literate identities within and beyond formal secondary school contexts.

References

Alvermann, D. E. (2001). Reading adolescents' reading identities: Looking back to see ahead. *Journal of Adolescent & Adult Literacy*, *44*(8), 676–690.

Baker-Bell, A. (2020). *Linguistic justice: Black language, literacy, identity, and pedagogy*. Routledge.

Cochran-Smith, M., & Lytle, S. L. (2009). *Inquiry as stance: Practitioner research for the next generation*. Teachers College Press.

Crenshaw, K. (1989). Demarginalizing the intersection of race and sex: A Black feminist critique of antidiscrimination doctrine, feminist theory and antiracist politics. *University of Chicago Legal Forum*, *1989*(1), 139–167.

Davies, B., & Harré, R. (1990). Positioning: The discursive production of selves. *Journal for the Theory of Social Behavior*, *20*(1), 43–63. https://doi.org/10.1111/j.1468-5914.1990.tb00174.x

Dyson, A. H., & Genishi, C. (2005). *On the case: Approaches to language and literacy research* (an NCRLL volume). Teachers College Press.

Engeström, Y. (2015). *Learning by expanding: An activity-theoretical approach to developmental research* (2nd ed.). Cambridge University Press.

Frankel, K. K. (2017). What does it mean to be a reader?: Identity and positioning in two high school literacy intervention classes. *Reading & Writing Quarterly: Overcoming Learning Difficulties*, *33*(6), 501–518. https://doi.org/10.1080/10573569.2016.1250143

Frankel, K. K., Becker, B. L. C., Rowe, M. W., & Pearson, P. D. (2016). From "what is reading?" to what is literacy? *Journal of Education*, *196*(3), 7–18. https://doi.org/10.1177/002205741619600303

Frankel, K. K., & Brooks, M. D. (2018). Why the "struggling reader" label is harmful (and what educators can do about it). *Journal of Adolescent & Adult Literacy*, *62*(1), 111–114. https://doi.org/10.1002/jaal.758

Frankel, K. K., Fields, S. S., Kimball-Veeder, J., & Murphy, C. R. (2018). Positioning adolescents in literacy teaching and learning. *Journal of Literacy Research, 50*(4), 446–477. https://doi.org/10.1177/1086296X18802441

Guthrie, J. T., Klauda, S. L., & Ho, A. N. (2013). Modeling the relationships among reading instruction, motivation, engagement, and achievement for adolescents. *Reading Research Quarterly, 48*(1), 9–26. https://doi.org/10.1002/rrq.035

Gutiérrez, K. D. (2016). Designing resilient ecologies: Social design experiments and a new social imagination. *Educational Researcher, 45*(3), 187–196. https://doi.org/10.3102/0013189X16645430

Gutiérrez, K. D., Morales, P. Z., & Martinez, D. C. (2009). Re-mediating literacy: Culture, difference, and learning for students from nondominant communities. *Review of Research in Education, 33*, 212–245. https://doi.org/10.3102/0091732X08328267

Harré, R., & Van Langenhove, L. (Eds.). (1999). *Positioning theory: Moral contexts of intentional action*. Blackwell.

Heath, S. B., & Street, B. V. (2008). *On ethnography: Approaches to language and literacy research* (an NCRLL volume). Teachers College Press.

Kress, G. R. (2010). *Multimodality: A social semiotic approach to contemporary communication*. Routledge.

Ladson-Billings, G., & Tate, W. F. (1995). Toward a critical race theory of education. *Teachers College Record, 97*(1), np. https://doi.org/10.1177/016146819509700104

Leont'ev, A. N. (1978). *Activity, consciousness, and personality*. Prentice-Hall.

Lerner, R. M., Lerner, J. V., & Buckingham, M. H. (2023). The development of the developmental science of adolescence: Then, now, and next–and necessary. In L. J. Crockett, G. Carlo, & J. E. Schulenberg (Eds.), *APA handbook of adolescent and young adult development* (pp. 723–741). American Psychological Association. https://doi.org/10.1037/0000298-044

Lewis, C., & Del Valle, A. (2008). Literacy and identity: Implications for research and practice. In L. Christenbury, R. Bomer, & P. Smagorinsky (Eds.), *Handbook of adolescent literacy research* (pp. 307–322). Guilford.

Lewis, C., Enciso, P. E., & Moje, E. B. (2007). *Reframing sociocultural research on literacy: Identity, agency, and power*. Routledge.

Lewis Ellison, T., Robinson, B., & Qiu, T. (2020). Examining African American girls' literate intersectional identities through journal entries and discussions about STEM. *Written Communication, 37*(1), 3–40. https://doi.org/10.1177%2F0741088319880511

McVee, M. B., Brock, C. H., & Glazier, J. A. (Eds.). (2011). *Sociocultural positioning in literacy: Exploring culture, discourse, narrative, and power in diverse educational contexts*. Hampton.

Moje, E. B., & Luke, A. (2009). Literacy and identity: Examining the metaphors in history and contemporary research. *Reading Research Quarterly, 44*(4), 415–437. https://doi.org/10.1598/RRQ.44.4.7

Moje, E. B., Overby, M., Tysvaer, N., & Morris, K. (2008). The complex world of adolescent literacy: Myths, motivations, and mysteries. *Harvard Educational Review, 78*(1), 107–154. https://doi.org/10.17763/haer.78.1.54468j6204x24157

Muhammad, G. E. (2018). A plea for identity and criticality: Reframing literacy learning standards through a four-layered equity model. *Journal of Adolescent & Adult Literacy, 62*(2), 137–142. https://doi.org/10.1002/jaal.869

New London Group. (1996). A pedagogy of multiliteracies: Designing social futures. *Harvard Educational Review, 66*(1), 60–92.

Paris, D., & Alim, H. S. (Eds.). (2017). *Culturally sustaining pedagogies: Teaching and learning for justice in a changing world*. Teachers College Press.

Street, B. V. (1984). *Literacy in theory and practice.* Cambridge University Press.

Vasudevan, L., Schultz, K., & Bateman, J. (2010). Rethinking composing in a digital age: Authoring literate identities through multimodal storytelling. *Written Communication, 27*(4), 442–468. https://doi.org/10.1177/0741088310378217

Vygotsky, L. S. (1978). *Mind in society: The development of higher psychological processes.* Harvard University Press.

7

HOW YOUTH CONSTRUCT LITERACY-RELATED IDENTITIES

The Role of Tracking and High-Stakes Testing

Julie E. Learned, Laura C. Dacus, and Kewsi Burgess

Introduction

The same young person wears many different hats on any given school day while navigating the diverse literacy demands across the curriculum. These "hats" can be understood as identities enacted through a young person's literacy practices. For example, as an algebra student during first period, the student might read a linear function with ease but then, the following period, struggle to make sense of a poem in English class. In addition to these literacy-related identities, the adolescent also enacts a multitude of social identities including, for example, racial and gender self-identifications. The student juggles these hats dynamically over the course of not only a school day but also a school year.

The kinds of learning identities and social positions that are available to students—which hats are available for the wearing and when—are shaped in large part by the organization of high schools. It is commonplace for schools to be organized into tracked content classes (e.g., remedial, mainstream, honors) and to focus on high-stakes test preparation. In this chapter, we assert that although youths construct and enact a variety of reading-related identities throughout school, tracking and high-stakes testing (HST) can position youths as static readers (e.g., proficient reader, struggling reader). Tracking and testing, then, as organizing features of many secondary schools, not only belie the dynamic nature of youth reading but also contribute to the deficit positioning of some young people as uniformly poor or struggling readers and learners.

To inform this discussion, we will first discuss the theories that undergird our perspective on literate identities and then share two research studies that examined how tracking and testing contributed to deficit literacy-related labeling and identities among youths—and how youth resisted and at times resourcefully

DOI: 10.4324/9781003271406-14

navigated this positioning. We argue that improving literacy learning opportunities and disrupting inequitable school systems necessarily involves critical examination of the "ability" positioning inherent in secondary school literacy-related tracking and HST.

Theoretical Grounding—How We Understand Literacy and Identity

We hold sociocultural perspectives on literacy (Scribner & Cole, 1981; Street, 1984). That is, we understand literacy not simply as discrete skills (e.g., word decoding) but as a social practice that individuals engage in for specific purposes and within particular contexts. Far from static or unidimensional, youth's literacy skills, practices, and identities manifest differently depending on context. That is, the dynamic interplay among disciplinary texts, people, and learning purposes contribute to youths' demonstration of literacy skill or difficulty (Learned & Moje, 2015).

Our view of literacy, then, requires a robust understanding of context. We see contexts not as places but as social environments that individuals construct through interactions (Erickson & Schultz, 1997). While contexts are not places, they are linked to the sites (e.g., math class) in which activities and interactions (e.g., collaborative problem solving) take place and objects (e.g., math textbooks) circulate (Latour, 1987).

Further, we view school contexts not as neutral but as inherently imbued with power relations (Gutiérrez et al., 2009). As teachers and students express power, they both take up and resist various social positions. Through these actions, they discursively construct themselves and enact identities (Davies & Harré, 1990). Being positioned as a struggling reader (Alvermann, 2001) impacts literacy learning (Franzak, 2006; Learned, 2018a); therefore, it is important to attend to positioning in school contexts.

These theories, by shedding light on the roles of context, power, identity, and positioning, help us to explicate the literacy experiences and perspectives of youth and teachers as they navigate secondary tracking and testing.

Brief Empirical Review–Literacy-Related Tracking, Testing, and Identity

Although young people exhibit various literacy skills, practices, and identities both within school (Frankel, 2016; Ivey, 1999; Learned, 2016, 2018b) and outside of school (Lam, 2009; Leander & Lovvorn, 2006; Moje, 2000), deficit and static labels such as "struggling reader" continue. These labels can compromise youths' literacy learning (see Franzak, 2006; Gutiérrez et al., 2009) not only by constructing deficit identities (Alvermann, 2001) but also by reifying the socially constructed categories of ability/disability (or proficiency/deficiency) and requiring students to be classified as such (McDermott et al., 2006). To resist the negative consequences of labeling and recast reading-related struggle more productively, researchers have put forth a variety of other modifiers (e.g., striving, improving, inexperienced readers) (Greenleaf & Hinchman, 2009). Despite these efforts, deficit-oriented labeling persists.

Reading achievement labels, and relatedly reading-related identities, persist because they are constructed, in large part, through school tracking. Tracking involves grouping students according to their post-secondary aspirations (e.g., college-bound, vocational track) or perceived learning ability (e.g., "advanced," "average," "slow"). In some states, students are tracked based on their predicted performance on high-stakes tests of reading and thus positioned to enact track-related identities (e.g., low reader) before even taking the test (see our discussion of Research Study #1). Since the 1920s, tracking has been a common practice in most schools (see, Oakes, 1995; Oakes et al., 2018). High schools tend to organize content classes (e.g., mathematics, science, English language arts (ELA)) into different "ability" tracks, ranging from lower (e.g., remedial) to higher (e.g., advanced) on the basis of academic history, family or student preferences, and/or teacher recommendations. Although the supposed purpose of tracking is to differentiate instruction, research has shown that it can undermine students' language and literacy learning (Callahan, 2005; Gamoran et al., 1995) and their overall academic gains (Brunello & Checchi, 2007). For instance, a classic study of tracking in two different school systems demonstrated that students across tracked classes possessed a broad range of skills and abilities, calling into question the philosophy of homogenous ability grouping that undergirds tracking (Oakes, 1995). Additionally, these practices disproportionately placed minoritized youths into lower tracks, leading to reduced opportunities for learning and lower academic performance. Today researchers continue to call for the scrutinization and disruption of tracking practices, and in this chapter, we consider this in relation to academic and literacy identities.

Similar to the research on tracking, many studies over the past two decades have raised concerns about the validity of HST and its tendency to constrain curriculum and instruction (e.g., Linn, 2000; Ravitch, 2010). This work has revealed the emotional toll that HST can take on students and teachers (e.g., Segool et al., 2013; Gonzalez et al., 2017) and the ways in which HST may be inequitable due to cultural bias (e.g., Luykx et al., 2007). Although scholars have called for more research on how teachers and students deal with these constraints, few studies have explored these considerations (e.g., Davis & Willson, 2015; Dutro & Selland, 2012; Triplett & Barksdale, 2005). Recently, Hikida and Taylor (2020) pointed to this gap and argued, "By remaining relatively silent on this work, the educational research community makes statements about the (lack of) possibilities for teachers and students to respond to and resist standardizing educational policies like HST" (p. 22). In both the case of testing and tracking, we argue that because teachers and youths interact more intimately with these dominant school structures than other stakeholders (e.g., policymakers), there is much to learn from studying their perspectives, responses, and resistance—and the role that testing and tracking play in youth literacy-related identities. Thus, we conducted two studies to address these gaps in research.

Research Methods

We conducted both studies in the same public high school in a Northeastern city. As the city's sole high school, Central High (all names are pseudonyms) was a vibrant mainstay of the community that served generations of racially and ethnically diverse residents. The school district participated in a federal program that provided free breakfast and lunch to all students. Central High's teaching staff was notably stable, with many educators working their entire careers in the school. The graduation rate hovered between 50% and 60%, and the state designated the school as "persistently struggling."

In the first study, Learned and Morgan (2018) examined the role of tracking in youths' perceptions of reading proficiency and difficulty over six months. Specifically, they examined how reading labels and identities—both struggling and proficient—were constructed and maintained through tracked ELA classes. Two years later, Learned, Dacus, and their colleagues (2020) conducted a second study examining adolescents' and educators' perceptions, reactions, and resistance to HST. Across multiple tracks and content areas, researchers traced participants' interactions with and about testing for an entire school year as educators and students prepared for, discussed, and eventually participated in test day.

Both studies focused on 11th grade and had 15 youth participants, as well as youths' content teachers. In each study, researchers used qualitative methods to observe classroom instruction, interview youth and teachers, and collect classroom artifacts (e.g., assignments). Then, researchers used constant comparative analysis (Glaser & Strauss, 1967) to iteratively code data to identify categories and themes relevant to the research questions. (For a detailed description of methods, please see each article.)

As we next discuss the studies' findings, we assert that youths' and teachers' perspectives—and ways in which they navigated and resisted tracking and testing—provide insight into the effects of these organizing features of secondary school, as well as suggesting promising, alternative routes toward school equity and meaningful literacy identities.

Research Study #1–Tracking and the Construction of Reading-Related Identities

The first study (Learned & Morgan, 2018) examined the role tracking played in youths' literate identities, their perceptions of reading proficiency and struggles, and their learning across content areas. Like many US high schools, Central High had hierarchically tracked classes: "Advanced Placement" (AP) was regarded as the highest and most rigorous track; "Honors" was considered mainstream placement and was subsequently the highest enrolled track; and "State Test" was considered the lowest track and focused on preparation for the graduation-dependent state exam. (Central High labeled this track with the assessment name, and we use "State Test" to protect anonymity.) In this study, researchers investigated the differences among tracks in ELA, including how reading proficiency and difficulty were conceptualized across tracks and how youths navigated deficit labeling as it related to their identities.

Instruction varied across the different ELA tracks. Overall, lower-level tracks tended to focus on test-taking skills and strategies and basic text recall, and higher-level tracks tended to focus on critical reading across complex texts, as well as evaluating authors' arguments. In this way, higher-level tracks were intellectually engaging and positioned readers as active meaning-makers, whereas lower-level tracks involved rote literacy skill and test practice and positioned readers less agentively. To illustrate these trends, we next discuss classroom artifacts (i.e., student work) from State Test, Honors, and AP (see Figure 7.1). Youths' literate identities were intricately intertwined with the work they did in tracked classes, and the following artifacts represent enactments of their identities at particular moments in time.

In State Test English, two focal youths, Jon and Opal, created a poster report on Samuel Adams, which included a biography and a timeline of events (see Figure 7.1). The assignment's goal was to recall and represent information during a nonfiction unit on American historical figures. According to Ms. Cober, the State Test teacher, Jon and Opal's poster met the project's aim and received a passing grade. While students met the objectives and demonstrated reading proficiency in terms of recall, the assignment neither fostered nor demanded critical analysis. For instance, asking for a critique or an evaluation of Samuel Adam's contributions to American society or an examination of how different authors discussed Samuel Adam's legacy may have supported the students to move beyond recall. Ms. Cober's goal for State Test English, however, was to prepare students to successfully pass the exam. She described that recalling and representing information were the skills tested on the ELA state exam. She reported, "Well, the way it stands right now … [my goal] is to get them through the test and graduated." Literacy-related instruction in this context was largely shaped by the exam, and exam performance had high-stakes implications for graduation.

In Honors English, reading proficiently involved identifying and analyzing central themes. Shannon, Maude, and Ariel, three students, used two literary texts to take a stand on a quote: "It is the challenge of literature to challenge and confront the values of a society" (see Figure 7.1). Asking students to read across texts, in this case *The Crucible* and *To Kill a Mockingbird*, to take and defend a position, rather than only recalling information, was a complex literacy practice central to Honors classes. Nevertheless, one similarity between State Test and

State Test English–Poster Report on Samuel Adams

Honors English–Presentation Notes Comparing The Crucible and To Kill a Mockingbird

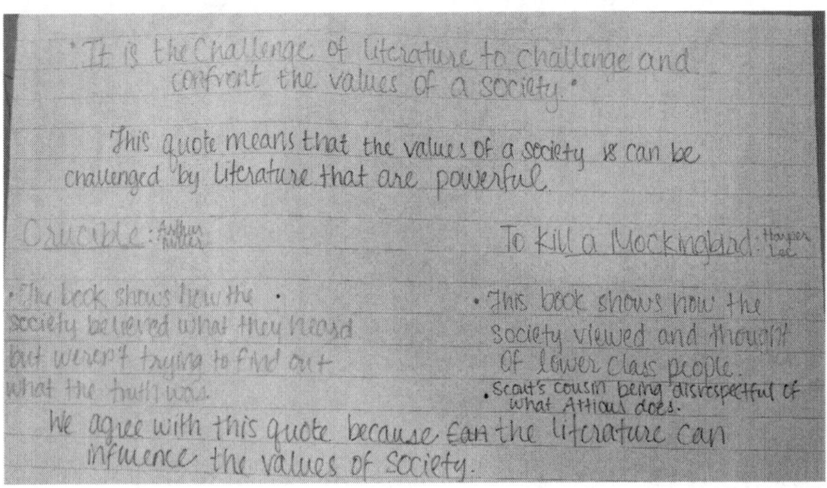

(*Continued*)

FIGURE 7.1 Classroom Artifacts

Advanced Placement English—Annotations on Hillary Rodham Clinton's 1996 Address to the Democratic National Convention

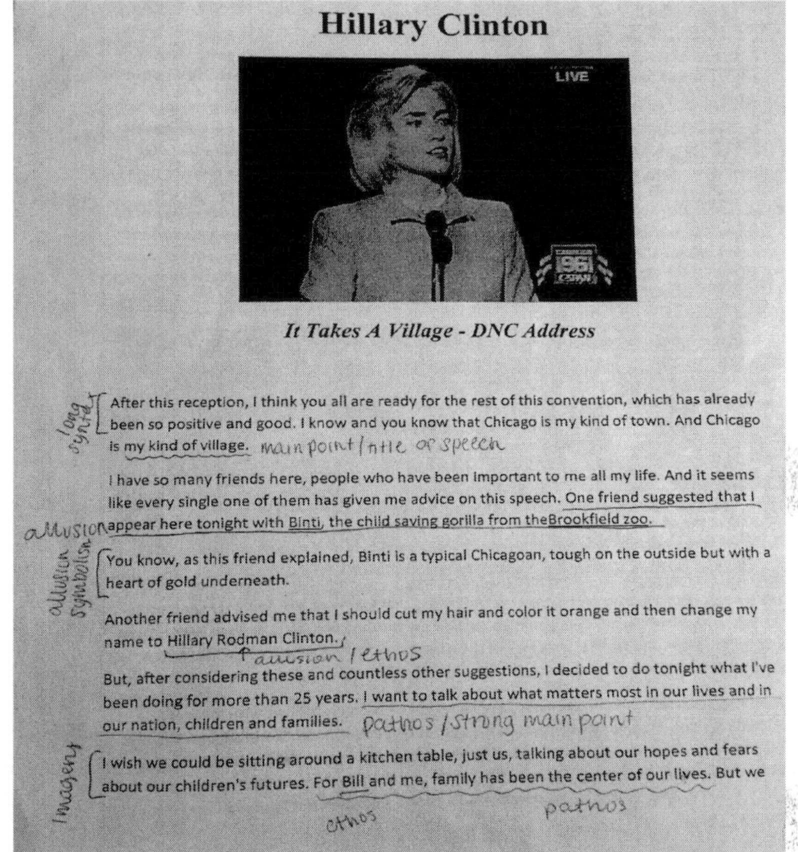

Hillary Clinton

It Takes A Village - DNC Address

After this reception, I think you all are ready for the rest of this convention, which has already been so positive and good. I know and you know that Chicago is my kind of town. And Chicago is my kind of village.

I have so many friends here, people who have been important to me all my life. And it seems like every single one of them has given me advice on this speech. One friend suggested that I appear here tonight with Binti, the child saving gorilla from theBrookfield zoo.

You know, as this friend explained, Binti is a typical Chicagoan, tough on the outside but with a heart of gold underneath.

Another friend advised me that I should cut my hair and color it orange and then change my name to Hillary Rodman Clinton.

But, after considering these and countless other suggestions, I decided to do tonight what I've been doing for more than 25 years. I want to talk about what matters most in our lives and in our nation, children and families.

I wish we could be sitting around a kitchen table, just us, talking about our hopes and fears about our children's futures. For Bill and me, family has been the center of our lives. But we

FIGURE 7.1 (Continued)

Note. Classroom artifacts from differently tracked English Language Arts classes. Adapted from "Constructing Reading Proficiency and Struggle Through Tracked Contexts," by J. Learned and M. Morgan, 2018, *English Teaching: Practice & Critique* 17(3), pp. 189-190. Copyright 2018 by Emerald Publishing Limited. Adapted with permission.

Honors was an emphasis on literacy skills tied to the state exam. When asked about his goals for students' learning, Mr. Jones, the Honors teacher said, "The first goal is, unfortunately, the state exam, like you have to focus on that piece because … it's there and it looms." Mr. Jones' reference to the exam as looming captures the ever-present, weighty influence it had across the school year in the mainstream Honors track.

AP teachers taught and demanded the most complex literacy practices and skills. For example, assignments often required students to evaluate a text or author's craft by analyzing literary devices and rhetorical appeals. Demonstrating reading proficiency in this context, then, meant cultivating and showing facility with a wide range of sophisticated literacy practices. For instance, one student, Alice, analyzed Hillary Clinton's speech to the Democratic National Convention in 1996. In her annotations of this speech, Alice identified not only the text's effectiveness at making a clear main point ("strong") but also how Clinton accomplished it ("pathos"). Alice enacted an authoritative identity critiquing the text. Ms. Miller, the AP English teacher, described the importance of such literacy skills and identities in students' lives outside of school:

> I really want the kids to come out [of AP] able to look at arguments and be able to decipher essentially what people are trying to sell them and why and to maybe look at their own ways in which they try to convince others and figure out stronger ways to go about it. Also to be more informed consumers just of information in general.

Ms. Miller's goal that students "be able to decipher essentially what people are trying to sell them" prioritized critiquing text, evaluating the author's purpose, and examining different perspectives. This kind of instruction positioned students as knowledgeable evaluators of text.

These classroom artifacts are representative assignments from the three ELA tracks, and they highlight how different conceptions of reading "proficiency" undergirded instruction. Rather than reading proficiency being held to a common high bar, it was constructed dynamically through the tracked contexts of ELA. And, although youths in each track demonstrated literacy "success" in terms of the goals outlined by the teachers and informed by the school tracking structure, reading with proficiency varied widely and ranged from decontextualized skills in State Test to complex critique in AP.

Also, across different ELA tracks, teachers' and students' perceptions of reading proficiency and difficulty were linked to student behavior, which participants described in terms of identities. For example, Devon, a focal student in State Test, described a struggling reader as "a person that slacks." Similarly, Shannon, a focal youth in Honors, described struggling readers as, "Not trying. Just not paying attention to what you're reading [...]. just laziness." The focus on students' behavior rather than instruction, mismatched curriculum, or poor text selection as the reason for literacy-related difficulty was evident in students' comments across tracks. Similarly, teachers attributed the differences between lower and higher tracks to students' identities or behaviors, rather than their skills or knowledge. When asked about the main difference across tracks, Ms. Miller, the AP teacher, said,

> I think that there's a large behavioral different expectation. AP is very focused and college- oriented [...] we put a lot of kids in State Test who are, you know, behavioral issues or truancy issues or just like the kids who will not pick up a pen.

Despite this emphasis on behaviors and identities as indicative of literacy difficulty or proficiency, it is notable that no students self-identified as struggling readers; rather, they resisted these deficit labels and identities. Although they used words such as "a person that slacks" and "laziness" when describing struggling readers, they did not describe themselves in those ways. This suggests that participants, even those in lower-tracked contexts, believed that they could improve their reading and were not defined as readers by those deficit labels.

This study showed the role that tracking played in perceptions of literacy and how literacy-related labels were constructed, navigated, and resisted by participants across tracks. Overall, findings suggest that tracking mediated youths' literacy-related identities, and students placed into lower tracks were positioned as "struggling" and had limited access to rigorous, engaging literacy instruction.

Research Study #2–Testing and Its Outsized Role in Literacy-Related Education and Identities

The second study (Learned et al., 2020) we review built on the findings from the first study (Learned & Morgan, 2018) and explored how youths and teachers at Central High negotiated and navigated the tensions associated with high-stakes testing (HST) during one academic year and how HST was a dominant context that mediated participants' ideas about and experiences with literacy teaching and learning. In this sense, this study suggests that HST, like tracking, impacts youths' literate identities by positioning students as particular kinds of readers and writers based on test performance.

At the time of the study, the school was experiencing significant state oversight that included visits from administrators and frequent collection of data to measure student progress. Researchers found that HST served not merely as a self-contained event with a clear beginning and end, distinct from the primary teaching and learning activities of the school year, but rather as a dominant context through which literacy and content learning were enacted and experienced. This context created conflict for the participants as their beliefs about education were sometimes at odds with what HST held them accountable for. Teachers felt that HST tended to narrow the curriculum and hamper learning while students described the emotional distress that can accompany HST and expressed various attitudes toward their usefulness as a measure of what they know and can do. Participants' efforts to negotiate the tensions and controversies associated with HST constituted this powerful social context. Although participants, particularly teachers, felt that HST had a reductive effect on teaching and learning and contributed to a high-pressure atmosphere, state mandates rendered them a virtually indisputable aspect of school life.

Students described their dislike of HST while also acknowledging the power these tests wielded over their academic lives and trajectories. Wilma, for instance, a student scheduled predominantly in classes geared toward preparation for year-end tests (i.e., State Test track) said,

> I feel like state tests show the potential in kids in general. I mean I don't like them, but I mean, I take them because I know that's what people look at. And that's how they, not define me, but see what I'm capable … and then teach me what I'm not capable of.

Although Wilma had negative feelings toward state tests, she recognized the weight placed on them as a proxy for her academic abilities and potential. The conflict and tension that students had to navigate come through in Wilma's comments: while she stopped short of saying these tests "define" her, she "know[s] that's what people look at" when assessing her knowledge and skill in a content area, suggesting that her test performance positions her as a particular kind of student and has implications for her literacy-related and academic identity.

Similarly, teachers struggled to manage tensions surrounding HST and described ways they sought to both stabilize and disrupt these conflicts. Mr. Gold, an English teacher with 22 years of experience, reported that state oversight prompted a curriculum redesign to align instruction more closely with the state test and the results were higher scores:

> And so while the data demonstrates that there's been an improvement, that's only a result of us teaching directly to the test, which is something we are loathe to do, but we've been forced to do through this new curriculum. And maybe that's what administration wants. I don't know. Our test scores have gone up.

Mr. Gold's statement shows the turmoil that teachers felt over being compelled to teach in ways that ran counter to their beliefs about literacy education. Although scores improved, Mr. Gold suggested that this was not indicative of improved learning for students; rather, it was a function of simply "teaching directly to the test." The test-driven context at this school required teachers to manage some degree of "doublethink"—that is, they had to allow mutually exclusive conceptions of learning to coexist despite evidence that such perspectives are incompatible. In this instance, Mr. Gold's beliefs about literary learning came into conflict with a curriculum designed to improve test performance; this requisite "doublethink" was evident in how Mr. Gold followed the required curriculum yet supplemented it with a "choice book" unit in which students could pick a novel to read based on their interests. In contrast to the required curriculum with its emphasis on standardization and achievement of specified benchmarks, Mr. Gold's "choice book" unit allowed students to choose texts that engaged their interests and experiences. Such instruction supported students' reading identities by positioning them as agents of their own literacy learning and development.

Ms. Violet, a science teacher, engaged in a sustained act of resistance through creating a different kind of science class, Forensic Science, that was not tied to any state tests. The class was a resounding success: Ms. Violet taught seven sections of it due to its popularity, and each of the focal youths who were enrolled reported that it was their favorite class. Ms. Violet compared the learning in her class to that of AP Biology:

> Next door is AP Bio. The kids I have would never sign up for AP Bio [but] I'm really doing a bio tech class… Look what they're doing, we're doing, like, chemical testing. We're doing six known solvents for an unknown. Basic chem lab. [My students] think it's fun because they're trying to solve for the evidence… So like a gel electrophoresis set they'll run over there in AP Bio … here we're going to do the same exact thing.

Ms. Violet found a way to resist the constraining effects of HST, and from her perspective, this class fostered learning and engagement in ways that test-driven curriculum and instruction could not. The result was that students had opportunities to step into more agentive literacy identities (e.g., forensic scientist), actually doing science rather than just learning about it for the sake of passing a test.

Eleventh-grade students had diverse opinions on the value of HST as a meaningful measure of their learning. At one end of the spectrum was Sandasi, an AP and Honors student, who said, "I definitely feel doing the state test is going to be a good reflection of what I know and what I don't know." At the opposite end was Abel, another AP and Honors student, who said, "The state test is basically … a joke." Despite these different stances on its usefulness, students agreed that it produced emotional distress and could have far-reaching effects on their experiences. For instance, Abel described how "[his] nerves were just like shaking" when he took the Global History state test, and this anxiety caused him to fail: "I just, like, froze and I messed up." Denice, a student in State Test English and State Test U.S. History, echoed Abel's feelings about the stress associated with HST and the negative impacts of failure: "[The tests] are too raw and they shouldn't be based on if you graduate or not because most people … aren't good test takers and have anxiety."

Faced with the distressing impacts of HST, students resisted in "sanctioned" ways, such as protesting HST in English essays, and "unsanctioned" ways, such as falling asleep during a lesson on multiple-choice test-taking strategies. Other students tried to stabilize the controversy that characterized HST by attempting to justify the tests' purpose. Damon was a student in State Test and Honors classes; when asked whether he considered the tests a good measure of his learning, he said,

> Yes, because … our teachers, they basically tell us what's going to be on the state test. So, they basically do the best that they can to prepare us…

> And they're kind of right because the stuff that we see in the state test is basically stuff that we learned in the year. So, we know what's coming and we know how to prepare for it, and I usually do well, so yes.

Damon's response shows how students had to engage in circular reasoning to make sense of the role HST played in their learning. He described how teachers teach to the test; students learn it; therefore, the test is a good measure of their learning. Damon's comments also reveal how learning and test performance become practically synonymous and difficult to disentangle within this HST context.

Overall, by placing student and teacher perspectives on HST in conversation with each other, this study helped to illuminate how HST became a socially constructed context that mediated literacy teaching and learning at this school. By defining reading and writing through a narrow frame, HST contexts reduced the range of literacy identities that students could enact and experience, often relegating youths to more passive roles as readers and writers.

Conclusions and Implications—What We Recommend for Educators and Researchers

Class tracking and standardized testing are interwoven and complex organizing features of secondary public schooling in the United States. Understanding what they mean for youth literate identities and learning is, thus, complicated. But this task is essential if we are to create equitable and meaningful literacy learning opportunities with and for all youth.

Conclusions Drawn from Our Studies on Tracking and Testing

The research we discuss in this chapter showed that Central High, like many schools and districts around the country, aimed to align its instruction and assessment to the now ubiquitous, if critiqued (e.g., Applebee, 2013), Common Core State Standards and its derivations. The first study showed that this standards-aligned instruction, which was intended to raise teaching to a common "high bar" across tracks, did not accomplish this. Instead, instruction tended to be more skill-based in lower tracks and more substantive and meaningful in higher tracks (Learned & Morgan, 2018). Indeed, "being a reader" or demonstrating reading proficiency, rather than being consistent or self-evident across tracks, was constructed through the social and instructional contexts of different classrooms. These variations in understandings of proficiency were reflected in and constituted through different instructional focuses across the tracks ranging from text recall in the lower tracks to text critique and evaluation in the higher tracks. Moreover, deficit discourses about reading struggle persisted across tracked contexts, and students and teachers attributed reading difficulty to students' attitudes and behaviors. This stance that students created difficulty through poor behavior appeared to detract participants' attention away from building literacy knowledge and practices, as well as enacting literate identities. Youth, however, never described themselves in negative terms, which suggests they resisted the deficit labels a literacy-related tracking system can generate.

The second study built on these findings by showing that test preparation efforts contributed to instruction and learning opportunities that differed across tracks (Learned et al., 2020). For example, State Test track classes, because it was their charter, spent more time than other tracks preparing for HST. Moreover, African American and Latinx youths were disproportionately scheduled into State Test classes, a demographic finding in line with a long line of research on tracking (Oakes, 1995; Oakes et al., 2018). Also, some urban schools have been systemically positioned to focus on HST (Jennings, 2010; Waitoller & Pazey, 2016) despite findings that such a focus is more likely to negatively impact the learning of students of color in working-class communities (e.g., Au, 2016; Blaise, 2018; Pandya, 2011). Our findings extend this line of work by calling for more attention to spaces within urban schools where the effects of HST may be exacerbated, specifically lower tracks focusing, somewhat exclusively, on test preparation. By taking up time and instructional attention, test preparation nudged out opportunities for youths to build disciplinary knowledge and enact sophisticated literate identities. The purpose of this study, as well as our chapter, is not to paint a picture of a failing school, as the state had designated Central High to be, but to shine a light on what test-driven, state-level accountability appeared to yield in one school—and how young people and educators resisted and persisted in these contexts.

Implications for Future Research—Understanding and Reimagining Tracking and Testing to Promote Literacy Learning and Identities

Broadly, we assert that more research is needed on the promising contexts that exist in urban schools to (1) counter "gap-gazing" at low test scores, which is associated with deficit-based perceptions of urban schools as "broken" or students as unmotivated (Ladson-Billings, 2006), and (2) imagine how educators, school communities, and researchers can together leverage those strengths to create meaningful secondary literacy teaching and assessment. At the same time, more research is needed on teachers' and young people's experiences and perceptions of literacy-related HST, particularly in urban settings (see Hikida & Taylor, 2020). Correspondingly, researchers need to move beyond documenting how tracking persists—to tackling *why* it persists—as a dominant, organizing feature of schools despite decades of research indicating its reductive effects (Oakes, 1995; Oakes et al., 2018). What are the institutional and policy mechanisms by which tracking is perpetuated and rationalized? Also, what role do literacy-related assessment and state accountability play in the persistence of inequitable tracking practices?

The studies' findings suggest that enacting literate identities—being a "good" or "struggling" reader—were indeed social categories with moral dimensions, and being a struggling reader was conceived of as deficient ("slacks," "lazy"). Yet, students across tracks described instances of experiencing difficulty with texts and said difficulty did not preclude someone from being a good reader. Many students also mustered motivation to prepare for HST even as they critiqued these tests. These were resourceful positions and practices. Future research, then, can investigate how youths achieve such a stance and how it mediates their literacy learning and identities. Pursuing these directions for research will support the creation of school contexts that invite all youth readers into inquisitive, critical, and agentive interactions with texts and each other.

Implications for Schools and Teaching—Navigating and Disrupting Tracking and Testing

Educators and youths resisted, sometimes productively, the deficit positioning inherent in tracked and high-stakes-testing contexts. However, we contend that students' and teachers' energy could be better spent cultivating meaningful learning—including literate identities—rather than managing the undue and research-documented burdens of tracking and testing. Therefore, we urge school leaders and policymakers to take steps to radically reorganize secondary schools into heterogeneous content classes as a fundamental step toward school equity. (Relatedly, we point to research that problematizes stand-alone reading intervention classes, and we call for rich disciplinary literacy instruction to be integrated into content classes (see Frankel et al., 2021; Learned et al., 2022).)

We also urge school leaders to rethink and reimagine HST. One key avenue into this work is for administrators and policymakers to investigate students' and teachers' perspectives about the purpose, usefulness, and effects of HST. In the studies we discussed, teachers and students had suggestions for different assessment models they thought would support literacy-related learning. Those included portfolio assessments of students' work, ongoing assessments throughout the year rather than year-end tests, and class-level assessments rather than state-standardized tests. Some educators and youths recommended doing away with traditional summative assessment altogether and instead engaging deeply with students' writing and work throughout the year.

Although these suggestions may sound dramatic if not unfeasible, we are living during a time when schools have demonstrated extraordinary agility and flexibility. The global health pandemic of 2020 initially spurred school closings around the world, and many schools canceled year-end testing, which before would have been unthinkable. As COVID-19 persists, the structures of American public schooling have changed perhaps more in the past two years than in the past few decades. Teachers and students have learned to interact remotely and digitally—in synchronous and asynchronous ways. Now most schools have returned to full in-person teaching but with safety measures in place. Other schools have adopted hybrid instructional models, which depend on technology for distance learning. Along the way, disparities in access to technology among both families and school systems have become more apparent.

These school-based systemic inequities have been laid bare at the same time as societal inequities regarding police violence and structural racism against people of color have been exposed more starkly. It is a moment of important social change, which is affecting our conceptions of schooling and its purpose, including assessments. The nimbleness and creativity with which many American schools have responded to this pandemic—including the ingenuity and resilience of students and families—even amid significant structural challenges and setbacks, opens an opportunity to consider what else might be radically and meaningfully changed, particularly when it comes to HST and tracking by perceived "ability."

Moving Forward Toward Meaningful Literacy Learning and Literate Identities

In conclusion, we believe that these research findings represent a clarion call to educators, policymakers, and researchers to seriously reevaluate the purpose, form, and outcomes of tracking and testing in secondary schools, particularly in urban schools experiencing state oversight as was the case at Central High. We assert that it is necessary to look beyond literacy-related labels and test scores to understand a more complex picture of secondary learning. Rather than viewing young people as defined by these surface-level measures of proficiency, we must attend to the various literate identities that youths enact, the "hats" that they wear on a given school day and across a school year. And we must ask which literate identities are systemically made available when and to whom, as well as examine how students take up, resist, and create literate identities. Paying attention to the perspectives of young people and teachers who are navigating assessment-driven, tracked contexts can and should inform the way forward toward more meaningful literacy learning.

Discussion Questions

1 How might tracking shape or influence youths' literate identities?
2 How does testing appear to shape or influence youths' literate identities?
3 How can teachers avoid teaching to the test in a test-driven context? How can teachers see and support youths' productive literate identities in such contexts?
4 How can school leaders and teachers resist school structures, such as tracking, if they promote deficit literacy-related identities? What are radical and subtle ways to advocate for change?

5 How can we center students' and teachers' voices and perspectives in future research on literate identities? What do we still need to know about the role of school structures such as testing and tracking in youths' literate identities and learning?

References

Alvermann, D. E. (2001). Reading adolescents' reading identities: Looking back to see ahead. *Journal of Adolescent and Adult Literacy, 44*(8), 676–690.

Applebee, A. (2013). Common core state standards: The promise and the peril in a national palimpsest. *English Journal, 103*(1), 25–33.

Au, W. (2016). Meritocracy 2.0: High-Stakes, standardized testing as a racial project of neoliberal multiculturalism. *Educational Policy, 30*(1), 39–62. https://doi.org/10.1177/0895904815614916

Blaise, J. G. (2018). The effects of high-stakes accountability measures on students with limited English proficiency. *Urban Education, 53*(9), 1154–1181. https://doi.org/10.1177/0042085915613549

Brunello, G., & Checchi, D. (2007). Does school tracking affect equality of opportunity? New international evidence. *Economic Policy, 22*(52), 781–861. https://doi.org/10.1111/j.1468-0327.2007.00189.x

Callahan, R. M. (2005). Tracking and high school English learners: Limiting opportunity to learn. *American Educational Research Journal, 42*(2), 305–328. https://doi.org/10.3102/00028312042002305

Davies, B., & Harré, R. (1990). Positioning: The discursive production of selves. *Journal for the Theory of Social Behaviour, 20*(1), 43–63. https://doi.org/10.1111/j.1468-5914.1990.tb00174.x

Davis, D. S., & Willson, A. (2015). Practices and commitments of test-centric literacy instruction: Lessons from a testing transition. *Reading Research Quarterly, 50*(3), 357–359. https://doi.org/10.1002/rrq.103

Dutro, E., & Selland, M. (2012). "I like to read, but I know I'm not good at it": Children's perspectives on high-stakes testing in a high-poverty school. *Curriculum Inquiry, 42*(3), 340–367. https://doi.org/10.1111/j.1467-873x.2012.00597.x

Erickson, F., & Schultz, J. (1997). When is a context? Some issues and methods in the analysis of social competence. In M. Cole, Y. Engeström, & O. Vasquez (Eds.), *Mind, culture, and activity: Seminal papers from the laboratory of comparative human cognition* (pp. 22–31). Cambridge University Press.

Frankel, K. K. (2016). The intersection of reading and identity in high school literacy intervention classes. *Research in the Teaching of English, 51*(1), 37–59. http://www.jstor.org/stable/24889933

Frankel, K. K., Brooks, M. D., & Learned, J. E. (2021). A meta-synthesis of qualitative research on reading intervention classes in secondary schools. *Teachers College Record, 123*(8), 31–58. https://doi.org/10.1177/01614681211048624

Franzak, J. K. (2006). Zoom: A review of the literature on marginalized adolescent readers, literacy theory, and policy implications. *Review of Educational Research, 76*(2), 209–248. https://doi.org/10.3102/00346543076002209

Gamoran, A., Nystrand, M., Berends, M., & LePore, P. C. (1995). An organizational analysis of the effects of ability grouping. *American Educational Research Journal, 32*(4), 687–715. https://doi.org/10.3102/00028312032004687

Glaser, B. G., & Strauss, A. L. (1967). *The discovery of grounded theory: Strategies for qualitative research*. Aldine.

Gonzalez, A., Peters, M. L., Orange, A., & Grigsby, B. (2017). The influence of high-stakes testing on teacher self-efficacy and job-related stress. *Cambridge Journal of Education, 47*(4), 513–531. https://doi.org/10.1080/0305764x.2016.1214237

Greenleaf, C. L., & Hinchman, K. A. (2009). Reimagining our inexperienced adolescent readers: From struggling, striving, marginalized to thriving. *Journal of Adolescent & Adult Literacy, 53*(1), 4–13. https://doi.org/10.1598/jaal.53.1.1

Gutiérrez, K. D., Morales, P. Z., & Martinez, D. C. (2009). Re-mediating literacy: Culture, difference, and learning for students from nondominant communities. *Review of Research in Education, 33*(1), 212–245. https://doi.org/10.3102/0091732x08328267

Hikida, M., & Taylor, L. A. (2020). "As the test collapses in": Teaching and learning amid high-stakes testing in two urban elementary classrooms. *Urban Education*. Advance online publication. https://doi.org/10.1177/0042085920902263

Ivey, G. (1999). A multicase study in the middle school: Complexities among young adolescent readers. *Reading Research Quarterly, 34*(2), 172–192. https://doi.org/10.1598/rrq.34.2.3

Jennings, J. L. (2010). School choice or schools' choice? Managing in an era of accountability. *Sociology of Education, 83*(3), 227–247. https://doi.org/10.1177/0038040710375688

Ladson-Billings, G. (2006). From the achievement gap to the education debt: Understanding achievement in U.S. schools. *Educational Researcher, 35*(7), 3–12. https://doi.org/10.3102/0013189x035007003

Lam, W. S. E. (2009). Multiliteracies on instant messaging in negotiating local, translocal, and transnational affiliations: A case of an adolescent immigrant. *Reading Research Quarterly, 44*(4), 377–397. https://doi.org/10.1598/rrq.44.4.5

Latour, B. (1987). *Science in action: How to follow scientists and engineers through society*. Harvard University Press.

Leander, K. M., & Lovvorn, J. F. (2006). Literacy networks: Following the circulation of texts, bodies, and objects in the schooling and online gaming of one youth. *Cognition and Instruction, 24*(3), 291–340. https://doi.org/10.1207/s1532690xci2403_1

Learned, J. E. (2016). "The behavior kids": Examining the conflation of youth reading difficulty and behavior problem positioning among school institutional contexts. *American Educational Research Journal, 53*(5), 1271–1309. https://doi.org/10.3102/0002831216667545

Learned, J. E. (2018a). Doing history: A Study of disciplinary literacy and readers labeled as struggling. *Journal of Literacy Research, 50*(2), 190–216. https://doi.org/10.1177/1086296x17746446

Learned, J. E. (2018b). Classroom contexts and the construction of struggling high school readers. *Teachers College Record, 120*(8), 1–47. https://doi.org/10.1177/016146811812000802

Learned, J. E., Dacus, L. C., Morgan, M. J., Schiller, K. S., & Gorgun, G. (2020). "The tail wagging the dog": High-stakes testing as a mediating context in secondary literacy-related education. *Teachers College Record, 122*(11), 1–47. https://doi.org/10.1177/016146812012201115

Learned, J. E., Frankel, K. K., & Brooks, M. D. (2022). Disrupting secondary reading intervention: A review of qualitative research and a call to action. *Journal of Adolescent and Adult Literacy, 65*(6), 507–517. https://doi.org/10.1002/jaal.1234

Learned, J. E., & Moje, E. B. (2015). School contexts and the production of individual differences. In P. Afflerbach (Ed.), *Handbook of individual differences in reading: Reader, text, and context* (pp. 177–195). Routledge. https://doi.org/10.4324/9780203075562-21

Learned, J. E., & Morgan, M. J. (2018). Constructing reading proficiency and struggle through tracked contexts. *English Teaching: Practice & Critique, 17*(3), 182–198. https://doi.org/10.1108/etpc-10-2017-0144

Linn, R. L. (2000). Assessments and accountability. *Educational Researcher, 29*(2), 4–16. https://doi.org/10.3102/0013189X0290020

Luykx, A., Lee, O., Mahotiere, M., Lester, B., Hart, J., & Deaktor, R. (2007). Cultural and home language influences on children's responses to science assessments. *Teachers College Record, 109*(4), 897–926. https://doi.org/10.1177/016146810710900403

McDermott, R., Goldman, S., & Varenne, H. (2006), The cultural work of learning disabilities. *Educational Researcher, 35*(6), 12–17. https://doi.org/10.3102/0013189x035006012

Moje, E. B. (2000). "To be part of the story": The literacy practices of gangsta adolescents. *Teachers College Record, 102*(3), 652–690. https://doi.org/10.1111/0161-4681.00071

Oakes, J. (1995). Two cities' tracking and within-school segregation. *The Teachers College Record, 96*(4), 681–690. https://doi.org/10.1177/016146819509600418

Oakes, J., Lipton, M., Anderson, L., & Stillman, J. (2018). *Teaching to change the world* (5th ed.). Routledge.

Pandya, J. Z. (2011). *Overtested: How high-stakes accountability fails English language learners.* Teachers College Press.

Ravitch, D. (2010). *The death and life of the great American school system: How testing and choice are undermining education.* Basic Books.

Scribner, S., & Cole, M. (1981). *The psychology of literacy*. Harvard University Press.

Segool, N. K., Carlson, J. S., Goforth, A. N., Von Der Embse, N., & Barterian, J. A. (2013). Heightened test anxiety among young children: Elementary students' anxious responses to high-stakes testing. *Psychology in the Schools, 50*(5), 489–499. https://doi.org/10.1002/pits.21689

Street, B. V. (1984). *Literacy in theory and practice.* Cambridge University Press.

Triplett, C. F., & Barksdale, M. A. (2005). Third through sixth graders' perceptions of high-stakes testing. *Journal of Literacy Research, 37*(2), 237–260. https://doi.org/10.1207/s15548430jlr3702_5

Waitoller, F. R., & Pazey, B. L. (2016). Examining competing notions of social justice at the intersections of high-stakes testing practices and parents' rights: An inclusive education perspective. *Teachers College Record, 118*(14), 1–24. https://doi.org/10.1177/016146811611801402

8

TRANSNATIONALISM, WRITING, AND IDENTITY WITHIN A CARIBBEAN CLASSROOM CONTEXT

Allison Skerrett

Introduction

Transnationalism refers to the phenomenon in which people maintain strong ties and feelings of belongingness to two or more nations. In today's world, transnational people undertake physical, virtual, and imaginative practices to traverse national borders to sustain their transnational lives, literacies, and identities (Levitt, 2001). This chapter examines how youth who lead transnational lives draw upon their transnational literacies and identities for composing in literacy classrooms. Data for this chapter come from an ongoing longitudinal inquiry into how Caribbean-originated youth engage and further develop their transnational identities and literacies as they traverse Caribbean and other geographies. Part of this study involved a four-month classroom-based inquiry in which the researcher (the author of this chapter) served as a teacher for a group of youth, aged 12–18, on the Caribbean island of Dutch Sint Maarten. In this work, I implemented a literacy curriculum informed by theories of literacy as social practice, a sociocultural approach to literacy instruction, and transnationalism.

One unit of study involved an Inquiry into Literate Lives in which students explored the concept of literacy as social practice, investigated into their literacy practices, and created multimodal compositions to display their literate lives. In this chapter, I examine the multimodal compositions of two of the transnational students who participated in the unit. I further explore the classroom interactions around the two focal students' presentations of their compositions on their literate lives. I do so to reveal how these two students drew upon and further bolstered their transnational identities through the creation and presentation of their compositions. I conclude with some observations of how, in this classroom, transnational identities and lives of a particular nature were privileged over other

DOI: 10.4324/9781003271406-15

configurations of transnational lives and identities. I propose the need for taking de/colonial perspectives when examining the writing and identities of transnational youth to raise critical awareness of how transnationalism can be rendered as an asset as well as how it can work to marginalize certain identities.

Literacy, Transnationalism, and Identity

Scholars based in the United Kingdom, the United States, and other dominant world nations, often working in colonialized contexts, have led the sociocultural turn in literacy (Scribner & Cole, 1978; Street, 1984). This theoretical turn toward *literacy as practice* critiques an autonomous view of literacy (Street, 1984), which is print- and text-centric and which conceptualizes literacy as a universal set of cognitive skills that can be taught the same way to any learner and in any context. Street offered a contrasting approach to the autonomous perspective, what he and others called an ideological perspective on literacy. This ideological perspective privileges individuals' and groups' social, linguistic, and cultural identities; their goals, values, and practices pertaining to literate activity; and technologies available to them for making meaning (Scribner & Cole, 1978; Street, 1984).

In a related vein, conceptions of multiple (multi) literacies and multimodality have advanced understandings of the semiotic resources used by people to construct and interpret meaning. One impactful essay is the New London Group's [NLG] (1996) theory of multiliteracies pedagogy in which they examined how different modes—oral, aural, gestural, spatial, and multimodal (this last a combination of modes)—can be used to design and redesign meaning. In relation to the composition process, theories of multimodality and multiliteracies have enabled the literacy field to expand its understandings of what "counts" as writing. Moving beyond a print-centric understanding of writing, acts of composition are now understood as bringing to bear the full repertoire of modes on the production of texts (Hull & Nelson, 2005; Kress, 2010). In line with these understandings, this chapter conceptualizes the writings of two transnational youth as multimodal compositions and examines how transnationalism and transnational identities are implicated in their composing work.

This analysis also makes use of positioning theory (Davies & Harré, 1990; Harré & van Langenhove, 1999) to facilitate insights into how transnational identities were negotiated during classroom interactions. Transnational identities refer to the dynamic ways in which people align with and invoke belonging to two or more nation-states. Such identities entail dynamic admixtures of national cultures, languages, and norms that are deployed by transnational people in order to be recognized as a member of, and accomplish particular goals in and across, the different national cultures they inhabit (Skerrett, 2018). The dynamism of transnational identities can be further understood through positioning theory. In keeping with positioning theory, identity is neither static nor singular. Each individual possesses a number of role identities or positional identities—positions that they understand themselves to occupy in and across social worlds. In positioning theory (Harré & van Langenhove, 1999), subject positions are always taken up in social groupings of at least dyads. If one person is positioned in a particular way, then others are positioned complementarily. Thus, positional identities are not only self-ascribed but assigned to individuals by co-participants in social practices within social worlds.

Importantly, subject positions can change from moment to moment within a given interaction. People can take up, reject, or mediate the positional identities assigned to them by others in their social worlds. Positioning theory thus allows for the agency of individuals. Davies and Harré (1990) propose that individuals have and do exercise agency in rejecting positions others have placed them into and repositioning themselves in terms of who they know themselves to be. As such, individuals agentively position and reposition themselves during their interactions with others (Harré & van Langenhove, 1999). This analysis considers how transnational identities were invoked and mediated by students in their compositions and related classroom interactions in which they shared their work.

Review of the Literature

The compositions of the youth explored in this chapter were generated from literacy instruction that took a sociocultural perspective on literacy teaching, learning, and practice. A sociocultural approach to literacy instruction centers learners' identities, literacy goals, values, practices, and technologies for making meaning in instructional planning (see Skerrett, 2020 for a comprehensive review of research that explores sociocultural approaches to literacy instruction). Additionally, a sociocultural approach to literacy instruction attends to the varied ways in which literacy takes form (multiliteracies practices) (NLG, 1996) and is learned, used, and adapted, within and among families, communities, and broader sociocultural contexts such as educational institutions (Skerrett, 2020; Scribner & Cole, 1978). The processes and outcomes of literacy teaching and learning guided by sociocultural theory emphasize community, increased student agency, strengthening literacies for academic and other purposes, and identity shifts (Skerrett, 2020; Hernandez-Zamora, 2010).

Sociocultural perspectives on literacy and identity have informed understandings of transnational youths' identities and associated literacy practices. Scholars have explored how transnational youth and adults engage in reading, writing, and other meaning making and communicative practices as a function of their transnational lives (e.g., de los Ríos & Seltzer, 2017; Pandya et al., 2015; Skerrett, 2018; Viera, 2019; Yenika-Agbaw, 2016). Within this research is a focus on how multimodal digital composing affords opportunities for youth to determine what, how, and with whom they will share about their transnational experiences and perspectives (Pandya et al., 2015). Scholars have raised cautions, as well, about how language and literacy practices associated with imperialist contexts can be privileged over language and literacy practices from marginalized contexts in literacy classrooms that serve transnational youth. Yenika-Agbaw (2016), in the context of Cameroon, and de los Ríos and Seltzer (2017), studying linguistically diverse students in urban US classrooms, exposed the endemic colonizing practices in English classrooms that continue to privilege Euro-Western knowledge and language practices in implicit and covert but still damaging, ways. Transnational people's literacy activities, or their transnational literacies, are imbued with the multiple cultures, languages, and ways of knowing, being, and doing that comprise their transnational lives and identities. Through the continual practice of literacy to develop, sustain, and strengthen their relationships and activities across borders, transnational people develop transnational identities.

Scholars have studied the writing of transnational youth and, in some cases, interviewed youth about their composing process or compositions, and identified aspects of transnationalism that have informed their writing. For example, I have noticed sociopolitical critiques of the dehumanizing practice of family separation in the writing of transnational youth (Skerrett, 2012; Skerrett & Bomer, 2013). Scholars have also pointed to how transnational youth writers draw on their multilingual and multimodal repertoires and transcultural knowledge as resources for composing (de los Ríos & Seltzer, 2017; Skerrett, 2012).

Across the extant literature on transnational youth and composing, then, there are rich examples of the productive and powerful ways transnationalism informs the writings of transnational youth. There has been less discussion, however, of the social practices and interactions in classroom contexts that intersect with the composing work of transnational youth. For example, little is known about how the peers of transnational youth within classroom writing communities understand and are affected by the transnationally infused compositions created by their transnational peers. Similarly, little is known about how transnational youth may intentionally or organically draw upon their socially situated knowledge of their classroom cultures and peers in developing compositions that reflect transnationalism. This chapter explores the compositions of two transnational youth within one classroom context, revealing how transnationalism came to bear upon their compositions. Additionally, by examining the youths' presentations of their compositions to their peers within a classroom context, this analysis generates insights about how the social context and interactions of/within the classroom afforded transactional space for transnational identities.

Methods

Data informing this chapter draw from an ongoing qualitative inquiry (Miles et al., 2013), begun in 2013, into the literacy lives of transnational youth with ties to the Caribbean. Data for this present analysis are culled from a four-month period of classroom teaching and research in a secondary English-speaking school on the island of Dutch Sint Maarten. (There are two separate nations that share the same land mass—Dutch Sint Maarten under the Netherlands Crown, and French Saint Martin, a French territory. Often the spelling "St." is used instead of Sint/Saint in referring to both nation-states.) I, the researcher/author, have had the privilege of conducting research at this school site since 2014, and I implemented the classroom-based study in spring 2016. I served as the literacy teacher to a group of students while also collecting data on the teaching and learning that occurred. Students engaged in an Inquiry into Literate Lives unit, a Reading unit, and a final unit that engaged them in developing reflective and intentional habits about growing their literate lives. Given the connection between literacy and identity, a central aspect of this work involved exploration of students' existing identities as literate people and how their identities shifted over the course of the study. This chapter examines data drawn from the Inquiry into Literate Lives unit.

Focal School Membership

Triumph Multiage School (TMS) (pseudonym) is located within an urban area of Sint Maarten. It is a fully privatized school opened in 2006 under the administration of a local Christian-based foundation. TMS averages a population of 50 students due to its small capacity and high student mobility. In 2015–2016, the year the study occurred, the school served 42 students. TMS is organized into two multi-age classrooms each with its own teacher: an elementary classroom serving students 5–11 years old, and a secondary classroom serving students 12 years and older. The school principal and its two teachers identify as Black Caribbean women with English as their primary language. The majority of students also identify as Black, Caribbean, and English speaking. However, the six youth research participants (who comprised the entire secondary class population during the year of the study) reflected the cultural, linguistic, and international diversity of Sint Maarten's population.

Students selected their own pseudonyms. Jekke is a Black young man born in the United States but raised across St. Martin/Maarten. Annemarie is a Guyanese-born young woman of Indian heritage. Peter is a Sint Maarten-born youth of Chinese parentage, Victoria and Sabrina are Sint Maarten-born young women with immigrant parents from other Caribbean islands, and Hector is a Sint Maarten-born young man whose father was from Honduras. All of the students led transnational lives, given family members spread across the Caribbean and other parts of the world. The students engaged in national border crossing across different Caribbean islands (e.g., Victoria) and across Caribbean islands, the United States, and Canada (e.g., Annemarie). Annemarie and Jekke were selected as focal students for this analysis because their identities as transnational persons with ties to the United States were more prominent in classroom social interactions and the literacy work they produced than any other students in the study. This situation made their cases ripe for analysis about how transnationalism and transnational identities may be implicated in classroom interactions and literacy learning.

As noted previously, I served as both researcher and literacy teacher in this study. I am a faculty member at a university in the Southwest United States whose focus is on secondary English education in culturally and linguistically diverse contexts. I identify as a Black, English-speaking woman of African-Caribbean origin who has lived in the United States for most of her life but who identifies as a transnational Caribbean-US person.

Literate Lives Unit

The Literate Lives unit (hereafter LLU) spanned three consecutive weeks (late January to mid-February, 2016). Classes met for 90 minutes for 4–5 days each week. This unit involved:

- Introduction of a guiding question, "How do you define literacy?"
- Facilitation of multiple class discussions through which students subsumed their autonomous-based definitions of literacy into an expanded ideological definition of literacy as practice.
- Student-created anchor charts of practices and activities that might involve or constitute literacy.
- Student-led inquiries into their own literate lives supported by the use of data-gathering tools, such as digital cameras and notebooks.
- Students' creation of multimodal products (such as PowerPoints and iMovies) to present on their literate lives to the classroom community.

Given the focus of this unit on exploring students' literate lives, students necessarily had to take stock of who they were as literate people, thus connecting literacy and identity.

Data and Analysis

Qualitative methodologies (Miles et al., 2013) were used to collect and analyze data. Data include audio- and video-recorded classroom observations (9 recordings of the LLU), field notes, teaching and learning artifacts, and interviews (one at the beginning and another at the conclusion of the LLU). In this chapter, the data of interest are the multimodal compositions that Jekke and Annemarie produced about their literate lives (a Prezi and a PowerPoint, respectively), transcription of the video-recorded classroom interactions of the students' presentations of their compositions, interview excerpts, and written field notes taken during class sessions, which were expanded on within four hours of leaving the classroom.

Data analysis occurred concurrently with, and also post, data collection. Analysis began with iterative reading of data (Glaser & Strauss, 2006) involving reading each piece of data, for example, a transcription of a video-recorded class session, straight through three times. Extensive notes were taken on initial impressions, thoughts, and questions about the data, including making rudimentary theoretical and research-related connections. For example, early observations of how students spoke to or about their peers in relation to particular practices, such as videogaming, or being connected to people and places outside St. Maarten, suggested that positioning theory (Davies & Harré, 1990) might be helpful for understanding the data. Such notes were made in the margins of texts, such as interview transcripts, lesson plans, and field notes; and in researcher notebooks when the data source was a digital one such as a photograph. Iterative reading facilitated progressive focusing (Glaser & Strauss, 2006), which, for the present analysis, entailed identifying data most pertinent to understanding how the youth engaged their literacy practices and identities, including those of a transnational nature, for multimodal composition.

During the process of iterative readings, inductive and deductive codes were generated. These codes were based in prominent ideas and themes in data related to Annemarie's and Jekke's cases, the theoretical frameworks, and the literature base. Examples of deductive codes included "transnational literacies," "identity," and "colonialism in education," which ultimately served as grand categories for the data set. Focused codes related to transnationalism included "traveling across Caribbean and US geographies," "online gaming" (in Jekke's case), and "world traveler" (in Annemarie's case), these last two codes signaling some of the identities the students held. Focused codes were then subsumed under the grand categories mentioned above, and in some cases, assisted in refining grand categories. Analysis then shifted to writing theoretical memos that considered research on transnational youth's multimodal compositions and theory and research related to transnationalism and identity (e.g., Pandya et al. 2015; Skerrett & Bomer, 2013). Doing so grounded the findings within scholarly and research-based perspectives (Corbin & Strauss, 2008) and facilitated insights into implications of the findings for literacy education and research.

Findings

Analysis of Jekke's and Annemarie's multimodal compositions found that both students used the practice of multimodal composing to foreground and strengthen their identities as transnational people to themselves and their peers. Analysis also pointed to the importance of the classroom (peer and teacher) positioning in interactions around the texts that Jekke and Annemarie composed in strengthening these two students' identities as transnational people. Finally, analysis indicated that the characteristics of the transnational lives and identities that Jekke and Annemarie claimed were assigned higher value than those of the transnational lives led by other students in the classroom.

Jekke's Composition: Literacy and Videogames

As noted earlier, Jekke was born in the United States but had been raised on Dutch Sint Maarten and French Saint Martin from the age of two. Jekke claimed his US citizenship as his national identity. Even though Jekke had not lived in the United States since the age of two, and did not spend extended time there, he was proud and emphatic about being an American. In our first interview, Jekke talked about frequent travels with family members across the Caribbean, such as to Saba, Curacao, and Antigua. Through his talk, he positioned himself as a transnational border-crossing person. Jekke also sought to distance himself from a Sint Maarten national and cultural identity. During classes and in other social interactions with his peers, Jekke sometimes made disparaging comments about the island and its people and culture. For example, he showed disdain for Carnival, calling it "stupid" (Fieldnotes, February 8, 2016) and announced often his intention of leaving the island upon high school graduation, "as soon as I can get off this island" (Field Notes, January 22, 2016). Jekke's understanding of his transnational identity, then, appeared to value the US context and culture of this identity and disparage the Caribbean contours of his transnational life and personhood.

As part of classroom conversations about the meaning of literacy, Jekke adapted his view of literacy as "being able to read and write" to a semiotic perspective that acknowledged that literacy involves the many modes through which people make and communicate meaning such as images and sound. He stressed, however, that for an activity or practice to be considered a literacy practice, it must involve reading and interpreting the written word: "There has to be reading in there to count as literacy" (Fieldnotes, January 19, 2016). This view of Jekke's represented the autonomous perspective of literacy that prioritizes the reading of print text as constituting literacy. However, Jekke's openness to other forms of mean-making modes also reflects tenets of the ideological perspective on literacy (Street, 1984).

Given his identity as an avid videogamer, Jekke's view of literacy was well aligned with his most treasured self-sponsored literacy. As a gamer who physically resided on Dutch Sint Maarten and French Saint Martin, Jekke often experienced technological constraints and intermittent Internet access. His parents were able to afford gaming systems for him, and he also had access to the Internet at home and school. Jekke also owned a laptop and a cell phone. However, he found it expensive to purchase sufficient bandwidth to make use of his phone as he wished to. Additionally, the broader infrastructure around technology on the islands created limited bandwidth and speed, and spotty access. This was the case both at home and at school.

Jekke's multimodal composition took the form of a Prezi with embedded videos linked to his YouTube Channel. His Prezi focused on his self-sponsored multiliteracies practice of videogaming. The data excerpt below is drawn from Jekke's presentation of his literate life as a gamer. Featured in this excerpt are

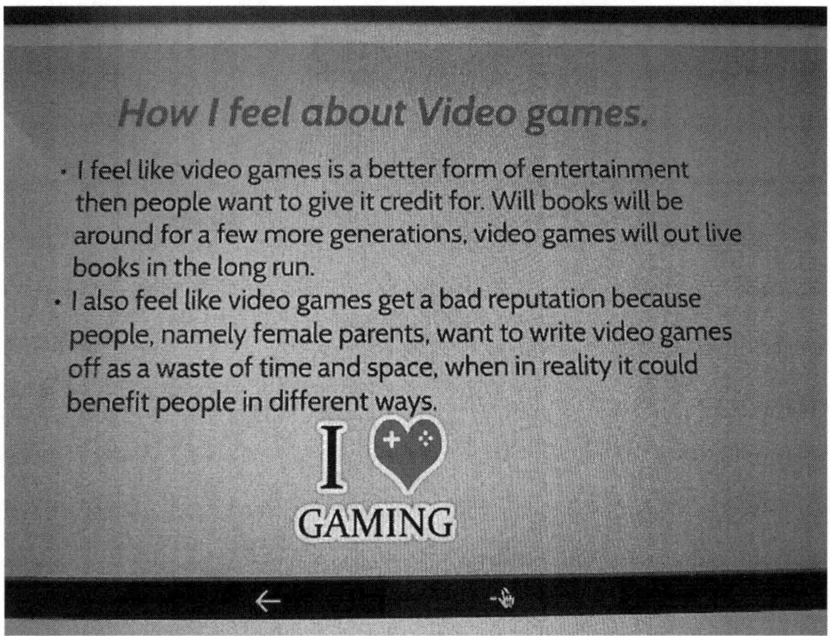

FIGURE 8.1 Jekke's PowerPoint Slide: "How I feel about Video games."

other students—Victoria and Annemarie—as well as me (Allison), as teacher-researcher. After presenting the excerpt, I engage in analysis of how Jekke's multimodal composition about his literate life as a gamer, and positioning practices during classroom interactions during his presentation, reflected his transnational identity and further assisted consolidation of this identity.

On his first slides (see Figure 8.1, which is the first slide of Jekke's Prezi), Jekke included written text that he also narrated in delivering his presentation. In this written portion, Jekke discusses his understandings of different social and ideological perspectives on videogames and argues for the value of videogames (Gee, 2007). He further argues that everyone plays videogames in their strictest definition as a digital game, and that the videogames that sometimes earn a negative reputation are those that are considered violent.

As Jekke delivered his presentation, students were highly engaged, evidenced in part by the social interactions during his presentation. For example, as Jekke read from his first slides, two students, Victoria and Annemarie, became animated about the specific videogames he mentioned:

JEKKE: Type of video games … now, video games are split into several gen, umm, genres. There's action, adventures, simulation, strategy, sports and action-adventures, and each genre has a sub-genre of their own, so in an action video game, there's like, fighting, or even platformer video games.

Some of these examples of action video games are Tekken 6 for Playstation 3, which is a fighting game, Halo 2 for the X-box, which is a first-person shooter game.

VICTORIA: Oh, yeah, Halo's a shooter.

JEKKE: Super Mario World, a platformer for the Nintendo, umm, for the Super Nintendo, and Pokemon Emerald, a game for the Game Boy Advance, which is a strategy game. … Then, my first-hand demonstration. Here is going to be a replay I have on Youtube, which has me, which has me playing as Fox McCloud from Starfox, fighting against Jigglypuff from Pokemon. I hope you enjoy it because…

ANNEMARIE: He did it, because he did it (laughs)

JEKKE: Because I enjoyed it.

VICTORIA: Jigglypuffs!

Jekke then clicks on a hotlink embedded in his presentation that should take him to his YouTube channel and one of the videos of himself gaming. However, given the unreliable Internet connection, Jekke was unable to access the video during his presentation timeslot as the Internet was down at that time. Below, as Jekke expresses frustration, I enter the interaction among him and his peers. In an effort to support Jekke, I offer my own lived experience, implicitly situated outside of the Caribbean, in which I too have been frustrated with digital technology. By juxtaposing Jekke's experiences and mine, I acknowledge and confirm our shared transnational identities within the classroom space. In essence, I offer Jekke a position as a transnational person, an identity position he accepts.

JEKKE: I don't know why it's [the video's] not playing.

ANNEMARIE: Is the Internet working?

JEKKE: Should be … it's connecting, just had to connect (inaudible question) … this is not loading.

ANNEMARIE: Take the plug out, pull the cord out and put it back in.

JEKKE: Okay, let me try it again.

VICTORIA: Are you going on YouTube?

ALLISON: That happens to me a lot when I do presentations, which is terrible because then it discourages you from putting video into your presentations because you're like "it's not gonna work –I'm gonna lose time, I'm gonna end up feeling nervous." It's just…-when it works it's…great and you're, like, so excited and happy, and then when it doesn't…

JEKKE: Then you're like, oh my god, why???

ALLISON: Yeah, you just feel awful.

[Jekke is trying to get the computer to work—inaudible dialogue about getting the computer to work]

JEKKE: Trying to get the video to load [awkward laugh]

JEKKE: Like, I was trying to end it on a high note, especially for me cause not many people actually watch my videos, so to actually have an audience watch it would have been nice.

Jekke's primary disappointment centered on the lost opportunity to perform his identity as a videogamer to his peers through showing a video of himself gaming. In the earlier portion of his presentation, he had already displayed a wealth of knowledge about gaming and so had already positioned himself successfully as a gamer. My remarks during Jekke's navigation of the technology, however, also brought attention to his identity as a transnational person. Above, I, as the literacy teacher and a transnational person, became part of the social interactions around Jekke's text that forwarded Jekke's identity as a transnational person. Neither Jekke nor I explicitly positioned other classroom members outside the identity of transnational. However, my expressions of familiarity with Jekke's technological challenges, coupled with the class' knowledge of my situatedness in the United States although a transnational person of Caribbean origin, may have further accentuated and prioritized the US elements of Jekke's identity as a transnational person. In the analysis to come, I will show how Jekke's peers, in classroom interactions, also positioned him as a transnational person with ties to the United States.

Annemarie's Multimodal Composition: Travel

The second text and interactions around it that I examine involves Annemarie's presentation of her Literate Life. Annemarie composed a PowerPoint on the topic of travel, which she greatly enjoyed. Given her family's middle-class status, and with family members living across Guyana, India, Canada, and the United States, Annemarie took frequent trips to different parts of the world. In sharing from her composition, Annemarie displayed her transnational identity. She also positioned Jekke as a transnational person with deep knowledge of and ties to the United States, and thus interactions around her text further advanced a value of transnational lives and identities that included a US component.

Annemarie's PowerPoint composition made use of found images on the Internet representing different Caribbean countries she had visited or had strong ties to—for example, the Guyanese flag. She varied uses of font style and size in the written portions of her composition in which she described aspects of and places in different countries she enjoyed. Toward the end of her composition, Annemarie described and compared her experiences of and views about the states of New York and Pennsylvania.

ANNEMARIE: ...and then this is my last two [places she spends time in], which is New York and Pennsylvania. New York. I mean, what is there not to love about New York. The city life, the people, different cultures, and the

24/7 delivery. So, you want pizza at like 3am? You gone get it. The random compliments. Simply kindness from everyone around you. Everyone and everything has such a good vibe.

JEKKE: For the tourists?

ANNEMARIE: Pardon?

JEKKE: For the tourists?

ANNEMARIE: Yeah, for the tourists. I mean you would know, right? Yeah. No, I said it with like you would know because you lived there.

JEKKE: No. I lived in North Carolina before.

ANNEMARIE: Ohhh. Okay. And, last but not least is Pennsylvania. I think Pennsylvania is one of the other under … under …

JEKKE: Underrated?

ANNEMARIE: Yeah. Underrated states …

In the above exchange, Annemarie makes a pointed effort to position Jekke as a cultural insider to the United States, thus reminding themselves and others in the classroom space of their shared transnational identities. While the theme of Annemarie's text is a transnational one, the recruitment of others who claim a transnational identity during the presentation of her composition is an additional, but overlooked practice, in which transnational students use their writing to display and strengthen transnational identities. In this exchange, Jekke corrects Annemarie that he had lived in North Carolina, and not New York. Thus, he qualifies the particularities of his transnational identity while accepting the broader transnational identities he and Annemarie share. Even though Jekke shared in an interview with me that he "doesn't remember" living in North Carolina—given he lived there from birth to two years old—he, and others in the classroom, recognize him as a transnational person of US citizenship. As Annemarie continues to share from her composition, Jekke creates another opportunity to display and enhance his US-based transnational identity.

ANNEMARIE: but Pennsylvania is quite different from the other states. … For me, even though it's like a two-hour drive away from New York, it's quite different because… from the other states. … because it's a lot more quiet and calming. The atmosphere brings peace. The weather most of the time is bearable. The food is different. Delicious.

PETER: [inaudible]

ANNEMARIE: [to Peter] *Delicious*. When I say the food is different… like my mom always cooks Guyanese food, so when you go to Pennsylvania, it's like more American and everything.

JEKKE: Do they still have sandwiches?

ANNEMARIE: [laughs] The activities are always fun. Whenever I go to Pennsylvania, I always…

Above, Annemarie emphasizes to a classmate, Peter, how delicious the food is in Pennsylvania, contrasting it with Guyanese food which she situates within the practices of her home in Sint Maarten. Peter, who does not forefront a transnational identity in the ways that Annemarie and Jekke did, is implicitly situated as a Caribbean-based person. Yet Peter is also transnational because he lives across Dutch Sint Maarten and French Saint Martin and maintains ties to China, his mother's homeland. Although Jekke earlier corrected Annemarie that he had lived in North Carolina only, his question to her "Do they still have sandwiches" serves to position him as a cultural insider in relation to Pennsylvania as well. Annemarie responds with laughter and does not question Jekke on the origins of his cultural knowledge. This response of Annemarie's could be read as a tacit social agreement between her and Jekke about the transnational identities they share vis-à-vis their other classroom peers.

Discussion and Implications

This chapter has examined how two transnational youth used writing as well as the social interactions around the texts they composed to display and enhance, to themselves and others, their transnational identities. Previous research on the writing of transnational youth has examined primarily the content and modes in their writing to understand how transnationalism, and its attendant literacy and linguistic repertoires, serve as tools or resources for their compositions (e.g., de los Ríos & Seltzer, 2017; Skerrett, 2012). Other research has explored the particular functions of writing in transnational life, for example, for political advocacy and to sustain relational ties (e.g., Viera, 2019). The present analysis indicates the importance of the social contexts and interactions in which the composing and sharing of texts created by transnational youth occur for these youths' articulation and strengthening of their transnational identities.

Given the ways in which transnational lives and identities that featured US contexts were privileged in the composing and sharing of texts in the classroom space of interest, it appears important to take a critical perspective when studying the literacies and identities of transnational youth. The Caribbean context and its peoples provide one example of the historical and continuing oppression of postcolonial/still colonialized contexts (Lavia, 2006). Transnationalism is an imaginative practice as well, and so it is worth considering the ways in which colonialism may be affecting the particular types of transnational identities and lifestyles that come to be privileged in local contexts as well as on a global stage (Appadurai, 1996). Although I, in my role as teacher, regularly challenged demeaning views shared by students on their Caribbean contexts and literacies, such as Carnival, a more explicit form of decolonizing literacy education may have gone further in promoting students' understandings and efforts to loosen the stronghold of imperialism on their transnational identities. Literacy education with transnational youth can benefit from integrating decolonial perspectives. Literacy research on transnationalism would, as well. This analysis of the compositions of two transnational youth and classroom interactions around these texts has provided one example of why it would be generative to apply a critical decolonial perspective in research on transnational people and related phenomenon. Doing so can help literacy scholars and educators not only celebrate transnational identities and literacies but also enable noticing, critiquing, and redressing of situations in which transnational literacies and identities may re/inscribe oppression.

Discussion Questions

1 What might it look like for a researcher to apply a critical decolonial perspective when examining the intersections of literacy, transnationalism, and identity? For example, in an interview situation, what types of questions might a researcher ask to help a transnational person examine their values and beliefs about the different national and cultural identities that comprise their transnational identities?
2 In this analysis, I have prioritized inquiry into the transnational dimensions of Annemarie's and Jekke's identities. However, other identities are salient for the students, for example, Jekke's identity as a gamer. What can be gained as well as diminished/lost when prioritizing particular identities in research? How might a researcher address the tension of telling a partial narrative of identity when the goal is producing depth of knowledge about a given phenomenon?
3 How might a teacher design an Inquiry into Literate Life unit, similar to the one described in this chapter, that ensures attention to identity? In other words, how might a teacher help students make connections between their literacy practices and their multiple identities? How might such attention to identity promote student learning?

References

Appadurai, A. (1996). *Modernity at large: Cultural dimensions of globalization.* University of Minnesota Press.

Corbin, J., & Strauss, A. L. (2008). *Basics of qualitative research* (3rd ed.). Sage.

Davies, B., & Harré, R. (1990). Positioning: The discursive production of selves. *Journal for the Theory of Social Behavior, 20*(1), 43–63. https://doi.org/10.1111/j.1468-5914.1990.tb00174.x

de los Ríos, C. V., & Seltzer, K. (2017). Translanguaging, coloniality, and English classrooms: An exploration of two urban bicoastal classrooms. *Research in the Teaching of English, 52*(1), 55–76.

Gee, J. P. (2007). *Good videogames and good learning: Collected essays on videogames, learning, and literacy.* Peter Lang.

Glaser, B. G., & Strauss, A. L. (2006). *The discovery of grounded theory: Strategies for qualitative research.* Aldine Publishing Co.

Harré, R., & van Langenhove, L. (Eds.). (1999). *Positioning theory: Moral contexts of intentional action*. Blackwell.

Hernandez-Zamora, G. (2010). *Decolonizing literacy: Mexican lives in the era of global capitalism*. Multilingual Matters. https://doi.org/10.21832/9781847692641

Hull, G. A., & Nelson, M. E. (2005). Locating the semiotic power of multimodality. *Written Communication*, 22, 224–261. https://doi.org/10.1177/0741088304274170

Kress, G. R. (2010). *Multimodality: A social semiotic approach to contemporary communication*. Routledge.

Lavia, J. (2006). The practice of postcoloniality: A pedagogy of hope. *Pedagogy, Culture & Society*, *14*(3), 279–293. https://doi.org/10.1080/14681360600891787

Levitt, P. (2001). *The transnational villagers*. University of California Press.

Miles, M. B., Huberman, M., & Saldana, J. (2013). *Qualitative data analysis: A methods sourcebook*. Sage.

New London Group. (1996). A pedagogy of multiliteracies: Designing social futures. *Harvard Educational Review*, *66*(1), 60–92. https://doi.org/10.17763/haer.66.1.17370n67v22j160u

Pandya, J. K., Pagdilao, K. C., & Kim, A. E. (2015). Transnational children orchestrating competing voices in multimodal, digital autobiographies. *Teachers College Record*, *117*(7), 1–32. https://doi.org/10.1177/016146811511700707

Scribner, S., & Cole, M. (1978). Literacy without schooling: Testing for intellectual effects. *Harvard Educational Review*, *48*(4), 448–461. https://doi.org/10.17763/haer.48.4.f44403u05l72x375

Skerrett, A. (2012). "We hatched in this class": Repositioning of identity in and beyond a reading classroom. *The High School Journal*, *95*(3), 62–75. https://doi.org/10.1353/hsj.2012.0008

Skerrett, A. (2018). Learning music literacies across transnational school settings. *Journal of Literacy Research*, *50*(1), 31–51. https://doi.org/10.1177/1086296x17753502

Skerrett, A. (2020). Social and cultural differences in reading development: Instructional approaches, learning gains, and challenges. In E. B. Moje, P. Afflerbach, P. Enciso, & N. Lesaux (Eds.), *Handbook of reading research* (Vol. 5, pp. 328–344). Routledge.

Skerrett, A., & Bomer, R. (2013). Recruiting languages and lifeworlds for border-crossing compositions. *Research in the Teaching of English*, *47*(3), 313–337.

Street, B. V. (1984). *Literacy in theory and practice*. Cambridge University Press.

Viera, K. E. (2019). *Writing for love and money: How migration drives literacy learning in transnational families*. Oxford University Press. https://doi.org/10.1093/oso/9780190877316.001.0001

Yenika-Agbaw, V. (2016). Textbooks, literacy, and citizenship: The case of Anglophone Cameroon. *Research in the Teaching of English*, *50*(4), 378–399.

9

"LEARNING TO CODE ... WITH A GOAL THAT I GET TO DETERMINE"

A Latina Girl's Literate Intersectional Identities at a STEAM Workshop

Tisha Lewis Ellison, Bradley Robinson, and Tairan Qiu

Introduction

Literate identities are central components in understanding youths' literate processes. Youth construct these identities in how they read and write based on their literate stories, cultural histories, experiences, and communities, but also in how they negotiate their social and multimodal texts and practices over time. Thus, to conceptualize youths' literate identities is to determine how they construct themselves as readers, writers, and users of language (Wagner, 2021). However, for minoritized and multilingual youth, their literate identities are often rejected in school-based practices and curricula (Enright et al., 2021). For instance, when youth engage in digital and science, technology, engineering, arts, and mathematics (STEAM)-related practices, their identities get entangled in those practices, which shifts the ways they conceptualize, process information, navigate, and negotiate their textual and literate experiences in online spaces (Alvermann, 2011; Lewis Ellison, 2014). What is most significant is that these learners use practices that are personally and culturally meaningful to their lives in ways that further stimulate their learning and creativity.

Within the ongoing creative spaces of digital and STEAM literacy practices, today's youth use digital texts to make sense of their world (Alvermann, 2011), rely on digital learning and relationships (Lewis Ellison, 2017), and support their multimodal compositions for classroom engagement and participation (Price-Dennis, 2016; Vasudevan et al., 2010). Research has explored how students of color, specifically Black and Latina/é/x girls, have already gained entry into how their digital and STEAM literacy practices (Greene, 2016; Lewis Ellison et al., 2020; Lewis Ellison & Qiu, 2023; Price-Dennis et al., 2017) and identity-laden

DOI: 10.4324/9781003271406-16

literacies (Price-Dennis, 2016) transcend how creative they are in out of school spaces. While discussions around Black (Muhammad & Haddix, 2016) and Latina/é/x girls in digital literacy studies are the least explored, Black and Hispanic women comprise 2% of those working in STEAM-related fields (National Center for Science and Engineering Statistics, 2015, 2017). However, research about Black and Latina/é/x girls' identities in STEAM continues to increase in literacy and computing fields (Ashcraft et al., 2017; Lewis Ellison et al., 2020; Scott et al., 2015). In this chapter, we acknowledge the nuances of the racial identities of individuals who identify as Latina/é/x or Hispanic. We use the terms "Latina," "Latiné," "Latinx," and "Hispanic" interchangeably to be inclusive of the multiple ways members of this prominent group identify themselves.

Furthermore, as we explored the literate identities of Black and Latina/é/x girls' digital and STEAM literacy practices (Lewis Ellison et al., 2020), specifically, how the multimodal texts they used and the literacy practices they engaged in shaped their learning, we noticed an omission that did not justly capture the salience and multiplicity of these Black and Latina/é/x girls. Because these girls are not monolithic in their abilities, speech, learning, identities, etc., we acknowledge that they come into being holding many identity and social markers that have interconnecting racialized, gendered, and classed identities that are equally significant. Given this importance to Black and Latina/é/x girls and young adults as well as to the digital/STEAM fields, we chose to extend the concept of literate identities to include literate *intersectional* identities from our first iteration of this framework (Lewis Ellison et al., 2020).

In this chapter, we illustrate the significance of this concept to understand Suzanna, an 18-year-old, Latina/Hispanic teenager, who participated in a STEAM workshop in 2018. We explore how her literate intersectional identities were supported and illuminated throughout the multimodal activities (e.g., creating a digital app, vision boarding, journaling) she engaged in with other Black and Latina/é/x girls. In addition, we highlight how her identity as a Hispanic youth became an impetus for her digital app topic and app creation based on Hurricane Maria in Puerto Rico in 2017. Therefore, we investigated the following question: *How did one Latina girl's digital design process affect her literate intersectional identities during a culturally affirming STEAM workshop for girls of color?*

We acknowledge literate intersectional identities as an important concept to identity and literacy fields. We aim to inform and provide ways that literacy researchers, in-service teachers, and community leaders can support minoritized and multilingual youth who may or may not participate in digital/STEAM contexts, but who want a well-rounded understanding of socially just, culturally sustaining, and humanizing pedagogy. The section below explicitly highlights the literate intersectional identities framework that guides our analyses and understandings of literacy and identity in cultural and multimodal ways.

Theoretical Framework

This study of Suzanna's literacy practices is rooted in sociocultural theories of literacy and identity, which have enabled us to explore how young people enact their identities through STEAM-based multimodal digital composing. Attention to the relations between literacy and identity, which Moje and Luke (2009) once termed "literacy-and-identity studies," has allowed scholars and practitioners to move beyond naïve, cognition-centered accounts of literacy to explore the racial (e.g., Curenton et al., 2022), gendered (e.g., Kelly, 2020), abled (e.g., Hikida, 2018), and neurodivergent (e.g., Kleekamp, 2020) implications of literacy as it is lived and learned. In this work, we are particularly indebted to Vasudevan et al.'s (2010) concept of literate identities and Crenshaw's (1989) notion of intersectionality, which we have synthesized as *literate intersectional identities* to illuminate how multifaceted identities compose and are composed through literacy engagements (see Figure 9.1). More specifically, this framework was critical in how we understood "the diverse ways in which histories, literacies, and identities traverse categories, communities, genres, and modes of meaning" through the texts used throughout this STEAM community setting with Black and Latina/é/x girls (Lewis Ellison et al., 2020, p. 6).

For Vasudevan et al. (2010), a literate identities perspective begins with the assumption that people's identities are inseparable from the social contexts within which they emerge. Because social contexts (e.g., classrooms) can serve to enable or constrain the development and expression of individuals' identities, it is crucial for scholars and educators to reckon with how the practice of literacy can similarly enable or constrain identity work. As Moje and Luke (2009) observed, "people's identities mediate and are mediated by the texts they read, write, and talk about" (p. 416), yet it is neither obvious nor inevitable that what young people are asked to read, write, and talk about in literacy-learning spaces always supports identity affirmation. Indeed, young people's literate identities—that is, their perceptions of themselves as readers, writers, speakers, listeners, and creators—are often constrained by the limited opportunities for identity affirmation provided to them by schooled literacy curricula (Vasudevan et al., 2010). In response, informal learning contexts like the *Dig-A-Girls: STEAM Workshop* can function as sites of resistance to identity-erasing curricula, spaces that nurture "possibilities for productive disruption" (Vasudevan et al., 2010, p. 446) through identity-affirming literacy engagements. While Vasudevan and colleague's notion of literate identities understands identity as multiple, complex, and fluid—identities are plural, after all—we argue that (literally) centering *intersectional* between *literate* and *identities* emphasizes the multiple lines of identity that mediate peoples' senses of themselves as literate beings. Crenshaw's (1989) original conception of intersectionality centered Black women to show how various stakeholders (e.g., second-wave feminists) laid claim to their experiences without working toward their liberation and flourishing. For instance, Black feminist theorists Crenshaw (1991)

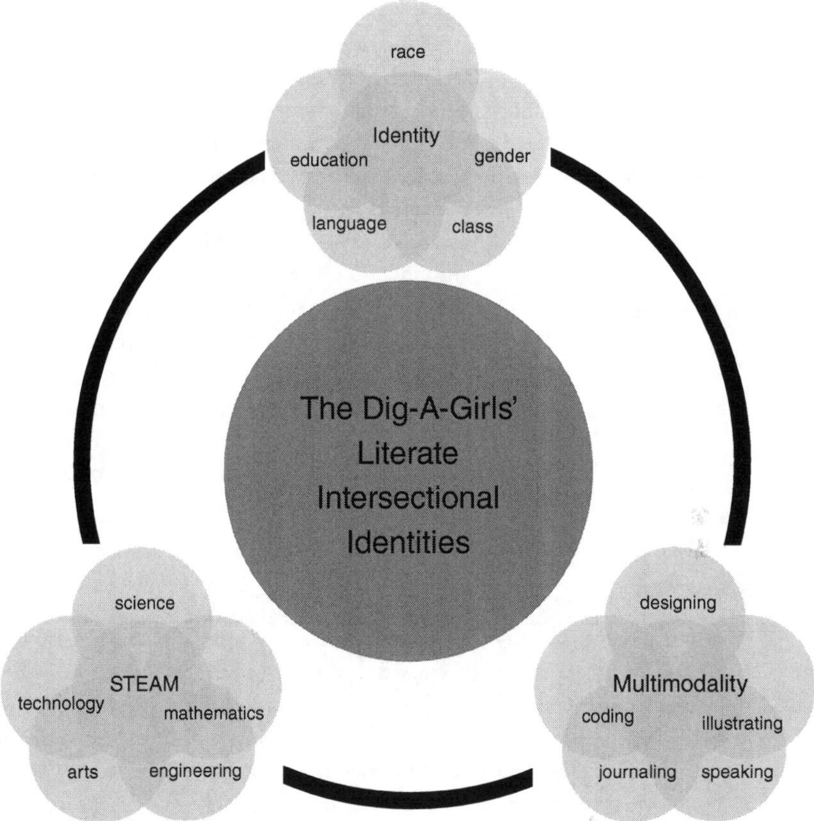

FIGURE 9.1 Literate Intersectional Identities Framework

and Collins (1998) argue that Black women's social locations and markers of power around race, sexuality, class, and gender are critical to report because it helps shape their experiences across social contexts. In fact, Scott (2002) stated that these "intersecting forces ... shed light on [an] individual's position within a social context, the norms of the environment, and the dynamics involved in maintaining those contextual standards" (p. 397).

In this chapter, we explore how Suzanna's literate intersectional identities within our STEAM workshop implicate racialized and intersectional experiences. Thus, literate intersectional identities for Black and Latina/é/x women and girls, in STEAM specifically, help to repudiate social constraints to their identity, such as oppression, struggle, and lack of access (Morton & Parson, 2018). Such "intersectional erasures," Crenshaw later noted, "are not exclusive to Black women" (2015, para. 6), positing an insight reinforced by an influential line of intersectional studies and scholarship (Cho et al., 2013). A literate intersectional identities perspective, we argue, wards off the risk of intersectional erasures in literacies research and education by centering the multifaceted nature of identity as it constructs and is constructed through the practice of literacy.

Figure 9.1 uniquely complicates the multiple intersections of literacies, identities, and practices, as well as the social markers that are represented across three strands of this work: identities, STEAM, and multimodality. The framework conceptualizes how these various lines of identity in practice inform and are enacted in and across literacies that are linked to how individuals understand themselves, how the world understands them, and how their histories and stories inform their worlds (identities). In addition, this framework captures the ways in which historically and socially marginalized identities in STEAM education and research must influence, and be made visible. Moreover, these identities should be positioned as pivotal, and as roles of engagement and interest. Lastly, this theory demonstrates how the various modes of meaning help to center the innovative ways literacies are used and utilized in practices beyond just reading and writing, to include speaking, listening, creating, and producing (multimodality).

Methodology

This work was based on a larger qualitative case study of ten Black, Bi-/multiracial, and Latina/é/x girls ages 10–18 who participated in Lewis Ellison's *Dig-A-Girls* STEAM Project in February 2018. *Dig-A-Girls* was a project for young elementary to high school girls who were interested in creating digital apps on topics of their choice during a two-day workshop. For this larger study, Lewis Ellison, along with Robinson and Qiu, was interested in how Black/African American and Latina/é/x adolescent girls engaged in a culturally affirming STEAM/digital literacy-related workshop, and how STEAM-related activities and digital tools/practices provided Black/African American and Latina/é/x adolescent girls with cultural and positive representations of themselves that fostered agency.

The girls were recruited using multiple distributions via emails and flyers sent to schools, libraries, community centers, and churches in a metropolitan city and its suburbs in the southeastern United States. In addition, flyers were distributed via social media sites (e.g., Facebook, Twitter, and LinkedIn), as well as through word of mouth. Interested parties were sent a 41-question Likert-type scale survey via Qualtrics, composed of fill-in-the-blank, open- and closed-ended, and rank-order questions regarding the following criteria:

- identified as Black/African American/Bi-racial/Latina/é/x
- was a girl between the ages of 10 and 18
- was interested in aspects of STEAM-related activities
- had little to no prior experience in coding or smartphone app development
- was available to attend two free full-day workshops in the metropolitan city

Ten girls were selected after emailing and calling their parents to share more about the *Dig-A-Girls* project and to confirm their interests. Data sources comprised 30- to 60-minute, semi-structured, audio-recorded interviews in their homes, libraries, a bookstore, and at Lewis Ellison's house. Additional sources included audio- and video-recorded observations, photos, printed journal entries, multimodal community journaling, digital apps, and 60- to 90-minute focus groups. Interview questions emphasized the girls' interests and hobbies at home and school, school experiences, career aspirations, STEAM interests, and race and gender experiences in STEAM subjects.

Our first iteration of this work (Lewis Ellison, et al., 2020) examined how three Black girls from the *Dig-A-Girls* project used journaling and interviews to better understand STEAM as part of their literate identities. Based on the problematic racial and gender disparities in STEM for Black and Latina/é/x, and Hispanic women, we explored how race, access, and the underrepresentation of women of color in STEAM helped them make sense of their self-assurance, self-awareness, agency, and interest in STEAM careers.

For this chapter, we highlight Suzanna, an 18-year-old high school senior, whose literate intersectional identities we observed as she created and discussed her digital app, which expressed deep, personal meaning related to Hurricane Maria in Puerto Rico in 2017. Suzanna had shared the effects of the hurricane where many of her family members (e.g., her grandparents) were currently living. She decided to focus her digital app primarily on fundraising efforts to support her family as well as other Puerto Ricans who still did not have cell phone communication accessibility and electricity, and those who faced damage to their land infrastructure.

Data used for this study focused on Suzanna's interview transcriptions, print journals, videos from the two-day STEAM workshops, and her digital apps to help us understand the following research question: *How did one Latina girl's digital design process affect her literate intersectional identities during a culturally affirming STEAM workshop for girls of color?*

This question and our methodological choices were informed by the literate intersectional identities framework and contribute to the field of Black and Latina/é/x and Hispanic women and girls in STEAM. For instance, through our approaches via print and multimodal journaling about STEAM, we amplified the girls' voices, and, more specifically, Suzanna's, to discuss how the racial and gender disparities in STEAM could potentially affect their personal and pre-work lives. We were knowledgeable about the agency and awareness the girls brought into the workshop which helped fortify and humanize their digital participatory choice cultures (Lewis Ellison, 2017) to choose digital app topics that they were passionate about, something that is rarely expressed in research.

In addition, through thematic coding (Miles et al., 2014), we developed four phases of coding (*Individual, Collaborative, Collapsed, and Broader themes*) that directly aligned with our data and framework to eventually end with these three themes: *self-assurance*, *self-awareness*, and *agency* (Lewis Ellison, et al., 2020). Each theme and approach were intentional to highlight the dimensions of intersectionality (identity, STEAM, and multimodality) and how the girls' literate intersectional identities were enacted in their journal writings, multimodal digital composing, creating of a digital app, discussions about the racial and gender inequities in STEAM, and how they spoke about themselves as girls of color to not only be interested in but to major in STEAM. Through these analytical moves, we came to understand how Suzanna's literate intersectional identities were illuminated through her participation in the Dig-A-Girls STEAM program.

Findings

Our study of Suzanna's mobile app development positions her intersectional identity as central to her digital composing process. We therefore pay particular attention to how her racial, gender, linguistic, and cultural identities came to bear upon the creation of her mobile app. In what follows, we offer an account of Suzanna's design process that centers her intersecting identities—a geek, a scholar, a young woman, a Puertorriqueña—and describe the identity-affirming potential of digital design for young people. We organize the findings by three concepts: STEAM, multimodality (e.g., linguistic, auditory, and visual), and intersectionality (e.g., language, race, and gender). Suzanna's design process, we will show, sits at the intersection of these intersectional concepts and highlights how digital composing affirmed her literate intersectional identities.

STEAM-Powered Identity Work

A high school senior, Suzanna brought to the Dig-A-Girls project a wealth of insight into the complex sociocultural factors influencing how science, technology, engineering, art, and mathematics are taught and learned in school. Throughout her years in the US public school system, she was keenly sensitive to the visibility of women in general, and women of color, as both students and teachers in the STEAM disciplines. "I think there's not enough encouragement for minority girls," she noted in an interview with the research team. Here Suzanna is pointing to a latent capacity, interest, and passion for STEAM as both a personal and professional endeavor in many girls of color, a latency ready to be awakened in identity-affirming learning contexts like the Dig-A-Girls workshop.

During her time at the workshop, Suzanna wanted to develop a mobile app that could connect her local Puerto Rican community with international charities working to support Puerto Rico in the wake of Hurricanes Irma and Maria, which ravaged the island in the late summer of 2017. "I think it would be really cool," she stated, "to have an app that was maybe focused on hurricane relief efforts in small, lesser-known territories." Such a project had the power to engage Suzanna's identity as a critical creator, one for whom building, developing, and researching are opportunities to build bridges between her local community and Puerto Rico, where much of her family lived.

Guided by the Workshop's lead instructor—a Black woman, engineer, developer, and cofounder of a STEAM camp for girls of color—Suzanna drew on a variety of STEAM literacies to design and deploy her mobile app, "Hurricane Relief for Puerto Rico." Using Code.org's App Lab program, for example, she coded the app's user interface by applying block based Javascript, integrating different numerical values to organize information within the app and to prompt user interactions. While engaged in such technical work, she was mindful of the app's aesthetic appeal, which she described as "minimalist" in her design journal, the aim of which was to focus user attention on the app's mission statement: "Our goal is to connect people with reputable charities to foster increased recovery efforts for Puerto Rico after the passage of Hurricane Maria and Hurricane Irma" (see Figure 9.2). Such a powerful "our" is significant, evoking as it does the Dig-A-Girls community, the local Puerto Rican community, and perhaps even the multitudes contained within Suzanna.

Multimodal Identity Work

During the Dig-A-Girls digital application workshops, the girls were provided with various opportunities and prompts to read and write multimodally.

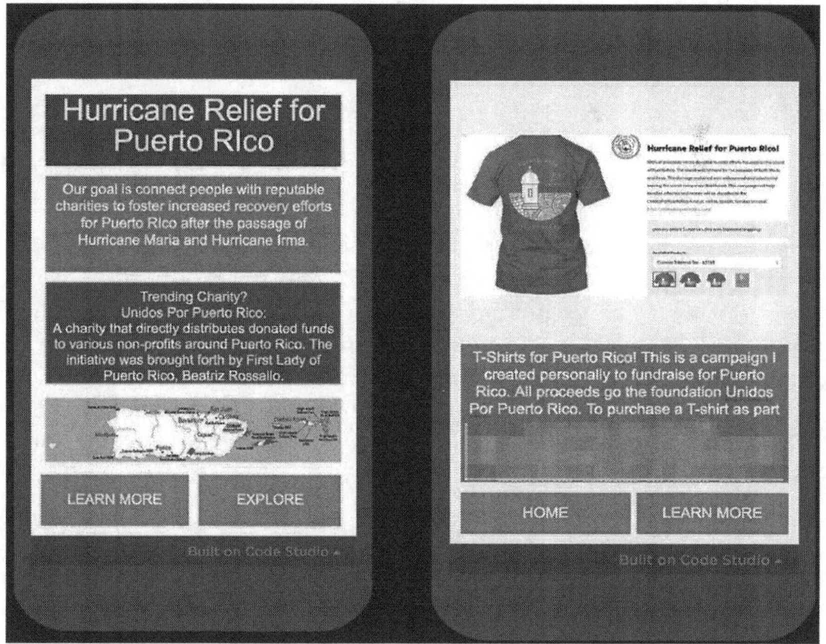

FIGURE 9.2 Suzanna's Collage of Digital App-Making Activities

For example, along with other femtors (female mentors) in STEAM who worked at a major broadcasting company where the workshops took place, the girls, their parents, and the research team jointly took part in crafting a Multimodal Community Journal (MCJ, Lewis Ellison et al., 2021). At the end of the workshops, the MCJ became a beautiful multimodal canvas of the hopes, dreams, affirmations, and solidarity of the Dig-A-Girls community. Suzanna was a part of the creation of the MCJ. Additionally, along with the other Black, African American, Latina/é/x, and Hispanic girls, Suzanna was prompted to (a) individually create a vision board in preparation for the application creation, (b) journal in any language and format in a tangible notebook, (c) include any multimodal text in her final application, and (d) engage in conversations about her identities and experiences related to STEAM.

In her interview, Suzanna mentioned that "creating comes naturally" for her. She expressed that she found it extremely rewarding to create things like diagrams and posters to illustrate concepts, because this process challenged her to connect different concepts and think more in-depth. The crafting of her digital application, from the vision board to the final product, was a creation process that engaged Suzanna's artistic, speaking, coding, and writing literacy skills. In her journal, she wrote: "I found that helping explain the process to my partner [another Dig-A-Girl] allowed me to further cement my knowledge of the lab and the details of using it." Suzanna found that each mode of literacy practice informed each other during her creation process of the digital application. Moreover, in her final application, she included pictures, written words, and website links to support her cause of raising money for recovery efforts in Puerto Rico. During our time with Susanna, she was constantly challenged to create with prompts that centered creating and meaning-making multimodally through listening, speaking, journaling, coding, and illustrating individually and in community with other girls and women of color.

The multimodal creation processes provided opportunities for Suzanna to explore, embody, and express her literate intersectional identities (see Figure 9.2). While her app expressed her Puerto Rican identity, what we want to emphasize is that the multimodal blending of colors, text, images, and links—all of which were structured by computer programming language—emerged at the intersection of intersections: STEAM, multimodality, and identity. Suzanna's multimodal composing, then, was not simply a young person leveraging modal affordances. Rather, multimodality itself, as an intersectional concept, reinforced and affirmed her literate intersectional identity.

Intersectional Identity Work

As we examined Suzanna's literate intersectional identities and literacies through the lens of STEAM and multimodality, we noted that her identities were crucial in how they shape and are shaped by her myriad literacy practices. These (intersectional) identities are rooted in the social contexts in which Suzanna navigated her literate life.

As a young woman, Suzanna was aware of the disparity between men and women in STEAM. She was working hard to challenge the inequities and stereotypes that girls/women face. In the interview, when asked about how she felt about the extremely low number of Hispanic girls in her science and computer class at school, compared to white men, she said: "It's not that they're not there. It's just that they may feel as though it should be left to other people to pursue that, or that it may be easier for them to pursue a different area of study." In this excerpt, Suzanna understood the reality of the low number of girls of color in the STEAM pipeline, and was actively considering the cause for this reality, in an effort to change it. Her action to take part in the Dig-A-Girls project was one of her efforts to increase the number of girls of color in STEAM.

In addition to identifying as a girl, her trans-geographic experiences across time also shaped her identities as a Hispanic woman and speaker of Spanish. The first language that Suzanna learned was Spanish. Although she only spoke Spanish in Spanish class at school, her mother tongue was integral to her keeping her relationship with her family in Puerto Rico. In the interview, Suzanna shared a sacred account of this relationship via her grandparents' patio:

> My grandmother had this very intricate patio in Puerto Rico that my grandfather had built for her before he died, and it's all made of tile, and it's all hand-laid mosaic tile, and cement that he had for her to put her plants in. And so the first one [hurricane] that came through, Irma, kind of just knocked down a couple of trees, but most of the concrete stayed intact. But when Maria came through, all of the trees are falling over, and the concrete is all torn up. The mosaic tile is torn up. She [her grandma] was very heartbroken about it. She actually came and spent the holidays with us, instead of staying over in Puerto Rico.

Upon telling us about the family stories and histories she heard about Puerto Rico, Suzanna revealed that she and her mom were talking about potential ideas for her digital app during their drive to our interview. They both thought it would be meaningful if Suzanna made an application to raise money for Puerto Rico's post-hurricane recovery efforts. She stated:

> So I definitely signed myself up for charity. I think there's a lot to be done there. I was brainstorming a couple of ideas with my mom in the car. We were talking about the app Charity Navigator, and that kind of like tells you where the money is going, how much of it goes and that sort of thing, and I would kind of like to do something like that ... for Hurricane Irma and Maria relief. Because my experiences with my friends wanting to donate money to Puerto Rico to help families there, they didn't know where to donate.

> They didn't know what place was reputable. And that sort of thing, so I think it would be really cool to have an app that was focused on Hurricane Relief efforts and smaller, lesser-known territories. To make sure that people can help out, the people who do want to help out, they know exactly where to go to help out. I feel like that would be really cool to set up. So it would be a small-scale Charity Navigator but for lesser-known territories.

In Suzanna's final application, she not only included facts about Puerto Rico, but she also included a link to a website that sold T-shirts that she designed and made. On the front of her T-shirt design, it read, "I [heart] Puerto Rico" On the back of the T-shirt, she wrote in Spanish, "solidaridad." Suzanna took an activist role in fundraising to donate to Puerto Rico through selling T-shirts and creating the digital application that included myriad donation outlets.

As shown above, to finalize her vision for her digital application, Suzanna engaged in storytelling with her mom and grandmother about memories of their past and aspirations for their futures. These intergenerational literacy practices guided her activist efforts in creating the application. Suzanna engaged in the remaking of her identities through digital practices in the Dig-A-Girls workshops while she made sense of her family histories and futures.

Discussion

Whereas conventional approaches to STEAM learning tend toward intersectional erasure—that is, they are shaped by discourses of neutrality, objectivity, and instrumentality and can marginalize identity—this chapter suggests that opportunities for identity-affirming literacy engagements can support deeply meaningful forms of technical innovation. Even though intersectionality is a theory focused on how oppressive systems uphold the power of white supremacy, it also helps us understand how Suzanna's intersectional identities function in shaping her literate life. As Crenshaw (2017) has observed, "intersectionality is a lens through which you can see where power comes and collides, where it interlocks and intersects" (para. 4). A literate intersectional identities perspective makes visible how the power circulating within disciplines and modalities can be leveraged to support intersectional affirmation. By centering Suzanna's literate intersectional identities, we have shown how the racial, ethnic, gendered, linguistic, and familial axes of her identity were nurtured through STEAM learning and multimodal digital design, which, crucially, we understand as intersectional practices in their own rights. While Suzanna was engaged in digital design for "lesser-known territories," digital design itself became a tool for expressing lesser-known territories of herself, a way to show how each dimension of her rich identity—female, designer, artist, Puertorriqueña—contributed to her technical innovation. A literate intersectional identities perspective therefore helped us understand that there is power at the intersection of STEAM, multimodality, and identity, a power that suffused the Dig-A-Girls: STEAM Workshop.

But how might researchers and practitioners leverage the concept of literate intersectional identities in their work? Our suggestion is to look for the intersections. Crenshaw's pioneering work with intersectionality greatly expanded how the social sciences in general, and education in particular, understand the relationship between power and identity. In our work, the concept of intersectionality has guided us toward seeing the intersections in STEAM and multimodality, which helped us appreciate how the intersectional nature of such concepts related to Suzanna's literate intersectional identities. Where else might such intersections be found (e.g., language learning, familial literacies, and video games), and how might they be generatively set alongside the insights of identity-forward, intersectional literacies studies? Similarly, we urge practitioners to look for the intersections in their curricula, classrooms, schools, and communities, not to mention themselves, and allow the intersections they find to inspire identity-affirming affiliations and collaborations. The *Dig-A-Girls: STEAM Workshop*, for example, was the product of intersectional identities—researchers, families, young people, STEAM professionals—joining together to sustain the cultures, interests, and hobbies of the Dig-A-Girls at the intersection of two urban streets.

Moreover, we urge practitioners and researchers to pay close attention to the multiple identities of the students and youth they teach or work with, and how these identities intersect and inform each other to shape their literacies. Suzanna was engaged in myriad opportunities to read and write multimodally on topics related to STEAM. These reading and writing practices (broadly defined) challenged Suzanna to (re)examine and (re)tell narratives and lived experiences that embody her literate intersectional identities as a coder, Hispanic girl, and activist. It is important to acknowledge that after Suzanna's participation in Dig-A-Girls, she graduated from her STEM high school and enrolled in environmental engineering at a research university. She graduated in spring 2022 and is continuing her academics in STEM in the fall. She wrote in a post-study statement about her experiences in the Dig-A-Girls workshop:

> My experience with Dig-A-Girls built my confidence and gave me the technical agency to create through code a program to help Puerto Rico in recovery from Hurricane Maria. Learning to code, and to code with a goal that I get to determine, opened my eyes to my ability to fill some of the gaps I was seeing in my community of peers and empowered me to take a chance and set up my own fundraiser.

In teaching and research, it is crucial for scholars and teachers to acknowledge the complexities of the identities and experiences our youth and children bring into school or research spaces, and to provide continuous opportunities and explicit support for them to explore these literate intersectional identities.

Discussion Questions

In closing, we challenge our readers to (re)consider the following questions in their teaching and research endeavors:

1. How can you extend the conceptualization of literate intersectional identities in your research and educational contexts?
2. What are your literate intersectional identities that shape your positionality, onto-epistemology, and philosophy for research and teaching?
3. What are some ways researchers and teachers can explore and leverage the intersectional literate identities of the people they work with?
4. How can researchers and teachers become humble listeners of the stories of the research partners and students whom we work with that shape their intersectional literate identities, to affirm and sustain their ways of knowing and being?

References

Alvermann, D. E. (2011). Moving on/keeping pace: Youth's literate identities and multimodal digital texts. In S. Abrams and J. Rowsell (Eds.), *Rethinking identity and literacy education in the 21st century* (pp. 109–128). Teachers College Press.

Ashcraft, C., Eger, E. K., & Scott, K. (2017). Becoming technosocial change agents: Intersectionality and culturally responsive pedagogies as vital resources for increasing girls' participation in computing. *Anthropology and Education Quarterly*, *48*(3), 233–251. https://doi.org/10.1111/aeq.12197

Cho, S., Crenshaw, K. W., & McCall, L. (2013). Toward a field of intersectionality studies: Theory, applications, and praxis. *Signs: Journal of Women in Culture and Society*, *38*(4), 785–810. https://doi.org/10.1086/669608

Collins, P. H. (1998) *Fighting words: Black women and the search for justice*. University of Minnesota Press.

Crenshaw, K. (1989). Demarginalizing the intersection of race and sex: A Black feminist critique of antidiscrimination doctrine, feminist theory and antiracist politics. In K. Maschke (Ed.), *Feminist legal theories* (pp. 23–51). Routledge.

Crenshaw, K. W. (1991). Mapping the margins: Intersectionality, identity politics, and violence against women of color. *Stanford Law Review*, 43, 1241–1299. http://www.jstor.org/stable/1229039

Crenshaw, K. (2015, Sept. 24). Why intersectionality can't wait. *The Washington Post*. https://www.washingtonpost.com/news/in-theory/wp/2015/09/24/why-intersectionality-cant-wait/

Crenshaw, K. (2017). *Kimberlé Crenshaw on intersectionality, more than two decades later*. News from Columbia Law School. Columbia Law School. https://www.law.columbia.edu/news/archive/kimberle-crenshaw-intersectionality-more-two-decades-later

Curenton, S. M., Harris, K., Rochester, S. E., Sims, J., & Ibekwe-Okafor, N. (2022). Promoting racial literacy in early childhood: Storybooks and conversations with young black children. *Child Development Perspectives*. Advance online publication. https://doi.org/10.1111/cdep.12440

Enright, K. A., Wong, J. W., & Sanchez, S. (2021). Gateway moments to literate identities. *Journal of Literacy Research, 53*(4). https://doi.org/10.1177%2F1086296X211052260

Greene, D. T. (2016). 'We need more "US" in schools!!': Centering Black adolescent girls' literacy and language practices in online school spaces. *The Journal of Negro Education, 85*(3), 274–289. https://doi.org/10.7709/jnegroeducation.85.3.0274

Hikida, M. (2018). Holding space for literate identity co-construction. *Journal of Literacy Research, 50*(2), 217–238. https://doi.org/10.1177/1086296X17751824

Kelly, L. L. (2020). Exploring Black girls' subversive literacies as acts of freedom. *Journal of Literacy Research, 52*(4), 456–481. https://doi.org/10.1177/1086296X20966367

Kleekamp, M. C. (2020). "No! Turn the pages!" Repositioning neuroqueer literacies. *Journal of Literacy Research, 52*(2), 113–135. https://doi.org/10.1177%2F1086296X20915531

Lewis Ellison, T. (2014). Digital ontologies of self: Two African American adolescents co-construct and negotiate identities through the sims 2. *Digital Culture & Education, 6*(4), 334–357.

Lewis Ellison, T. (2017). Digital participation, agency, choice: An African American youth's digital storytelling about Minecraft. *Journal of Adolescent and Adult Literacy, 61*(1), 25–34. https://doi.org/10.1002/jaal.645

Lewis Ellison, T., Robinson, B., & Qiu, T. (2020). Examining African American girls' literate intersection identities through journal entries and discussions about STEM. *Written Communication, 37*(1), 3–40. https://doi.org/10.1177%2F0741088319880511

Lewis Ellison, T., Robinson, B, &. Qiu, T. (2021, April 10). *African American and Latinx Girls' Compositions of Multimodal Community Journaling as Artifactual Literacies about STEAM* [Conference Presentation]. *American Educational Research Association 2021 Annual Meeting*. Virtual Meeting.

Lewis Ellison, T. & Qiu, T. (2023). From Black girl exclusion to Black girl empowerment: Understanding one adolescent Black girls' digital and STEAM literacy practices as empowering, liberatory, and agentic. *International Journal of Qualitative Studies in Education, 36*(3), 465–486.

Miles, M. B., Huberman, A. M., & Saldaña, J. (2014). *Qualitative data analysis: A methods sourcebook*. Sage.

Moje, E. B., & Luke, A. (2009). Literacy and identity: Examining the metaphors in history and contemporary research. *Reading Research Quarterly, 44*(4), 415–437. https://doi.org/10.1598/RRQ.44.4.7

Morton, T. R., & Parsons, E. C. (2018). #BlackGirlMagic: The identity conceptualization of Black women in undergraduate STEM education. *Science Education, 102*(6), 1363–1393. https://doi.org/10.1002/sce.21477

Muhammad, G. E., & Haddix, M. (2016). Centering Black girls' ways of knowing: A historical review of literature on the multiple literacies of Black girls. *English Education, 48*(4), 299–336. https://www.jstor.org/stable/26492572

National Center for Science and Engineering Statistics. (2015). *Women, minorities, and persons with disabilities in science and engineering: 2015 (Rep. No. NSF 07-315)*. National Science Foundation.

National Center for Science and Engineering Statistics. (2017). *Women, minorities, and persons with disabilities in science and engineering: 2017 (Rep. No. NSF 13-304).* National Science Foundation.

Price-Dennis, D. (2016). Developing curriculum to support Black girls' literacies in digital spaces. *English Education, 48*(4), 337–361. https://www.jstor.org/stable/26492573

Price-Dennis, D., Holmes, K., & Smith, E. (2015). Exploring digital literacy practices in an inclusive classroom. *The Reading Teacher, 69*(2), 195–205. https://doi.org/10.1002/trtr.1398

Price-Dennis, D., Muhammad, G. E., Womack, E., McArthur, S. A., & Haddix, M. (2017). The multiple identities and literacies of Black girlhood: A conversation about creating spaces for Black girl voices. *Journal of Language and Literacy Education, 13*(2), 1–18.

Scott, K. (2002). "You want to be a girl and not my friend": African American/Black girls' play activities with and without boys. *Childhood, 9*(4), 397–414. https://doi.org/10.1177/0907568202009004003

Scott, K. A., Sheridan, K. M., & Clark, K. (2015). Culturally responsive computing: A theory revisited. *Learning, Media and Technology, 40*(4), 412–436. https://doi.org/10.1080/17439884.2014.924966

Vasudevan, L., Schultz, K., & Bateman, J. (2010). Rethinking composing in a digital age: Authoring literate identities through multimodal storytelling. *Written Communication, 27*(4), 442–468. https://doi.org/10.1177/0741088310378217

Wagner, C. J. (2021). Literacy and identities. In G. Noblit (Ed.), *Oxford research encyclopedia of education* (pp. 1–23). Oxford University Press.

SECTION IV

Literate Identities Across Childhood and Adolescence

Introduction to Literate Identities Across Childhood and Adolescence

Christopher J. Wagner, Katherine K. Frankel, and Christine M. Leighton

Introduction

As children and adolescents grow they develop in remarkable ways that include dramatic changes in their abilities to use language and literacy. Over time children and adolescents make and remake their literate identities as they shape and reshape who they are and who they are becoming in relation to language and literacy. Children and adolescents play active roles in constructing and "rewriting" their literate identities as they change in their literacy interests, practices, goals, and experiences with literacy in and out of school. These changes draw attention to the critical role that time plays in the development of literate identities, and the ways that past experiences and future expectations shape children's and adolescents' literacy practices and identities. This consideration of time and change is central to conceptualizing how children and adolescents are "becoming" readers and writers.

Examining how and why literate identities change is an important aspect of understanding their role in learning. Broadly speaking, schools are not a consistently positive influence on literate identities. Though most children demonstrate a strong interest in reading and writing and positive assessments of their literacy ability at school entry, there is a general decline in students' attitudes and interest in literacy over time (Bates et al., 2016; McKenna et al., 1995; Morgan et al., 2008). The importance of understanding how and why literate identities change is made more urgent by the correlation between literate identities and literacy practices, and the profound ways that literate identities and literacy achievement are intertwined for learners across all grades (Harackiewicz et al., 2008; Marsh et al., 2005).

DOI: 10.4324/9781003271406-18

Theorizing Identities Across Childhood and Adolescence

Time is an essential aspect of the human experience and the construction of identities. The literate identities of children and adolescents exist in and across moments of time that shape who they are becoming as readers and writers (Compton-Lilly, 2014; Vygotsky, 1978). Literate identities are both informed by past histories and continuously constructed and reconstructed toward new possibilities and futures. The different ways that time can be conceptualized in identity research, including how literate histories, trajectories, and possibilities are accounted for by researchers, matters to how literate identities are understood.

In one approach, time may be regarded as a variable that is accounted for through the age of participants, the duration of a study, or as a factor in quantitative analyses. From this perspective time is one of many influences that may be considered in the study of literate identities. Alternatively, time may be centered to examine identities as temporal constructs that are embedded within the passage of time and shaped by change, memory, and other related constructs that are integral to experience and learning (Compton-Lilly, 2015; Lemke, 2000). Considering time in either of these ways raises further questions about how to theorize time and development in identity research.

For example, researchers may consider time as a singular, linear construct that is constant across children and experiences. Alternatively, researchers may consider time as multidimensional, exploring how time can be differently constructed and variably shaped by notions of memory, lived experience, and other subjective aspects of the human experience (Adam, 2000; Schatzki, 2006). Time can likewise be considered in ways that connect it to spaces and the movement of bodies both physically and experientially (Bakhtin, 1981). These views can complicate notions of time and how it is connected to context and lived experience, and open possibilities to consider how time is connected to the changing bodies of children and adolescents.

Time is likewise implicit in the construct of development, which attends to change in children and adolescents as they grow. Developmental perspectives have attempted to both provide normative accounts of how changes occur over time (e.g., Erikson, 1980; Harter, 2012), and at other times to deconstruct and critique such models (Langer-Osuna & Nasir, 2016). Often these models of identity have emphasized ways that developmental changes may mediate children's capacities for constructing identities. Though there may be reasons to consider whether cognition or other aspects of development influence identity processes, there is likewise a risk in assuming that children of some ages may lack key capacities to construct identities (Starmans, 2017).

Exploring time, change, and development requires researchers to consider what tools both identity and developmental theories provide and how they can be brought together. Many developmental theories have not attended to diversity and culture in development, including the roles of language, race, and culture on identity construction or the roles of differing cultural models of literacy across school, home, and community contexts (Langer-Osuna & Nasir, 2016; Wagner, 2021). Taking a developmental lens to identity studies requires researchers to attend to such issues of diversity and culture, and to consider when new or revised theories may be needed to examine literate identities across time.

Research Methods Across Childhood and Adolescence

Studying change and development in literate identities requires the use of research methods that are designed to collect data at multiple points in time. Longitudinal research designs provide the most intuitive and straightforward approach to exploring questions of time, change, and development. Longitudinal studies follow one or more research subjects over an extended period of time to document how subjects' identities change or develop. This may include how various experiences, influences, and other factors shape the ways children and adolescents construct literate identities, engage with literate communities, and develop literate practices that inform who they are becoming as readers and writers.

Cross-sectional research designs look at different developmental or time points to understand ways identities change or differ across age groups. Though similar to longitudinal designs in some respects, cross-sectional studies differ in that they look at different research participants who are at different stages of development or life, rather than following a single set of research subjects across time. Cross-sectional studies can typically be conducted in less time than longitudinal studies because the research subjects are not followed across time. Though this can ease some of the logistical challenges of researching identities across time, cross-sectional studies cannot provide the same degree of information about change and causation that can be drawn from longitudinal designs.

Both longitudinal and cross-sectional studies present methodological needs and challenges for researchers. This begins with a need to consider the ways that children and adolescents and their literacy practices change as they develop as readers and writers. This includes ways that children can produce more extended writing samples as they grow as writers, or ways that reading often moves from an oral practice in childhood to an internal and silent practice as readers grow toward adolescence. Accounting for these changes requires concurrent changes in data collection procedures that are responsive to children's development and that view children as dynamic and not static beings.

Though considering how data collection is responsive to children's development is a first step, researchers must also consider how other aspects of research studies are designed to account for time and development. For example, researchers may need to consider how data will be interpreted that involves memory, recollection, and other related constructs that may present differences between linear and recalled notions of time. Other issues raised by longitudinal study designs include the need for ongoing consent of participants as they become more independent and may have changing views on their role in research. These challenges highlight the need for robust theorizations of identity and time that can guide researchers in understanding and making decisions about the design of studies.

Chapters in This Section

This section includes three chapters that look at literate identities across time. In two of these chapters, the authors follow one or more students across time to explore how literate identities change and how time functions as a contextual factor in understanding literate identities as histories and trajectories. In the other chapter, the authors look at different children and adolescents at moments in time to examine how age, grade, development, and other concepts associated with time inform how researchers understand literate identities and their role in literacy learning. By taking up both longitudinal and cross-sectional approaches to researching literate identities, these chapters illustrate the potential and necessity of understanding literate identities as a process that is bound and informed by constructs of time and change.

In Chapter 10, Compton-Lilly considers three children through the lens of three different theories (intersectionality, figured worlds, and assemblage) to explore the complexity of identity "becomings" across childhood and adolescence. Compton-Lilly follows these children from first grade to 12th grade in longitudinal portraits that show the multiple ways that change occurs in their identities and to counter views of identities that are tied to rigid developmental expectations. Though language and literacy may at times seem central and at other times peripheral to these children's becomings, Compton-Lilly shows how literate identities are bound up in the multiple and complex identity processes that children and youth engage in, and serve as both an identity on their own and a tool to the construction of other identities.

The multiple theoretical approaches Compton-Lilly uses to explore change and development in these case studies complicate the relationship between identities and time. The presentation of each case through the lens of a single theory shows both the critical roles of these different identity theories and how theoretical choices shape what is seen about identities and time. Through this approach, Compton-Lilly constructs an argument for why multiple theories and complexity are needed in identity research by showing how any one theory presents only a partial portrait of a person's identities, and how these partial portraits must be considered within a broader view of who children and adolescents are becoming.

In Chapter 11, Kabuto examines data on a child and parent collected across a decade to consider the ways identities are shaped by the special education system through processes of labeling. Kabuto draws on the concept of "becoming labeled" to describe how children construct multiple intersectional identities that are shaped by problematic discourses and structures around concepts like normalcy and standardization. By considering how these ideas play out across time, Kabuto provides insights into how children and families negotiate "becoming labeled" in the special education system and ways that students are agentive in the process of constructing, challenging, and reifying identities.

By critiquing fixed notions of ability that are grounded in deficit perspectives of children, Kabuto raises critical questions about what is "normal" in how learning and ability are conceptualized in school spaces. Through attention to the "sociocultural, non-chronological nature of time," Kabuto captures the ways that a child and parent align themselves with and challenge the labels assigned by the school and the special education system over time. Kabuto shows how identity processes are not decontextualized, momentary occurrences, but are instead informed by the past and "re-experienced" as students navigate school and literacy experiences.

In Chapter 12, Enriquez, Kontovourki, and Johnson present four vignettes that explore embodiment, or the roles of bodies, texts, and objects, and literate identities across a range of grade levels. In these vignettes the authors show how bodies are impacted by the material artifacts and spaces involved in reading and writing, and at the same time how children and adolescents use their bodies to exert agency in constructing and performing literate identities. The authors center the material and physical aspects of the body in space to consider how children and adolescents exist as doers of literacy in physical bodies and environments.

These vignettes draw on ethnographic and case study methods, showing how different methodological tools can bring to light various aspects of children's and adolescent's bodies and identities. Rather than positioning embodiment as an alternative to theories that view identities as discursively constructed, the authors instead show how material and physical spaces and acts extend discursive understandings of identities across ages and time, and in ways that challenge normative constructs of development. The authors' readings of these children's and adolescent's experiences complicate and disrupt understandings of identities and of literacies, asking researchers to see literacy and identities as entanglements of the material and human worlds.

Across these chapters, the authors show how considering time as a contextual factor can expand what researchers know about literate identities in childhood and adolescence. In some cases this focus on time challenges ideas about development and the linear constructs of age, grade levels, and academic progression that are common in schools. Kabuto raises questions about what is considered developmentally "normal" by critiquing fixed notions of ability that are grounded in deficit perspectives of children. Compton-Lilly similarly sets out to present narratives that counter views of identity that are tied to fixed trajectories and timelines, while Enriquez and colleagues draw attention to the body, which is itself a site of change and development.

The focus on time in these chapters highlights a need to consider development and change in ways that are complex and create space for variability and nuanced understandings of growth and learning as multifaceted and nonlinear processes. The range of theories used by the authors in these chapters, including critical theories that question common presuppositions about learning and development, points to a continued need for new ways of looking at identities and theories that challenge assumed or "established" knowledge about identities and the literate lives of children and adolescents. Together the chapters in this section are examples of both the challenges and opportunities open to researchers to explore how children and youth are becoming readers and writers across time.

References

Adam, B. (2000). The temporal gaze: The challenge for social theory in the context of GM food. *The British Journal of Sociology*, *51*(1), 125–142. https://doi.org/10.1080/000713100358462

Bakhtin, M. M. (1981). *The dialogic imagination: Four essays* (C. Emerson & M. Holquist, Trans.). University of Texas Press. https://doi.org/10.2307/40136453

Bates, C. C., D'Agostino, J. V., Gambrell, L., & Xu, M. (2016). Reading recovery: Exploring the effects on first-graders' reading motivation and achievement. *Journal of Education for Students Placed at Risk*, *21*(1), 47–59. https://doi.org/10.1080/10824669.2015.1110027

Compton-Lilly, C. (2014). Introduction: Conceptualizing past, present, and future timespaces. In C. Compton-Lilly & E. Halverson (Eds.), *Time and space in literacy research* (pp. 1–16). Routledge. https://doi.org/10.4324/9781315795829

Compton-Lilly, C. (2015). Time in education: Intertwined dimensions and theoretical possibilities. *Time & Society*, *25*(3), 575–593. https://doi.org/10.1177/0961463x15587837

Erikson, E. H. (1980). *Identity and the life cycle*. W. W. Norton.

Harackiewicz, J. M., Durik, A. M., Barron, K. E., Linnenbrink-Garcia, L., & Tauer, J. M. (2008). The role of achievement goals in the development of interest: Reciprocal relations between achievement goals, interest, and performance. *Journal of Educational Psychology*, *100*(1), 105–122. https://doi.org/10.1037/0022-0663.100.1.105

Harter, S. (2012). *The construction of the self: Developmental and sociocultural foundations* (2nd ed.). Guilford Press.

Langer-Osuna, J. M., & Nasir, N. S. (2016). Rehumanizing the "other": Race, culture, and identity in education research. *Review of Research in Education*, *40*, 723–743. https://doi.org/10.3102/0091732x16676468

Lemke, J. (2000). Across the scales of time: Artifacts, activities, and meanings in ecosocial systems. *Mind, Culture, and Activity*, 7(4), 273–290. https://doi.org/10.1207/s15327884mca0704_03

Marsh, H. W., Trautwein, U., Lüdtke, O., Köller, O., & Baumert, J. (2005). Academic self-concept, interest, grades, and standardized test scores: Reciprocal effects models of causal ordering. *Child Development*, *76*(2), 397–416. https://doi.org/10.1111/j.1467-8624.2005.00853.x

McKenna, M. C., Kear, D. J., & Ellsworth, R. A. (1995). Children's attitudes toward reading: A national survey. *Reading Research Quarterly*, *30*(4), 934–956. https://doi.org/10.2307/748205

Morgan, P. L., Fuchs, D., Compton, D. L., Cordray, D. S., & Fuchs, L. S. (2008). Does early reading failure decrease children's reading motivation? *Journal of Learning Disabilities*, *41*(5), 387–404. https://doi.org/10.1177/0022219408321112

Schatzki, T. R. (2006). The time of activity. *Continental Philosophy Review*, *39*, 155–182.

Starmans, C. (2017). Children's theories of the self. *Child Development*, *88*(6), 1774–1785. https://doi.org/10.1111/cdev.12951

Vygotsky, L. S. (1978). *Mind in society: The development of higher psychological processes*. Harvard University Press.

Wagner, C. J. (2021). Reading identities as a developmental process: Changes in Chinese-English learners from prekindergarten to kindergarten. *Bilingual Research Journal*, *44*(2), 174–188. https://doi.org/10.1080/15235882.2021.1942324

10

LONGITUDINAL IDENTITY CONSTRUCTION

Intersectionality, Figured Worlds, and Assemblage

Catherine Compton-Lilly

Introduction

In this chapter, I draw on three theoretical perspectives to explore the complexity of longitudinal identity becomings for three children as they move from grade one through high school. I intentionally adopt the terms "becomings" and "identity becomings" to avoid meanings associated with chronological models that measure, track, and compare the rate and nature of change across children, cultures, and classrooms. For me, given the various dimensions of becoming that scholars could track, becomings are always plural. The complexity of identity becomings is remarkable—not only in terms of its unique and contextualized nature but also considering the nuances, considerations, experiences, and cultural and historical messages that contribute to children's becomings.

By drawing on three theoretical frames, I question the adequacy of any one framework for describing and depicting the becomings of a particular child. I argue that all three of these theoretical framings are equally as relevant to each of the three children, and accordingly I randomly selected one theoretical framing to apply to each case as described below. Thus, I draw on theories of *intersectionality* (Crenshaw, 2017; Ladson-Billings, 2021) to discuss data related to Gabby, a Mexican American child whose family immigrated to the United States at least three generations ago. I draw on theories of *figured worlds* (Holland et al., 1998) to discuss the case of Lupita, a first-generation Mexican American girl. Finally, I reference Deleuze and Guattari's (1988) discussion of *assemblage* to explore becomings for Adam, who immigrated to the United States from Morocco as a kindergartener.

I maintain that the immigrant status of each child's family provides a unique and powerful context for considering becomings as each child negotiated

DOI: 10.4324/9781003271406-19

language, culture, race, culture, and gender. This focus on immigrant children does not suggest that identity becomings for native-born American students are simple. Instead, the political and social complications that surround immigration in the United States highlight the negotiations made by children in immigrant families and provide insight into the nature of becoming for all children.

While I highlight instances of literacy and reveal how literacy was operationalized, I do not constrain my analysis to literacy practices. If anything, my longitudinal research has revealed how literacy is deeply intertwined with family, friends, schooling, and technology. Thus, literacy is one of many tools that children and adolescents use to write and rewrite themselves as readers, writers, and people. Thus, literacy is more and less salient across the three cases.

A Longitudinal Methodology

In this longitudinal collective case study, I follow Gabby, Lupita, and Adam from first grade through high school. The full longitudinal study includes nine families who have immigrated to the United States from around the world. The research question that framed the full study was admittedly broad: *How do children in immigrant families become literate and construct literate identities?* Families were solicited through a convenience sample involving myself, a team of graduate students, and local educators. I intentionally chose Gabby, Lupita, and Adam as the focus of this chapter, since they were the children that I have worked with directly. Early data from other cases were primarily collected by graduate students. Gabby and Adam participated in the project for 13 years and graduated from high school in June of 2021. Lupita joined the project the year after Gabby and Adam and is in her senior year of high school.

Research team analyses draw on interviews with Gabby, Lupita, and Adam, and their mothers, siblings, and teachers. Data include observations at home and school, artifacts created by the children (e.g., writing samples, self-portraits, maps, and photographs), and conversations about those artifacts. During the first year of the study, members of the research team visited the children five times at home and five times at school. During years two through eight, we visited each space three times. In year nine, I moved to a different state and personally visited each space twice annually. Data were designed to highlight the spaces that the families have occupied across time (i.e., home/neighborhood/school and native country/country of residence). Each year, we invited the children to complete the same or similar tasks. For example, we asked children to draw annual self-portraits to explore change and continuity in how they depicted themselves. Semi-structured interviews focused on school experiences, interests, literacy achievement, and literacy engagements.

For each case, we coded interviews and field notes using an established set of a priori codes reflecting our research foci (e.g., child identity, home literacy practices, or school literacy practices). Interviews and field notes were subsequently subjected to a grounded analysis resulting in additional codes (e.g., pop culture or technology). Artifacts were reviewed in relation to the emerging code set and evolving themes. In many cases, patterns suggested by interviews and observations were echoed in artifacts. At other times, artifacts complicated emerging themes.

However, our coding of these data was only partially helpful in identifying longitudinal patterns. In order to attend to change, consistency, and nuance across time, we intentionally attended to how children spoke and presented themselves across time. We considered the drawings they made, the photographs they took, and the activities they pursued. As I looked across data and identified long-term patterns, I recognized the multidimensional nature of each child's becomings. As noted, I believe that all three theoretical framings are equally relevant to each case. Thus, as I commenced writing this chapter, I wrote each child's name on a piece of paper and blindly drew it from a basket. I then blindly drew each of the theoretical framings from the same basket and matched the first name drawn with the first theory drawn.

Theorizing Becomings

Over the past 40 years, sociocultural researchers have increasingly recognized people's identities as multiple, negotiated, and involving power and positioning (McCarthey & Moje, 2002). In contrast to defined developmental trajectories of change (Erikson & Erikson, 1981; Mead, 1934), contemporary scholars have not only identified multiple conceptions of identity (Moje & Luke, 2009) but also have named a range of complexities that inform and affect identity (Gee, 2018; McAdams, 2001; Mishler, 2004; Wortham, 2006). Some of these conceptions focus on layered aspects of identity that locate people in terms of multiple identity positionings (e.g., race, gender, social class, and educational status). Intersectionality theory—discussed below in relation to Gabby—is an example. Other theories focus on how people operate within contexts that include assumed roles and relationships, as well as expected roles. These figured worlds are discussed in relation to Lupita. Finally, some theories of identity recognize the vast range of experiences, activities, and engagements with people, things, and ideas that affect becomings in rhizomatic and idiosyncratic ways. Theories of assemblage are referenced in Adam's case to illustrate his eternally emergent becomings.

While I draw on theories of identity, I purposely use the term "becomings" not only to highlight the multiple directions and varieties of change that simultaneously emerge, sustain, and falter but also to intentionally counter conceptions of identity that are tied to developmental expectations, trajectories, and timelines. I view becomings as inherently contextualized, individualized, and unpredictable across conceptualizations that highlight layered dimensions (intersectionality), cultural assumptions (figured worlds), and rhizomatic and idiosyncratic assemblages.

Intersectionality and Becomings

Theories of intersectionality highlight the complexity of individual identity becomings. As Delgado and Stefancic (2001) explained, "Intersectionality means the examination of race, sex, class, national origin, and sexual orientation and how their combinations play out in various settings" (p. 51). For example, the identity negotiations of African American women are different from those of African American men and white women, which in turn inform different lived experiences and positionings. The experiences of families that have immigrated to the United States can be viewed through an intersectional lens. For children, "naturalized hierarchies of gender and age" (Collins, 1998, p. 65) are relevant, as are intersectionalities of race, social class, language spoken, and nationality. Critical Race Theorists (e.g., Delgado & Stefancic, 2001; Ladson-Billings, 2021) have used intersectional understandings of experiences to understand how historical inequities are sustained across time.

Although investigations of intersectionality are often applied to adolescents and adults, elsewhere we have argued that young children also engage in intersectional identity becomings (Compton-Lilly et al., 2017). Investigations of identity becomings for children in immigrant families often highlight multidimensional, syncretic, and hybrid aspects of identities as children engage in various linguistic, literate, and cultural practices (Gregory et al., 2004; Souto-Manning, 2013). In particular, scholars explore the literacies children take up and practice across home, school, and community (Gregory et al., 2004). These becomings entail the simultaneous, "intermingling or merging of culturally diverse traditions" (Duranti & Ochs, 1997, p. 172), which inevitably entail intersectional dimensions (e.g., gender, race, socio-economic status, religion, and language). Because children in immigrant families simultaneously encounter assumptions about who they are as raced, gendered, and resourced learners as they move across home, school, community, and peer spaces, intersectional becomings are particularly significant.

Recognizing becomings as intersectional not only highlights the complexity of becomings but also situates becomings within power-laden contexts that carry long histories of privilege and inequity. Below, I explore three data sets for Gabby related to elementary school, middle school, and high school. Notably, these data represent what occupied Gabby's attention at particular moments. Admittedly, I was limited by what Gabby and her mother discussed and shared. Gabby's longitudinal becomings are a million times richer, deeper, and more complex than this sampling, and even my full 13-year data set might suggest. Regardless, I present these glimpses into Gabby's becomings to explore how dimensions of becomings intersected across time.

Gabby's Becomings During Her Elementary Years

Across the 13-year study, Gabby and her mother described Gabby as a "Tomboy." When Gabby was in first grade, her mother shared photographs of Gabby as a toddler sitting in a chair that resembled a large pink butterfly. I was surprised. Gabby's mother explained, "[That] was when I could get her to wear pink. Now I can't... We don't do girl clothes at all." The entire time I have known Gabby, she has consistently worn over-sized, dark-colored sweatshirts, T-shirts, and sweatpants passed down from her older brothers.

Across the interviews, Ms. Rodriguez often commented on Gabby's attire, identifying possible signs that Gabby might be becoming more feminine. In second grade, her mother reported she was "slowly coming out of it [being a 'Tomboy']" saying, "the other day she asked me to pierce her ears." Gabby's mother then moderated her comment saying, "But I still can't get her to put [on] the girl clothes … if anything looks remotely girly, fringy, she's not going for it." By grade four, Ms. Rodriguez noted that Gabby wanted "to dye her hair," and across the next two years her hair went from a bright red, to orange, to blue. Blonde or pink were never candidates. That same year, Gabby surprised us when she begged her mother for a curling iron. Yet when asked to choose between the curling iron and a set of LEGOs, Gabby chose the LEGOs. Gabby's mother continued to lament, "She has no, like girly attentions but, I mean, I was a Tomboy for many years." As Gabby explained, "I'm a Tomboy I like to stick around my brothers."

Gabby's Becomings During Her Middle School Years

Gabby's interest in LEGOs was evident in grade three when she started using them to make animals and construct buildings. This interest continued alongside an emerging fascination with the video game *Minecraft* as Gabby moved into middle school. *Minecraft* is a video game that could be described as a digital version of LEGOs. *Minecraft* invites players to build 3D worlds, including buildings, cities, and terrains. Notably, these interests were limited by the high cost of the LEGOs, the *Minecraft* app, and its required Android or iOS device. Ms. Rodriguez explained that a friend had given them a used set of LEGOs but that she could not afford more, saying, "[It's like] thirty-two bucks for one of those buckets," and then, "they have like this tiny box of Mario [LEGOs for] fifty bucks. And I'm like, no way." Gabby's engagement with Minecraft was limited to what she could do on her mother's cell phone—watching videos of other people playing the game. However, this did not curb her enthusiasm.

When Gabby was in sixth grade, I recalled her earlier practice of using LEGOs to make animals and I brought her a set of LEGOs that could be used to build a farm complete with animals. Gabby was excited and immediately poured the LEGOs onto the floor. As she dug through the pieces, she pulled out the pink LEGOs, that could be used to make a pig. She placed them in a pile commenting, "I'm leaving all the pink [LEGOs]… This is going to go bye-bye … I don't want these." Amused, I suggested that we get rid of the pink Legos. While Gabby decided to keep them, she made it clear that they would be used sparingly.

Her love of LEGOs was complicated by the pinkness of the pieces to the degree that even the possibility of making an animal was over-ridden by their pink-ness.

Gabby's Becomings During Her High School Years

By grade ten, Gabby described herself as "bi" and was dating a female classmate and later a formerly female-identifying classmate who was transitioning to male. She reported that she now had a PlayStation on which she could actually play *Minecraft*. Gabby's self-proclaimed goal was to become a welder. While she had considered becoming a veterinarian, she explained, "that takes too many years of school" while with welding, "you can just go straight into it and make good money." She was taking a series of introductory classes at her high school and explained, "I just really liked it. The teacher said I have a natural talent." She loved, "the way the metal heats up and melts and stuff, it's just satisfying."

It reportedly did not bother Gabby to be the only girl in her introductory shop classes and she was excited to take the official welding class in spring of 2021 but could not when schools closed due to the Covid-19 pandemic. While she completed high school in a twice-a-week, self-paced, alternative program, she reported, "the only thing that I'm bummed about with COVID is [that in] 11th grade I was going to take a welding class." At our final interview, Gabby proudly reported that she had gotten a part-time job, "working at the library—stocking shelves." She noted, "I feel like for a job it would be pretty easy."

Gabby's Intersectionality and Becomings

These data only touch on a small set of the intersectional dimensions that have informed Gabby's becomings. While I could have written about race, nationality, language, or age, gender and social class were particularly salient as I considered Gabby's case. Gabby's early claims of being a "Tomboy," later self-identification as "bi," and actions that accompanied these self-positionings were enacted through activities described above (e.g., preferring her brothers' clothes and dreams of becoming a welder) and others not reported (e.g., love of sports, self-described tough-ness, and preference for male friends). However, Gabby's gender negotiations occurred alongside limited economic resources (e.g., access to LEGOS and *Minecraft*, hand-me-down clothes, and fees needed to play sports) that further defined possibilities and opportunities.

Notably, Gabby's intersectional becomings were not simply the imposition of cultural and familial norms. Gabby resisted her mother's encouragement to dress in more feminine ways. She was selective in what she would take up (e.g., rejecting pink LEGOS), and she found work-arounds when needed (e.g., watching *Minecraft* videos rather than playing the game). Gabby also found advocates who supported her non-traditional interests and proclivities, including her mother who supported her "bi" becoming, her high school shop teacher who encouraged her to pursue welding, and a literacy researcher (me) who brought her sets of LEGOS and books about *Minecraft*.

Lupita's Figured Worlds and Becomings

Holland and her colleagues (1998) proposed figured worlds to explore how cultural experiences and agency situate and inform people's becomings. They describe figured worlds as a "socially and culturally constructed realm of interpretation in which particular characters and actors are recognized, significance is assigned to certain acts, and particular outcomes are valued over others" (p. 52). Drawing on a rich range of sociocultural theories (e.g., Vygotsky, Bakhtin, and Bourdieu), Holland and her colleagues worked at the intersection of sociocultural reckonings to argue for the complexity and multi-dimensionality of identity construction. They described their theorizing of identity as challenging "a coherent, unified, and ordinary subject" (p. 8) while highlighting how humans are "bounded" to established social and cultural practices and yet capable of collective and individual movement in new directions "led by hope, desperation, or even playfulness, but certainly by no rational plan" (p. 7). In short, alongside social and cultural influences are acts of agency, which are not always conducted with a clear plan in mind. Holland and her colleagues describe agency as "frail, especially among those with little power" (p. 5), while reminding scholars that agency happens "daily and mundanely, and it deserves our attention" (p. 5).

Particularly salient to Lupita and her family—who immigrated to the United States just before Lupita was born—are the "improvisations" (Holland et al., 1998, p. 18) that Lupita's parents made as they negotiated life in a new country and community. As Holland and her colleagues reported, "the improvisations of the parental generation are the beginning of a new habitus for the next generation" (p. 18). Like Critical Race Theory and theories of intersectionality, figured worlds recognize identity becomings as "situated in historically contingent, socially enacted, culturally constructed 'worlds'" (p. 7) that inform how people operate. However, improvisations and agency operate within these spaces as "socially powerful, cultural discourses and practices" which "position people and provide them with resources to respond to the problematic situations in which they find themselves" (p. 32). Through these enactments and discourses "people tell others who they are, but even more important, they tell themselves and then try to act as though they are who they say they are" (p. 3).

Lupita's Becomings During Her Elementary School Years

Language was a big part of Lupita's figured world of home and school. As the oldest sibling, Lupita was the first child to attend school in the United States and the first to learn to read and write in English. Our early field notes regularly captured

Lupita helping mom with English words and clarifying our interview questions. Members of the research team noted that "although Lupita answered the [interview] questions in English she did not always understand what the questions meant" and often "searched for English words." Lupita's father confirmed that she knew "more words and things in Spanish." That same year, her teacher noted, "She speaks English, but really doesn't always seem to understand everything. But she doesn't say [anything] … she just makes you think she does [understand]."

While in first grade Lupita reported that she did not "want to speak in Spanish [at school]" and wanted "to speak English to show my mom." By third grade, she was more ambivalent about learning to read and write in English. By then, her younger sisters were attending dual language classrooms where they were learning to read and write in Spanish and English. Lupita described learning to read in English as "muy dificil" ("it's really hard"), noting the "need to use this language, that language, any language, only English or Spanish." She explained that other people in her home read "Spanish books" and that English books were "boring" and gave her "headaches."

Lupita's Becomings During Her Middle School Years

In middle school, Lupita attended a special program for students who spoke Spanish but had not participated in the dual language program. Lupita was excited to take classes in Spanish, saying, "We just speak Spanish. We write in Spanish. I take Spanish classes!" Reflecting on differences between elementary and middle school, Lupita reported that elementary school was

> difficult and we speak a lot in English and they don't teach you any Spanish … at middle school it's different because they're like Spanish classes and you get to learn more and write more, even you get to speak more of your language.

She explained, it's "like part of my culture and my language." Lupita lamented, "I can't remember some of the Spanish, so I need to do that Spanish class."

By middle school, language use in the home was more fluid. Lupita described her mother as enjoying Spanish books, her youngest sister as preferring English books, and another sister as enjoying books in both Spanish and English. Lupita reported that her mother generally read in Spanish and added that she wanted to "read more in English so she can learn more and speak better." When we asked Lupita if she would have preferred learning to read and write in Spanish, Lupita initially identified a preference for Spanish, but then corrected herself saying, "actually both … because I want to get the opportunity to get farther for my future." When asked to write about herself, Lupita wrote, "I have a lot of family and I am a Latina. I am proud that I am a Latina."

Lupita's Becomings During Her High School Years

By high school, Lupita was committed to becoming fully bilingual. Her commitment reflected her future goals, which included "getting ready for college" and being able to "travel someday." To prepare for college, Lupita joined various clubs and programs designed to support Spanish-speaking students. In tenth grade, she took a Spanish class designed for Spanish-speaking students. Lupita found the class challenging, reporting that "I speak a different type of Spanish." A year later Lupita described the class as a "whole new experience" saying "it kind of messed me up a little" since the Spanish that they were taught was "Spain Spanish." Lupita continued, "you have to focus on how the verbs are, the non-verbs, and adjectives. And I'm just like, 'Whoa! Whoa! Whoa! I thought I knew Spanish.'"

As she moved into high school, Lupita increasingly compared her proficiency with Spanish and English. She reported that her parents sometimes teased her:

> From what my parents tell me, I was like, "So Mom, Dad, I have a question. It's a serious question." And they're like, "Yeah. What's up?" Do I speak good in English or Spanish? And they were like, first laughing, they're like, "None." And my sister was just like, "Yeah, You don't speak very well in Spanish or English." I'm like, "Oh, no. Don't be so rude. Don't over-exaggerate." Yeah, but there's some words that I don't know. And sometimes I translate it bad[ly] and that's why I kind of want to improve.

While recognizing that her family members were teasing, Lupita worried, "I'm losing my language and losing my pronunciation in the way of verbs, nouns, and all that and that's why sometimes at home they make fun of me." Lupita's parents intentionally tried to help her to improve her Spanish by sending her "texts messages, or news, and songs [lyrics]" in Spanish.

Across the interviews, Lupita often reported steps she was taking to improve her Spanish-speaking abilities, including reading stories and newspapers in Spanish, communicating with relatives in Mexico, and purposely using Spanish with bilingual friends. During twelfth grade, Lupita regularly read aloud in her Spanish-speaking church, conscientiously practicing these readings before each service.

As Lupita reflected back on her school experiences, she had mixed feelings about not attending a dual language school. She explained:

> Since I've been in an English[-speaking] public school, I never had that experience of bilingual [education]. And so, that kind of affected me because now schools teach [me] English as a second language... They're busy teaching you English, but they don't teach you anything in your first language, Spanish.

As Lupita noted, "I feel like it's messed up." She then added, "But at the same time, it's good because you get to improve your English more." Overall, Lupita appreciated the advantages her sisters had in attending dual language schools. She explained, "My hypothesis is that if I attended a bilingual elementary school, my Spanish would be much better and I think I would be able to learn better ... getting everything that they taught me inside of my head."

In grade 11, Lupita reported that participation in her Spanish-speaking church felt "nice because people get to reunite their families, and talk Spanish." That same year, she explained,

> Spanish is more my roots, my blood and English is just like a new [up]coming person for me. I have to see how to write it better or how I can speak it better, or what to apply because they both provide different meanings ... especially when it comes to religion because ... as a Spanish-speaker, we believe in one thing and the rest of the people believe in the other.

Lupita's Figured World and Becomings

For Lupita, language practices played a huge role in her figured world at home and at school. For example, speaking, reading, and writing in English were valued at school and home, especially since the family was newly arrived in the United States and Lupita's mother was just beginning to learn English. In the early years of the study, Lupita was often relied on to translate for her mother.

As Lupita grew older, additional possibilities informed Lupita's figured world. Specifically, Lupita aspired to attend college and came to recognize the affordances of being bilingual. Alongside these academic goals, Lupita also began to recognize the bilingual abilities of her sisters who had attended dual language programs. Not only was she concerned about "losing" her Spanish, but she also recognized that her younger sister's bilingual abilities made her a better translator for her mother. Lupita also became increasingly proud of her Latina heritage and her Spanish-speaking church. Thus, across the 13 years, we witness agency and improvisation as Lupita negotiated tensions among languages, family, school, future plans, culture, and belonging. Specifically, Lupita took steps to learn Spanish—linking herself to family, community, and her church.

Significantly, Lupita's becomings took place during a particular historical moment. The dual language school that her sisters attended opened only after Lupita had enrolled in school and was learning to read in English. Not only did the dual language program create different school experiences for Lupita's siblings, but it also created a revised figured world for Lupita. As Lupita observed her sisters becoming bilingual, she witnessed the affordance of bilingual education complicating the viability of only learning English. Becoming bilingual honored her family, her community, her faith, and had positive implications for her future. Thus, over time, Lupita's figured world shifted as new possibilities became available and Lupita agentially worked to become fully bilingual. Specifically, Lupita was becoming increasingly facile with Spanish, her sisters and her mother were learning more English, and the boundaries that separated home and school, English and Spanish, were becoming increasingly permeable.

Assemblages and Becomings

To make sense of Adam's becomings, I explore assemblages of things, activities, images, and texts referenced by Adam across the 13-year project. Deleuze and Guattari (1988) defined assemblages as evolving intersections and relationships among everything that constitutes existence. While assemblages can be territorializing when particular ways of seeing the world become dominant, they are always subject to re-organization, redirection, and replacement leading to new intersections of meaning and understandings. Drawing on the "stuff" of people's experiences, Deleuze and Guattari challenged scholars to move beyond the categories, binaries, and reified models for making sense of the world. They described assemblages of ideas, activities, interests, concerns, experience, and knowledge that operate within flows of continual movement and shifting intensities. These assemblages serve and constitute meanings, affects, relations, and understandings, including understandings about self.

Change over time and becomings are understood as rhizomatic—moving in unpredictable and unintentional directions as underground and emerging, as non-hierarchical, and as continually forming, reforming, and taking new directions and ever-emerging courses. Deleuze and Guattari (1988) argued that the past and the future always operate in the present. Thus, the present is not constituted by a sequence of past experiences but by multiplicities of processes, experiences, hopes, and possibilities (Williams, 2011). These permeable notions of time challenge generally accepted notions of development and learning that privilege causal and linear models, learning goals, curricular mappings, and assessment measures. In short, Deleuze and Guattari viewed time as involving multiple processes that do not contribute to singular, definable identities. As Willams noted, "no one travels forward in time as that self, same thing or person" (p. 16).

While sociocultural analyses entail links between events, actions, interactions, and experiences with the goal of producing coherent narratives. Deleuze and Guattari (1988) proposed other possibilities. Specifically, while drawing on the notion of assemblage, I resist constructing a coherent narrative of Adam's becomings. Instead, I treat his becomings as an assemblage of activities, things, people, and ideas that constantly emerge. Adam's assemblage entails various interacting and/or diverging processes, events, activities, and perspectives, which are articulated, represented, and/or expressed at particular points in time. These can only be conceptualized as "temporary resting place(s)" (Murris, 2021, p. 230) from which Adam expresses who he is and who he believes he is becoming. Fleeting meanings, while represented in the present, always draw upon Adam's fluid recognitions of the past, including the past experiences of families, and friends, as well as his knowledge of larger social histories (Deleuze & Guattari, 1988). Notably, Adam's meaning-making in the present also involved envisionments of possible futures, which like tracings of the past were continually subject to revision, reiteration, and rejection.

Adam's Becomings During His Elementary School Years

In his six-year-old self-portrait, Adam drew his smiling face accompanied by a bright-yellow sun and the outline of birds in the sky. When asked about the drawing, Adam explained,

> I was looking in the sky and dreaming that I was in Morocco that there was eleven birds and two trees and I loved my grandma that died and right now she is with Allah and I made a big smile on Eid [*Day of Celebration*] and that's all.

Adam's self-portrait and talk invoked joyous memories of sunny days in Morocco, a past Eid Celebration, and his grandmother's passing. Across the longitudinal study, Adam's Muslim faith was a recurring motif that assumed different forms and led in various directions. In second grade, Adam participated in the Eid ul-Adha celebration with his uncle in which the men slaughtered a sheep. Adam was excited and recounted the gory details of the slaughter. He reported, "We said Bismillah (In the name of Allah) and cut the sheep's throat quickly with a sharp knife. My uncle cut out the stomach and took the inside organs out." Adam reported, "I pulled down the sheep's skin." As he concluded his account, he proudly proclaimed, "Now, I'm a man." In third grade, when asked to draw a picture of Morocco, Adam drew a picture of "the world's second biggest mosque and nice scenery of Morocco."

When asked in fifth grade to draw a map of his school, Adam indicated the cardinal directions on his drawing. Adam explained, "My teacher told me where North is and I just figured out the rest. So that is North, East, South East, West [Adam pointed to the directions on his map as he spoke]." Recognizing the importance of directionality to Adam as a Muslim, I asked him if he prayed during school and he responded "No" explaining, "I would but it is not like the right times because when we have the first prayer, it is during school. I have that during math and sometimes during the test, so I can't." Tensions were apparent in the pride Adam displayed in his Muslim heritage alongside dominant school practices.

Adam's Becomings During His Middle School Years

As Adam's elementary school years ended, Adam became increasingly politically aware and often spoke about historical and political events. For example, in fifth grade, Adam attended a "rally for Palestine" at the state capital. Adam was concerned about the historical annexation of Palestinian territory by Jewish people. He noted that Palestinians had lived on the land for "more than like 2000 years." He worried that so many Palestinians had been recently killed by Jewish settlers saying, "they don't have the right to kill a few million [people]." In fall of middle school, Adam wrote an argumentative essay about Syria and worried that his classmates did not realize "there's a ***civil war*** in Syria and Palestine:"

> I mean if you ask a normal student in my school about what's happening in Palestine, they wouldn't even know. Like me and my friend … we went around and asked some students about what they think about Syrian refugees here in America. And most of them said they [refugees] should definitely stay.

By eighth grade, Adam was highly critical of President Trump. When asked about living in the United States, he named "Trump" as the primary problem saying, "he spreads a lot of hate." Concerned by Trump's rhetoric, Adam reported, "It's already started. People have been doing things—burning Mosques, spreading hate, beating people up."

Adam's Becomings During His High School Years

Across the high school interviews, Adam wrote and spoke about Muslim Chinese people interned in imprisonment camps, Yemeni people facing starvation, and the continued American bombing of Syrian civilians. When Notre Dame Cathedral burned, Adam compared the media attention paid to Notre Dame within the silences surrounding the burning of Mosques in other parts of the world.

It was during high school that Adam's critical consciousness extended to business and the environment. In tenth grade, Adam and his friends drafted a proposal for an Islamic shopping center, saying, "if you look at our malls right now, they're predominantly like white goods, you know like Sears, Kohls, stuff like that … there's an Asian mall in California." They proposed buying and renovating a building and establishing small shops inside. "The goods would be Islamic." In eleventh grade, Adam planned to organize a club for immigrant students. He explained, "a majority of my friends are immigrants." Club members would discuss "world problems … like global issues" with a focus on environmental issues. He described global climate change as a "major problem" and envisioned "a committee to build rain gardens" to reduce flooding. He noted that the United Kingdom has implemented a similar system saying, "I don't know why it's not a worldwide thing." Adam's interest in global issues contributed to his interest in studying international history.

Adam's Assemblages of Becomings

While it might be tempting to locate Adam's becomings as simply reflecting Muslim values of compassion or as a commitment to social justice, these efforts to story Adam's becomings are antithetical to Deleuze and Guattari's (1988) conceptions of assemblages and time. Assemblages always entail rhizomatic changes that emerge in multiple directions and redirections, involving unique mergings of activities and meanings, as well as past, present, and envisioned experiences. These formings and reformings are unpredictable and reiterative as past experiences and future possibilities inform meanings made and actions taken in the present.

As Williams (2011) explained, Deleuze and Guattari (1988) were interested in how people draw on assemblages of experiences to become and re-become new people across moments in time. All of what Adam shared was articulated, represented, and expressed at a particular point in time, which must be recognized as a "temporary resting place" (Murris, 2021, p. 230) from which Adam expressed who he was and who he was becoming. Thus, in telling Adam's story I am not identifying categories, binaries, models, or trajectories. I am merely recognizing the complex, emergings, mergings, and scatterings of ways of being and becoming. Across time, Adam is not simply engaged with his Muslim faith, aware of anti-Muslim sentiments, a member of the global Muslim community, politically aware, business-oriented, and environmentally concerned. He is simultaneously all of these and much more. Across the interviews, these various aspects gain/lose momentum, emerge/disappear, and reoccur with fluctuating intensity. Thus, a coherent storyline is resisted and Adam's experiences of being and becomings are simply observed. Adam is Adam and carries with him a vast range of past experiences, ideas, encounters, possibilities, and current moments.

Discussion and Conclusions

As illustrated across these analyses, scholars have drawn on a range of theories to challenge linear and developmental trajectories. Each conceptualization highlights complexities that inform and affect becomings. For Gabby, we explored intersectional aspects (Crenshaw, 2017; Ladson-Billings, 2021) of becomings related to gender and social class, which came together in unique ways and informed who Gabby was becoming and how she operated in her daily life. Figured world theories (Holland et al., 1998) highlighted expectations that people bring to contexts, including roles, relationships, and types of experiences.

In Lupita's case, we observed her negotiating languages at home, in school, and in terms of who she was becoming as an emerging bilingual speaker. Finally, Deleuze and Guattari (1988) provided a fluid notion of assemblage to recognize the vast range of experiences, activities, and engagements with people, things, and ideas that comprised Adam's becomings. Unlike the other accounts, which invite coherent accounts of becomings, assemblage theory is explicitly rhizomatic and idiosyncratic. The goal is not to document and explain development but rather to appreciate the complexity and beauty of Adam's becomings.

Literacy—as an identity marker—is presented differently in each account. In Gabby's case, traditional notions of literacy were barely mentioned—with the exception of the *Minecraft* books I gave her—while Gabby was deeply engaged with multimodal texts (e.g., *Minecraft* videos). Lupita often spoke about learning to read and write in English and Spanish and the literacy practices that she used to improve her abilities with Spanish (e.g., reading Spanish stories, newspapers, and church readings). Adam used writing to express his views on Syria and make plans for an Islamic shopping center. While these literacy practices are intriguing, there are significant literacy practices that I have not mentioned. Gabby read fanfiction. Lupita loved books with Latina protagonists, and Adam was involved with a youth book club at the Mosque. Of particular interest is when and how participants invoked literacy to mark their literate becomings.

As noted above, my application of particular theories to particular cases was purposely random and any of the three theories could be applied to each of the three cases. This methodological and theoretical move was purposeful and contributes to the argument that I make across this chapter. First, there are various challenges to linear developmental accounts. These challenges come from different theoretical spaces (e.g., Critical Race Theory, anthropology, and metaphysical philosophy) and attend to different aspects of becomings (e.g., intersectionality, social and cultural spaces, and emerging assemblages).

Second, multiple theories are needed to make sense of the scope and the complexity of people's becomings. Some readers might be tempted to ask, which theory is correct? Or which theory I would recommend? My answer will always be, "that depends." The theory you choose must be determined by which theory helps you to explore aspects/dimensions of becomings that have captivated your attention and answer your research question(s). In short, I argue that becomings are so complicated, contextualized, and personal that no single theory will ever be sufficient. However, each theory helps us to see and consider something that matters for students and for researchers.

Finally, by placing these theories side-by-side, we recognize and celebrate the complexity of human lives. Once we witness this complexity, it is difficult to judge other people, deny their humanity, and refuse to hear the range of voices that comprise their worlds. Thus, I would encourage researchers and educators to honor the complexity of identity becomings and to seek multiple ways of documenting and respecting all students.

Discussion Questions

1 Identify a dimension of becomings for children, teachers, or parents that interests you. Which of the theoretical frames discussed in this chapter might be useful for exploring your research questions or interests and why?
2 What other identity framings might be useful and what questions might they address?
3 What are the instructional implications of different ways of conceptualizing identity? What do these frames offer educators?

References

Collins, P. H. (1998). It's all in the family: Intersections of gender, race, and nation. *Hypatia, 13*(3), 62–82. https://doi.org/10.1111/j.1527-2001.1998.tb01370.x

Compton-Lilly, C., Papoi, K., Venegas, P., Hamman, L., & Schwabenbauer, B. (2017). Intersectional identity negotiation: The case of young immigrant children. *Journal of Literacy Research, 49*(1), 115–140. https://doi.org/10.1177/1086296x16683421

Crenshaw, K. W. (2017). *On intersectionality: Essential writings.* The New Press.

Deleuze, G., & Guattari, F. (1988). *A thousand plateaus: Capitalism and schizophrenia.* Bloomsbury Publishing.

Delgado, R., & Stefancic, J. (2001) *Critical race theory: An introduction.* New York University Press.

Duranti, A., & Ochs, E. (1997). Syncretic literacy in a Samoan American family. In M. B. B. Schieder (Ed.), *Discourse, tools and reasoning: Essays on situated cognition* (pp. 169–202). Springer. https://doi.org/10.1007/978-3-662-03362-3_8

Erikson, E., & Erikson, J. (1981). On generativity and identity: From a conversation with Erik and Joan Erikson. *Harvard Educational Review, 51*(2), 249–269. https://doi.org/10.17763/haer.51.2.g211757u27732p67

Gee, J. P. (2018). Affinity spaces: How young people live and learn on line and out of school. *Phi Delta Kappan, 99*(6), 8–13. https://doi.org/10.1177/0031721718762416

Gregory, E., Long, S., & Volk, D. (2004). *Many pathways to literacy: Young children learning with siblings, grandparents, peers and communities.* Routledge. https://doi.org/10.4324/9780203521533

Holland, D. C., Lachicotte, W. S., Skinner, D., & Cain, C. (1998). *Identity and agency in cultural worlds.* Harvard University Press.

Ladson-Billings, G. (2021). *Critical race theory in education: A scholar's journey.* Teachers College Press.

McAdams, D. P. (2001). The psychology of life stories. *Review of General Psychology, 5*(2), 100–122.

McCarthey, S., & Moje, E. B. (2002). Identity matters. *Reading Research Quarterly, 37*(2), 228–238. https://doi.org/10.1598/rrq.37.2.6

Mead, G. H. (1934). *Mind, self, and society.* University of Chicago Press.

Mishler, E. G. (2004). *Storylines.* Harvard University Press.

Moje, E., & Luke, A. (2009). Literacy and identity: Examining the metaphors in history and contemporary research. *Reading Research Quarterly, 44*(4), 415–437. https://doi.org/10.1598/rrq.44.4.7

Murris, K. (Ed.). (2021). *Navigating the postqualitative, new materialist and critical posthumanist terrain across disciplines: An introductory guide*. Routledge. https://doi.org/10.4324/9781003041177

Souto-Manning, M. (2013). *Multicultural teaching in the early childhood classroom: Approaches, strategies, and tools, preschool-2nd grade*. Teachers College Press. https://doi.org/10.1080/15348431.2014.944705

Williams, J. (2011). *Gilles Deleuze's philosophy of time: A critical introduction and guide*. Edinburgh University Press.

Wortham, S. (2006). *Learning identity: The joint emergence of social identification and academic learning*. Cambridge University Press.

11

BECOMING (UN)LABELED

Challenging Socially Constructed Notions of Normalcy in Literate Identities

Bobbie Kabuto

Introduction

Over the past 20 years, a mounting body of contemporary research argues that we need to move away from paradigms that perpetuate ideas of "fixing" children to "fixing" the education system as one historically built on unequal access to learning (Ball, 2012; Greene, 2007; Sauer & Lalvani, 2017; Willis, 2019). There is no better example of this evolving mindset than the US special education system. Researchers have illuminated how the special education system ranks and sorts students based on fixed notions of ability that socially construct the literate identities of students who are classified through the system. The special education system has, until recently, done little to recognize how ability, intelligence, and success are constructed within a matrix of instructional structures and external and legal policy decisions that describe academic and grade-level performances (Ball, 2012; Tomlinson, 2012). I argue that the special education system creates a cultural model of literacy that informs how literate identities are defined by dichotomizing what "normal" and "not normal" literacy learning looks like over time (Gee, 2002). As a result, students within the system take up or challenge identities of normality, otherness, and struggle (Wortham, 2006.)

This growing body of research, particularly in the area of critical disability studies, has highlighted that there is a master narrative on disabilities that focuses on deficit and medical perspectives of ability that ignore justice- and equity-oriented approaches to education (Goodley & Tregaskis, 2006). This master narrative not only labels students, it also disables families (Rogers, 2007). Families do not always have the same perception and approach to the classification process in school and believe that being classified with learning disabilities lowers teachers' expectations, develops social stigmas of their children, and perpetuates

DOI: 10.4324/9781003271406-20

the notion of otherness, which positions their children differently from those without disabilities (Kabuto, 2020; Sauer & Lalvani, 2017). While this aforementioned research addresses the intersection of family and special education structures and the structural inequities within the special education system, there is little research that takes a longitudinal look into how families navigate and negotiate becoming labeled through the special education system.

In this chapter, I will discuss the dynamic, contested, and temporal nature of identity within the context of time through a longitudinal case study of Carole and her daughter Christie, who was identified with multiple disabilities, including speech and language, hearing, and visual. Carole and Christie participated in a longitudinal study *Revaluing Readers and Families* that documented the family's reader and literate identities through transgenerational processes (Kabuto, 2009, 2016). Through theoretical and methodological discussions of identity and time, this chapter will address how literate identities were socially constructed within two special education structures: the classification process and the educational services with built-in curricular structures. These structures were designed to not only organize educational experiences over time but also have internal power structures that define and privilege certain types of learners and marginalize others through tracking systems (Ball, 2012).

Becoming Labeled as Identity Construction over Time

Critical disability studies is grounded in a social constructivist perspective that draws on notions of power and privilege to suggest that disabilities are given meanings within sociopolitical contexts (Lalvani, 2015; Lalvani & Douglas, 2013). Adding a critical view to disabilities dismantles common deficit and medical orientations to disabilities, replacing those narratives with ones that highlight themes of oppression and control (Lalvani, 2015). Through this perspective, I argue that disabilities can reside in and evolve out of social practices that define and defend the concept and culture of a disability within the context of families and schooling (Kabuto, 2016, 2020).

Research taking a social constructivist approach to disabilities has emphasized how they are reified within the matrix of structures of the special education system (Tomlinson, 2012). Studies have uncovered the special education system as a site of struggle and contestation among students, families, and school systems through the hidden tracking structures that lead to unequal power relationships and, ultimately, educational inequalities (Compton-Lilly, 2017; McDermott, 1996; Taylor, 1991; Tomlinson, 2012). These tracking systems, ranging from sorting students into reading levels to placing students in special classes (e.g., reading, speech, or self-contained classrooms), generate culturally defined meanings of what it means to be a "struggling" or "special education" student. Other studies focus on how educational testing can be a "making" of disabilities through limitations in addressing linguistic, cognitive, social, and cultural diversity (Everatt et al., 2014; Geva, 2000; Vellutino et al., 2004). More generally, the move to standardized assessments, whether at the state, district, or classroom levels, creates singular and privileged views of what and how students should learn in school, disenfranchising historically marginalized students including students identified with disabilities (Willis, 2019).

Therefore, *becoming labeled* is a term that I use to forefront how participation in the special education system is not neutral and involves cultural models, or taken-for-granted schemas, storylines, and theories that describe what is "typical" and "normal" (Gee, 2002).

Students and families who enter the special education system, whether willingly or not, learn to navigate it and, through that process, construct a myriad of intersectional identities that encapsulate identities of struggle (Hikida, 2018; Kabuto, 2016), otherness (Kabuto, 2020; Lalvani, 2015), and normality (Ball, 2012; Kabuto, 2020). These identities evolve over time as students and their families engage in a variety of social practices connected to the special education system.

Therefore, the process of becoming labeled is a social one resulting from one's ongoing participation in a system connected to ideologies of normalcy, standardization, and ranking individuals into categories that had led to the disproportional representation of students across race, gender, language, and ability (Artiles et al., 2002; Martin, 2014).

The temporal process of becoming encapsulates social and personal transformation within social and cultural spaces over short and long timescales (Compton-Lilly, 2011; Lemke, 2000). As individuals engage in similar, repeated activities over longer timescales, like yearly English Language Arts testing or moving to the next grade level, they move between that past and the present. In doing so, they work to make sense of their experiences so that past experiences mediate present and future ones (Compton-Lilly, 2011; Kabuto, 2016, 2020). Compton-Lilly (2011) describes this phenomenon as how time acts as a context so that individuals draw on, abandon, and revive their experiences to create meanings that are not represented through "simple, linear and chronological landscapes" (p. 248).

Sorokin (1943) discusses the nonlinear, sociocultural nature of time. In an enlightening discussion of the plurality of time across the social and physical sciences, Sorokin (1943) outlines the different ways that time is defined. More importantly, Sorokin effectively illustrates how these different conceptions of time can be confused and conflated within sociocultural contexts, particularly in the discourses that individuals employ to make sense of their lived experiences. As Sorokin (1943) argued, "Observation shows that persons equally old according to the physical clock are physiological at quite different stages of development" (p. 164) yet the special education system is built on a paradigm that privileges a linear progression of learning to normalize age- and grade-level expectations. We treat words like *age*, *grade*, and *year* as static, neutral numbers connected to terms like *childhood*, *adolescence*, and *adulthood*, when these temporal words are, in fact, words with sociocultural and political meanings. In what follows, I will discuss the temporally constructed nature of identity as illustrated through the study of Carole's and Christie's discourses as they storied Christie's experiences in becoming labeled and, eventually, unlabeled.

Revaluing Readers and Families

Christie and her mother Carole participated in ten-year longitudinal study *Revaluing Readers and Families* (Kabuto, 2009, 2016) through a revisiting framework. *Revaluing Readers and Families* was designed to explore how school-based concepts define notions of reading ability and intersect and reconstruct family structures and perceptions of themselves as literate individuals. Christie and Carole were one of seven families who participated in the study and one of two who I followed over time. Classified with a speech and language disability by the time she was two years old, Christie's case study provides insights into how the family understood themselves against labels like "struggling reader" and "learning disabled" as they began to redefine Christie's abilities in school over time. Examining Christie's experiences over time highlights how she understood herself as a literate individual defined and marginalized by the special education system.

I first met the family when Christie was in kindergarten. They began participation in the study when Christie was in first grade (Phase 1), and I revisited them when Christie was in third grade (Phase 2). My last revisit was when Christie was in the 11th grade (Phase 3). Table 11.1 shows the data that were collected as part of the study and the corresponding data analyses that occurred over the three phases of the study. As part of the larger study, the data included Family Retrospective Miscue Analysis (Family RMA; Kabuto, 2009). Family RMA involves families orally reading and reflecting on their reading. I have written about the potential of Family RMA in revaluing the reading identities of families through Christie and Carole's participation (Kabuto, 2009). Family RMA was repeated with different texts at each phase of the study. Other data provided a context within which to situate the reading and reflecting events that were part of the Family RMA procedures. These data included the collection of school-based documents, reading and informal interviews, and observations and reflexive note-taking. For purposes of this chapter, I will focus on the reading and informal interviews through a temporal discourse analysis.

Revisiting Framework

Studying Christie's experiences required a revisiting framework that considered the temporal nature of discourses and experiences. As Sefton-Green and Rowsell (2015) explained, revisiting involves returning to a research site or participants to "grapple with how the people they met again dealt with different

TABLE 11.1 Study Data and Corresponding Analyses

Data	*Phase 1 (10 Sessions; 10 hours)*	*Phase 2 (10 Sessions; 10 hours)*	*Phase 3 (4 sessions; 5 hours)*	*Analysis*
Christie's Grade	*1st Grade*	*3rd Grade*	*11th Grade*	
Data Collection	All 10 Sessions	All 10 Sessions	All 4 Sessions	
Interviews Reading Interviews Informal Interviews	All 10 Sessions	All 10 Sessions	All 4 Sessions	Content Analysis, Temporal Discourse Analysis
Observations and Reflexive Note-taking	All 10 Sessions	All 10 Sessions	All 4 Sessions	Thematic Coding
Miscue Data from Oral Readings and Retellings Child Parent	5 out of the 10 sessions	5 out of the 10 sessions	Sessions 2 and 3	Miscue Analysis
Family RMA Child-focused RMA Parent-focused RMA	5 out of the 10 sessions	5 out of the 10 sessions	Sessions 3 and 4	Discourse Analysis

perspectives in time, how stories from the past are mobilized in the present, and how future aspirations are imagined and enacted in talk" (p. 3). Revisiting allows researchers to study how participants contend with transformations in their experiences over time, or how they "re-experience." For instance, both Christie and Carole drew upon their past educational experiences to make sense of Christie's academic performances not only within events within shorter timescales, like reading and reflecting on a book, but also on longer timescales from grade to grade. As they engaged in activities and talked about their experiences around disability labels, they began to construct larger narratives of ableism that informed how Christie enacted identities that challenged or supported those narratives. As Compton-Lilly (2011) argued, families "repeatedly returned to some stories while neglecting and forgetting others or framed some stories as examples of larger patterns" (p. 248).

Christie's case study exemplifies how the family understood their experiences around school-based concepts through the context of time (Compton-Lilly, 2011). While this may be the case, I was also concerned with the sociocultural nature of time and how it mobilized meanings through a methodological discussion of the temporal nature of discourses. Building on a temporal discourse analysis (Compton-Lilly, 2015), I focused on how discourses connected to time indexed sociocultural meanings that were used to construct narratives and literate identities through the process of becoming.

Temporal Discourse Analysis

Compton-Lilly (2017) explicated how temporal discourse analysis can show how individuals situate themselves across time as they tell their past learning histories. By using temporal discourse analysis, Compton-Lilly (2017) explained how certain motifs, such as special education, the construction of success/failure, and notions of ability/normalcy, reoccur and are evidenced within an individual's discourse over time. Expanding temporal discourse analysis to include the sociocultural nature of time, the data were analyzed to consider how discourses related to time referenced school-based timeframes (e.g., first grade), synchronized special education routines (e.g., Committee on Special Education meetings), and provided a point of reference for or entry into understanding and discussing their children's learning and progress in school (e.g., reading grade level).

The temporal data analysis included coding transcribed interviews for forms (utterance type) and functions (meanings) of discourse (Gee, 1999). As I coded the data through the lens of sociocultural time, it became evident that words that represent temporal meanings—such as "now," "in X grade," or "this year"—did little to represent time in a chronological manner. In particular, the use of the word *year* presented a fascinating look into how the word was defined by the school calendar and the rhythm of educational activities connected to the special education process as Carole and Christie storied their experiences and tried to make sense of them over time. Temporal utterances, therefore, reflected time-bending, sociocultural meanings as Carole and Christie, who was more independent in storying her experiences as an 11th-grade student in Phase 3 of the study, narrated their experiences in becoming (un)labeled.

There were two notable findings that came out of Christie's case study. First, Christie took more agency in narrating her educational experiences as she moved from a young child to an adolescent. In Phase 1 and 2 of the study, Carole's voice dominated the narrative when describing and planning Christie's educational experiences. As Carole released more control to Christie, she became more independent in telling her stories and challenging how the school planned her education. The second finding from the temporal discourse analysis illustrates how the use of the word *year* over the phases of the study exemplified the sociocultural, nonchronological nature of time in relation to past, present, and future. The data analysis showed that the word *year* increased per session over each phase of the study and indexed events across longer timeframes. This finding highlighted how Carole and Christie used discourses to align Christie's identity with a classification label and, at the same time, challenged the deficit-oriented ways that the classification defined her ability and sense of self as a capable adolescent who experienced educational struggles since entering kindergarten. Here, I will focus on two interrelated themes that connected with the sociocultural use of the word *year* in the process of becoming (un)labeled.

The Classification Process

When I first met Carole and Christie, Carole provided an extensive explanation of Christie's educational and developmental history through a stack of documentation, including her Individualized Educational Program (IEP), work samples, and test scores. These materials were manifestations of the classification process, which Christie began at a young age. Christie started receiving speech services from the time she was 18 months old. Although Christie said her first words at an early age, her speech development appeared to halt and Carole described that Christie went silent.

Christie attended a special education preschool for a short time and, not feeling that Christie was benefiting from the environment, Carole removed her from the school. In addition, Christie was diagnosed with a "lazy eye" and wore a patch on her right eye for three years and underwent surgery for both eyes to correct the condition. Carole regularly expressed her concern over Christie's overall academic progress and described Christie as an "enigma" because she felt that Christie did not fit into a label of an extreme learning disability, although she was tested with a low IQ.

From Phase 1 to Phase 2, the word *year* increased to connect Christie's experiences with the classification process between the two phases. These connections, in particular, highlighted Carole's expressed frustration at different parts of the classification process. Testing was a regular point of contention for Carole because testing results over time did not show a clear picture of Christie's progress or needs. During Phase 2 of the study when Christie was in third grade, Carole discussed Christie's testing:

> They had the psychological (testing) **this year**. They came up with about what I would say 1.6 grade. The results weren't really that far off from first grade. She was on par more or less around first grade. I actually tested her at the end of kindergarten because she was going into first grade. I had it for the CSE (in first grade). What I really wanted to show them was where she was in the **new school year**, which was first grade.

As demonstrated in this dialogue, Carole associated testing with academic years in order to keep track of Christie's progress. In addition, Carole regularly expressed skepticism when it came to school-based testing that was part of the classification process. Carole paid to have Christie evaluated in order to compare the results from the private testing with those found by the Committee of Special Education (CSE).

Carole and a family advocate, hired by Carole, attended the CSE meetings to advocate for Christie. During the CSE meetings, the committee discussed Christie's language and psychological testing results, academic progress, and changes in educational programs. As the above dialogue illustrates, Carole was proactive in gathering information to bring to the CSE meetings and would express her disdain for services that she felt did not meet Christie's needs, which I will explore further in the next section.

Over time, however, Christie began to advocate for herself and started attending her own CSE meetings with the support of Carole in eighth grade. In Phase 3 of the study, Christie's use of the word *year* often linked to a point back in time when she received curricular placements that resulted from the review of her IEP. Making connections to the past assisted Christie in making sense of her lived experiences in Phase 3. Middle school appeared to be a particularly challenging time for Christie when the CSE tried to place her on a life skills path that provides students with vocational skills as an alternate route to graduation. Students who graduate high school on a life skills path receive a "local diploma" and career development and occupational studies credentials.

Christie was unhappy with her placement in life skills. Recognizing that her classes were being switched from academic classes to life skills classes, Christie said, "I don't want to be in life skills, end of story. I don't belong there. I'm different. You don't see how much different I am." When I asked her to elaborate more on why she is different, Christie responded, "I socialize a lot and I catch my speech delay and my dyslexia, my reading problem and my math problem. But I told them, 'You're not going to change anything what I want.'" What Christie wanted the most was to graduate with an academic high school diploma, even if it meant that she would graduate high school between 19 and 21 years of age. Christie explained, "**This year** was a real opportunity to put me in that normal class, but I know now… I've realized that I have … to have a couple of **years** to progress, because I'm really graduating I'm 20, 21 or 19."

As Christie storied her experiences in Phase 3, she provided unexpected insights into how she identified herself in relation to the classification process. While Christie said that she has dyslexia, formal documentation from the school or private evaluators that identified Christie with dyslexia did not exist. Christie associated the term with her struggles with reading and her classification with a language disability. When I asked Christie to tell me about her language disability in Phase 3, she replied, "My dyslexia, you know. I know (the words) but I can't say the words." For Christie, aligning her struggles with dyslexia was a way for her to understand her struggles with reading and, more importantly, why she could not master how to be a successful student in school.

Christie's discourses dichotomized what were "normal" and "not normal" educational experiences that reflected unequal tracking systems resulting from the classification process. The life skills path was not normal to Christie, and she positioned herself differently than those who were tracked into that path.

Christie argued that she should receive curricular structures that she deemed "normal" and rebuked the stigma of what it means to be identified with a learning disability. Christie felt capable and argued for educational services and curricular structures that would give her the chance to succeed in high school and graduate with an academic high school diploma.

Educational Services and Curricular Structures

Carole described the classification process and Christie's educational struggles in tandem with the types of services she received and the curricular structures embedded within those services. In narrating Christie's experiences, Carole used the word *year* to describe a continuous flow of experiences in Christie's changing reading instruction. In Phase 1, for example, Christie was in first grade and her reading instruction focused predominantly on the Wilson Program. Carole expressed frustration with the Wilson Program and how Christie was removed from previous instruction with the literacy specialist in the school. This change was based on a CSE decision, which initiated a change in Christie's IEP. Carole described,

> She [Christie] now works with a special education teacher who throws Wilson at them because that's what comes up for reading purposes based on the initial evaluation. She was participating in the group reading in the classroom **last year** and the **beginning of this year**.

Carole's exasperation indexed how curricular decisions were made with little input from Christie and Carole, although she attended CSE meetings. Carole felt that the Wilson Program was prescribed based on Christie's special education identification label and did not consider her overall educational needs as a student with goals and aspirations.

In Phase 2 when Christie was in third grade, Carole was still advocating for Christie to work with a reading specialist and was able to have reading instruction integrated into Christie's IEP. Carole said, "I met her [the reading specialist] at the evaluation. They finally gave it to us after all this asking … at the **end of the year**. It'll be the last six weeks of school." While Carole was successful, she expressed her ire at receiving the service at the end of the school year, not knowing if she would have to fight for the service again in the following academic year. Christie, in fact, did not receive reading assistance the following year.

By the time I met with Christie and Carole in Phase 3 when Christie was in the 11th grade, Carole had stepped aside and Christie took more control in negotiating her educational services, as I earlier described. Christie, again, used the word *year* to connect back to past experiences to help contextualize her current experiences fighting the tracking system that attempted to place Christie on a life skills path. She explained how her struggles in math in the 11th grade were connected to her middle school experience, when she was placed in basic math in preparation for the life skills track. Christie explained,

> Yeah. And I'm bad in math now – it's like I'm in Algebra. But math will take me a while to practice, because I've been in basic math and also the life skills. So that's going to be 10 times worse, because middle school destroyed me. Like the **whole year** in middle school, because I have to be in life skills.

In Phase 3 of the study, Christie attended a reading support class that she felt did little to help her. Christie described, "English is doing simple work like read a passage with like two sentences (and) fill in a questionnaire. That's easy enough. It's level 2 reading and I don't want to do that." Christie explained that if she did not advocate for herself to be removed from the life skills path, she would have had learned janitorial work and had a different experience in school than she was having, "If I gone there (life skills) like **last year**, I would have to do it (janitorial work) like every day."

Over time, Carole's and Christie's discourses emphasized the lowering of academic expectations as Christie progressed through school. Advocating for Christie's ability to learn meant that both Carole and Christie needed to fight the hidden curricular structures that separated students into those who were deemed capable and those who were not. Christie summarized below how educational services and curricular structures connected to the classification process reproduced disjointed perspectives of "normalcy" and "special" so that special was not normal.

> People recognize me this way … the special needs kid. I'm a shy person and they think I'm special needs. They knew me in the past. They knew me in a special ed class and it hurts me. And I'm telling them you don't know about me. I'm trying to show everything in my heart.

Becoming (Un)Labeled

In this study, temporal discourses that addressed the sociocultural nature of time were salient in the process of becoming labeled with disability classifications. These temporal discourses coordinated Christie's experiences, thoughts, and feelings as she participated in the special education system. Examining Christie's discourses over time illustrates that her identity as a reader and literate individual became tied to identities of struggle. Research by Compton-Lilly (2011) describes similar situations in which students become engulfed into the special education system and have to learn how to negotiate "a school system filled with expectations and tracked instructional experiences" (p. 16) and "heavy-handed discipline, low expectations, special education placement, retention, and racism" (p. 16), all of which inform one's sense of themselves as being successful or not.

Examining Christie's experiences over time illustrates how she used discourses to enact conflicting identities to challenge educationally prescribed negative labels of being a struggling student with a learning disability, while positioning herself as a learner with a disability, in particular with dyslexia. Christie's case study highlights that, in order to become unlabeled, she also needed to go through the process of becoming labeled. The process of labeling was a process of identity transformation in which Christie's identity, as a reader and literate individual, evolved as she was socialized into the cultural model of special education. Within the cultural model of special education, Christie learned that people are categorized into those who are "normal" and those who are not. Carole and Christie's experiences mirror those of other families who express feelings of otherness, frustration, stress, and rejection (Haley et al., 2018; Lalvani, 2015).

Becoming unlabeled describes the process by which Carole and Christie rejected how the special education system constructed notions of normalcy and the negative implications of what it means to struggle in school (Lalvani, 2015). By engaging in the process of becoming unlabeled, Carole and Christie were also engaged in the process of "the care of the self" in becoming a different kind of person (Ball, 2012). Ball describes the care of the self as,

> That is, an art or technology of living, a set of practices through which we establish a relationship to ourselves of self-examination and determination artfulness, and through which some possibilities of freedom may be achieved, at least temporarily.
>
> *(p. 125)*

Becoming labeled with a disability was ongoing, reinforced each school year with educational planning on the part of the family and structures designed to reify notions of those who are capable and those who are not. In other words, becoming labeled with a disability was a socially constructed phenomenon as Christie participated in special education structures, like CSE meetings, educational evaluations, special classes, and educational tracking systems. The longer she participated, the more her literate identity became associated with the "label of a disability," or how discourses related to special education indexed educational oppression and social and academic stigmas that would cause Christie to go on an alternative educational route and graduate at an older age when compared to non-special education peers. Christie described being bullied because her school was a "normal school" and that her classmates told her that she "should not be in this school." Concepts of normalcy and the social other that manifested themselves through educational services linked to the special education label dominated Carole's and Christie's narrative.

While Carole engaged in educational planning to support Christie through the special education system, Carole, and later Christie, rejected the deficit-oriented approach of a system that tried to "remediate" her through a tracking system. It was the intersection of the tracking system and the family's educational planning where there was evidence of the complex and dualistic ways that identity enactments may cause individuals to act in relation to how they perceive themselves in a system.

The sense Christie had for herself did not conform to the deficit-oriented narratives of being labeled with a disability. Christie refuted the idea that she was "different," or as she put it, the "special needs kid." Her sense of herself as a capable student and learner who needed help caused her to push back on the educational system and voice her reticence in being one of, as Christie said, "those kids." Over time, Christie began to engage in a different type of identity enactment specifically tied to how she recognized the ways in which the US special education system has hidden tracking systems that reproduce societal inequalities that limit access to learning and educational opportunities. Christie felt herself struggle, not because of her disability, but because the system did not have a place for her to grow, develop, and meet the goals she set for herself.

The temporal nature of becoming (un)labeled required a way of looking at discourses as changing and evolving over time and experiences. In this chapter, I looked specifically at the word *year* as a sociocultural connector that linked experiences over longer timeframes. Throughout the three phases of the study, Christie's and Carole's sociocultural use of the word *year* was aligned with educationally defined notions of time (i.e., grade level, movement to the next grade, testing timeframes, and CSE meetings). As the illustrative examples in this chapter demonstrate, the term had little to do with mathematical notions of time connected to development or progression. In addition, the word *year* was often accompanied by other types of temporal words that brought together two past timeframes. For instance, when describing her 11th-grade experiences in math, Christie returned to her experiences in middle school, when the CSE tried to place her on the life skills path which incorporated "basic math." Time acted as a context for Christie to make sense of her experiences in Phase 3 of the study when she talked about how being placed in life skills had had a negative impact on her. Occurrences in the present are not decontextualized activities; instead, they often reflect a re-experiencing of connected or related activities. Each time activities are re-experienced, they are given new and renewed meanings.

Implications

The number of students between the ages of 3–21 classified with disabilities continues to increase (U.S. Department of Education, 2021). According to the National Center for Education Statistics, 14.1% of the students between the ages of 3 and 21 were classified with a disability in 2018–2019, the highest percentage since the organization began collecting data. Despite the exhaustive efforts of Response to Intervention (RTI)—legislation designed to confront the over-identification of students to special education—the percentage of students being classified has increased over the past ten years, with the largest increase in the classification of a specific learning disability (Fuchs & Fuchs, 2006; U.S. Department of Education, 2021; Willis, 2019).

Taken within this growing national trend, Carole and Christie's case study adds to the literature that discusses how the process of classifying and labeling, as well as its associated practices, can have negative social and emotional impacts on families over time (Kabuto, 2020; Lalvani & Douglas, 2013; Sauer & Lalvani, 2017). Parents may not be seen as equal school partners and encounter barriers and entanglements within a system that privileges families with financial means who can advocate for their children (Haley et al., 2018; McDermott, 1996). In addition, Christie's long-term experiences around success and struggle reflect "experiential and instructional deficits rather than biologically based cognitive deficits" (Vellutino et al., 2004, p. 167). Christie will grow into adulthood and, as research (Kabuto, 2020) has proposed, will continue to carry the weight of negative identities that may shape how she raises her own children. In order to support the healthy literate identities of families for generations to come, more attention needs to be placed on addressing the system, rather than the child.

Discussion Questions

1. Are there benefits to becoming classified in the special education system? If so, how do these benefits act in tandem with the process of becoming labeled? If no, why?
2. Are there ways that we can advocate for educators to teach in the cracks of systems built on curricular tracking to disrupt the formation of negative identities that may result from the process of becoming labeled with a disability?
3. How can future research take a critical and justice-oriented stance to the study of disabilities and literate identities? How can we use research from identity frameworks to advocate for the creation of spaces in which students who have been labeled with learning disabilities can reimagine their future potentials through positive and healthy literate identities?

References

Artiles, A. J., Harry, B., Reschly, D. J., & Chinn, P. C. (2002). Over-identification of students of color in special education: A critical overview. *Multicultural Perspectives*, *4*(1), 3–10. https://doi.org/10.1207/s15327892mcp0401_2

Ball, S. (2012). *Foucault, power, and education*. Routledge.

Compton-Lilly, C. (2011). Literacy and schooling in one family across time. *Research in the Teaching of English, 45*(3), 224–251.

Compton-Lilly, C. (2015). Revisiting children and families: Temporal discourse analysis and the longitudinal construction of meaning. In J. Sefton-Green & J. Rowsell (Eds.), *Learning and literacy over time: Longitudinal perspectives* (pp. 61–78). Routledge.

Compton-Lilly, C. (2017). *Reading students' lives: Literacy learning across time*. Routledge. https://doi.org/10.4324/9781315641201

Everatt, J., Reid, G., & Elbeheri, G. (2014). Assessment approaches for multilingual learners with dyslexia. In D. Martin (Ed.), *Researching dyslexia in multilingual settings* (pp. 18–35). Multilingual Matters. https://doi.org/10.21832/9781783090662-005

Fuchs, D., & Fuchs, L. S. (2006). Introduction to response to intervention: What, why, and how valid is it? *Reading Research Quarterly, 41*(1), 93–99. https://doi.org/10.1598/rrq.41.1.4

Gee, J. P. (1999). *An introduction to discourse analysis: Theory and method*. Routledge.

Gee, J. (2002). A sociocultural perspective on early literacy development. In S. B. Neuman & D. K. Dickinson (Eds.), *Handbook of early literacy research* (pp. 30–42). Guilford Press.

Geva, E. (2000). Issues in the assessment of reading disabilities in L2 children—Beliefs and research evidence. *Dyslexia, 6*(1), 13–28. https://doi.org/10.1002/(SICI)1099-0909(200001/03)6:1<13::AID-DYS155>3.0.CO;2-6

Goodley, D., & Tregaskis, C. (2006). Storying disability and impairment: Retrospective accounts of disabled family life. *Qualitative Health Research, 16*(5), 630–636. https://doi.org/10.1177/1049732305285840

Greene, J. P. (2007). Fixing special education. *Peabody Journal of Education, 82*(4), 703–723. https://doi.org/10.1080/01619560701603213

Haley, K., Allsopp, D., & Hoppey, D. (2018). When a parent of a student with a learning disability is also an educator in the same school district: A heuristic case study. *Learning Disability Quarterly, 41*(1), 19–31. https://doi.org/10.1177/0731948717690114

Hikida, M. (2018). Holding space for literate identity co-construction. *Journal of Literacy Research, 50*(2), 217–238. https://doi.org/10.1177/1086296x17751824

Kabuto, B. (2009). Parents and children reading together: The possibilities of family RMA. *The Reading Teacher, 63*(3), 212–223. https://doi.org/10.1598/rt.63.3.4

Kabuto, B. (2016). The social construction of a reading (dis)ability. *Reading Research Quarterly, 51*(3), 289–304. https://doi.org/10.1002/rrq.135

Kabuto, B. (2020). Parental perceptions of learning disabilities. *The Educational Forum, 84*(3), 242–257. https://doi.org/10.1080/00131725.2020.1737997

Lalvani, P. (2015). Disability, stigma and otherness: Perspectives of parents and teachers. *International Journal of Disability, Development, and Education, 62*(4), 379–393. https://doi.org/10.1080/1034912x.2015.1029877

Lalvani, P., & Douglas, L. P. (2013). Historical perspectives on studying families of children with disabilities: A case for critical research. *Disability Studies Quarterly, 33*(3). https://doi.org/10.18061/dsq.v33i3.3209

Lemke, J. (2000). Across the scales of time: Artifacts, activities, and meanings in ecosocial systems. *Mind, Culture, and Activity*, 7(4), 273–290. https://doi.org/10.1207/s15327884mca0704_03

Martin, D. (2014). Introduction. In D. Martin (Ed.), *Researching dyslexia in multilingual settings* (pp. 1–17). Multilingual Matters. https://doi.org/10.21832/9781783090662-004

McDermott, R. (1996). Acquisition of a child by a learning disability. In S. Chailkin & J. Lave (Eds.), *Understanding practice: Perspectives on activity and context* (pp. 269–305). Cambridge University Press. https://doi.org/10.1017/cbo9780511625510.011

Rogers, C. (2007). Disabling a family? Emotional dilemmas experienced in becoming a parent of a child with learning disabilities. *British Journal of Special Education, 34*(3), 136–143. https://doi.org/10.1111/j.1467-8578.2007.00469.x

Sauer, J., & Lalvani, P. (2017). From advocacy to activism: Families, communities, and collective change. *Journal of Policy and Practice in Intellectual Disabilities, 14*(1), 51–58. https://doi.org/10.1111/jppi.12219

Sefton-Green, J., & Rowsell, J. (Eds.). (2015). *Learning and literacy over time: Longitudinal perspectives.* Routledge.

Sorokin, P. (1943). *Sociocultural causality, space, time: A student of referential principles of sociology and social science.* Duke University Press. https://doi.org/10.2307/2571463

Taylor, D. (1991). *Learning denied.* Heinemann.

Tomlinson, S. (2012). *A sociology of special education.* Routledge.

Vellutino, F. R., Fletcher, J. M., Snowling, M. J., & Scanlon, D. M. (2004). Specific reading disability (dyslexia): What have we learned in the past four decades? *Journal of Child Psychology and Psychiatry, 45*(1), 2–40. https://doi.org/10.1046/j.0021-9630.2003.00305.x

U.S. Department of Education, National Center for Education Statistics (2021). *Digest of education statistics, 2019 (NCES 2021-009).* https://nces.ed.gov/fastfacts/display.asp?id=64

Willis, A. I. (2019). Race, response to intervention, and reading research. *Journal of Literacy Research, 51*(4), 394–419. https://doi.org/10.1177/1086296x19877463

Wortham, S. (2006). *Learning identity: The joint emergence of social identification and academic learning.* Cambridge University Press.

12

LITERATE IDENTITIES AND/IN THE BODY

Tracing Embodiments of Literacy Across Grade Levels

Grace Enriquez, Stavroula Kontovourki, and Elisabeth Johnson

Introduction

Imagine a so-called "struggling" reader, writer, speaker, or listener. Really, close your eyes and envision that student in as clear detail as possible. What are they doing with the text at hand? How are they responding to it, holding it, moving it, working with it? Are they seated at a desk? Standing before an audience? Lying on the rug? Sitting next to someone else? What are their hands, lips, eyes, and limbs doing? How do their voices sound? What do they actually look like? Now, imagine the same for a "good" reader, writer, speaker, or listener. What do you envision? More importantly, how can we talk about identity—"struggling reader," "good writer," "engaging speaker," "active listener," etc. —without recognizing the role of the body?

Indeed, discussions about identity fall short if we neglect the materiality of what comprises identity—the concrete makeup of how we look, what we wear, how we move, and what our bodies engage with by virtue of being a physical body located in a physical space. Discussions about literate identities necessitate contemplating the role our bodies play in forming and challenging what it means to be a literate being. How, then, do theories of embodiment illuminate what we perceive about students' literacy identities?

To start, we acknowledge that the term *embodiment* has been used widely in many fields, referring to both general macroanalysis descriptions (e.g., "she is the embodiment of strength") and specific discourse about the human body. We clarify: "Broadly speaking, *embodiment* refers to an ontological, experiential and/or material quality, expression or representation of discursive reality" (Johnson et al., 2021, p. 71). Literacy scholars have used the term in both ways to counter the long-standing, but myopic, treatment of literacy as only a cognitive matter.

DOI: 10.4324/9781003271406-21

In either case, embodiment is used to push past a Descartian split between the mind and body. Throughout the twentieth century, this split rendered the body invisible and insignificant, constructing literacy into something disconnected from the physical realities of our lives. Positioning bodies as central to knowledge production, however, works to decolonize constructions of literacy and literacy identities (González Ybarra & Saavedra, 2021). Therefore, understanding literacy and literate identities as embodied allows us to reimagine possibilities for teaching and perceiving literacy learners in more robust and equitable ways.

Theories of Literacies and Embodiment

In the past three decades, literacy scholars have turned toward embodiment theories to address the complexities of literacy that cognitive approaches and socially situated practices did not consider. One set of theories built upon sociocultural and critical turns, acknowledging that sociocultural context, discourse, and power influence how literate bodies look and act. Think of a teacher explaining to students that a "good reader" builds their stamina for quiet, independent reading or that a "good writer" proofreads their work before submitting it, and consider the ways in which children themselves strive to be recognized as such. Such practices discipline bodies into an ideal literate being whose body aligns with what context-specific dominant discourses deemed preferable. At the same time, students internalize those discourses, sometimes complying with them, sometimes rejecting them, and sometimes subverting them to establish their own understandings of what a literate identity means and is. Thus, a literate identity is one that could be simultaneously disciplined (by others) and disciplining (of the self and others) (Luke, 1992).

Other theorists regarded bodies, and identities accordingly, as texts that are socioculturally constructed and therefore can be "read" and "rewritten" through social discourse (Hagood, 2005; Mallozzi, 2016). We see this "reading" occurring whenever someone enters a room wearing the "wrong clothes" or having a different body type, as well as whenever someone exhibits the "right" kind of body or clothing. Scholars have also underscored that our bodies are constantly feeling and sensing while we engage in literacies, mediating the texts we encounter with our personal and sociocultural histories, experiences, and ways of making meaning (Jones, 2013; Lewis & Dockter Tierney, 2011). Think of the incredible anxiety that arises, for some, around public speaking or being cold called to read aloud.

More recently, the relationship between literacies and embodiment has taken a post-discursive turn. Socio-material, transliteracies, and posthumanist approaches explore how meaning is generated through the intra-action and flows of activity among human bodies and non-human entities, such as clothing, sound, paper, media, and screens (Burnett et al., 2020; Zapata, et al., 2018). Still another body of research considers the constant mobility of bodies across time, space, modalities, and discourses (Leander & Boldt, 2013; Wager & Perry, 2016). For instance, as researchers follow how young bodies, objects like cameras and chairs, physical spaces like staircases, and print-based text ideas come together, they trace new meanings that are being created but also acknowledge boundaries drawn around what a multimedia text could possibly become (Ehret & Leander, 2019), hence pointing to the indeterminacy of identity and the entanglement and assemblage of human and non-human bodies existing together beyond discourse.

Theories of embodiment thus complicate, extend, and ground what a literate identity entails. Moreover, because our bodies change over time and in different contexts, our identities (including literate identities) are also in constant flux. In this sense, embodiment theories challenge the notion that literacy and literate identities can ever be determined by focusing solely on cognitive, skill-oriented understandings of literacy. Currently, political discourses are shifting the pendulum back toward a reductive phonics-centered approach to reading, particularly through the "simple view of reading" (Snow, 2018) and the "science of reading" (Godwin & Jiménez, 2020). A lens of embodiment therefore also works to decolonize conventional understandings of literacy that exclude opportunity and growth, especially for Black, Brown, Indigenous, and dis/abled learners, who too often are pigeonholed as "struggling," "underachieving," or "at-risk." Embodiment theories assert: "Silent and vibrant, bodies have always been the material entity through which we experience the world, citing institutional histories of injustice and inequity in accessing social goods and services" (Kontovourki et al., 2020, p. 381). Looking at literate identities as embodied thus considers how particular identities are produced and constricted, while always engaging the possibility to be rethought and remade.

Putting Theory to Work: Vignettes of Embodied Literate Identities

Scholarship on the relationship of literacy and identities has long shifted the focus away from psychological accounts of linear development with an endpoint reached at maturity to the perception of multiple, shifting identities enacted across a developmental trajectory as well as in different contexts (Moje & Luke, 2009). In sharing vignettes across four contexts and grades, we complicate the latter by paying attention to the power of bodies, texts, material objects, and discursive forces like long-held assumptions that determine people's identities, values, and actions. Rather than implying that one's literate identity evolves over time, viewing identities as embodied highlights how they are mediated by and inscribed on children's/youth bodies that feel, act, and intra-act along with other material bodies (e.g., objects, furniture, physical spaces) and nonmaterial stuff (e.g., discourses regulating what literacy and being literate is), constantly being shaped, negotiated, and morphed. As you read each vignette, note how things, bodies, and words converge, diverge, bounce, and layer up amid dominant discourses of age-appropriate, grade-appropriate, or leveled reading, performance, and "literacy" research. When we look at all the other movements and things entangling to make meaning and be, the discursive limits of levels, ages, and identities bend and bleed.

All vignettes are based on our research in K-12 classrooms. While the first three vignettes rely on observations and interviews, the secondary school vignette zooms in on intra-actions across a literacy researcher, research documents, and a youth participant in a school space. Integrating a vignette about a literacy research process conjures embodied intra-actions less visible in earlier vignettes, inviting imaginative re-readings beyond the frames of earlier vignettes. As you read a*nd re-read*, ask yourself: How do bodies, texts, and things move to render and bend literate identities in my worlds?

Kindergarten: Constructing Literate Identity at the Start

On a snowy January morning, Grace visits Melanie, a Kindergarten teacher in a racially, ethnically, linguistically, and socioeconomically diverse urban school district. An Asian American middle-class cisgender female university researcher and teacher educator, Grace had been visiting Melanie's class since the start of the school year as part of a qualitative collaborative case study exploring how teachers and students enacted critical literacy learning, including how their bodies were engaged in such teaching and learning. In this example, Grace collaborated *with* Melanie (a public school teacher and research participant) to construct understanding from multiple perspectives. The students are spread across the classroom, working in small groups at various literacy center activities. One group uses headphones to listen to an audiobook, another occupies the rug as they stage a dramatic performance of *The Very Hungry Caterpillar* (Carle, 1981), and another group plays a "spin, say, and record" sight word game. Melanie, a Black middle-class cisgender female, conducts a guided reading lesson with a fourth group at a corner table. It is the first day she is using the guided reading approach with this class.

Alex, a five-year-old White boy and child of Bulgarian immigrants, plays the spinning sight word game with Harry, Zane, and Eli. The group's energy and conversation are animated, with Alex exclaiming, "Booyah!", "Kapow!", and "I'm going to win!" each time he gets another word to add to his game card. At one point, Zane announces, "I think I'm catching up [to Alex's lead]!" Harry, a quieter boy among the group, asks, "Am I doing a good job?" Alex looks at Henry's game card, gives him a thumbs up, and says, "Yes, you are. I think you have more than me now!"

Soon afterward, Melanie calls out the names of Alex, Eli, and two other students to join her at the corner table. As Alex arrives, he asks, "Okay, why am I here?" Melanie responds, "Well, let's guess. This is a reading block, so we're going to read." She distributes four copies of *Merry-Go-Round* (Mohr, 2010), a children's book with a predictable pattern written for leveled reading instruction, and begins the guided reading lesson. After conducting a picture-walk with students, highlighting vocabulary words, and asking for plot predictions, Melanie asks students to "whisper-read" to themselves. Alex and Eli watch Melanie for several minutes as she works with the other students until she reminds them to start whisper-reading. "Oh!" they exclaim and begin reading aloud quickly. Melanie reminds them to *whisper*-read and to begin with the cover of the book.

After ten minutes, Melanie stops the group. She swaps their books for dry-erase marker boards and asks them to write the word *ride*. After showing them how one can erase the first letter and replace it with *s*, *h*, and *w* to spell other words, she asks the group to write the four words she just spelled on their own marker boards before going back to their literacy centers. Alex is the last to finish and says, "I'm a slow poke." Melanie replies, "No, you're not. You're taking your time." Nonetheless, Alex sighs and watches longingly as the others return to their small groups.

Vignette Analysis: Our Reading of the Event

In schools, literate identities are forged early on as students learn the discursive expectations for our bodies to engage in the desired actions and performances of an ideal reader, writer, speaker, etc. (Luke, 1992). Alex is constructing a literate identity that already hinges on a deficit mindset ("I'm a slow poke") despite exhibiting prowess at the sight word game just moments before. Embodiment theories problematize the essentializing of one's entire being into a single identity; instead, they emphasize the multiple and constantly shifting, feeling, and sensing identities within all of us and the numerous ways bodies can be read by others. Thus, Grace needed to triangulate sources of data and consider the positioning of Alex's body in the constant circulation of bodies, discourses, and materials around him. Framing this study as a collaborative case study allowed Grace to consult with Melanie about additional sources of data (i.e., student work and interviews) that would illuminate and layer the construction of Alex's literate identity.

Applying a lens of embodiment also helps to highlight the flows and entanglements of human and non-human bodies intra-acting to construct a more nuanced literate identity for Alex. In both activities, Alex is reading words, though the purposes, movements, social interaction, and work with physical materials differ. The material components of the game (a spinner, game pieces, game cards) compel him to take charge of his sight word work, while the material components of the guided reading lesson (a prescribed book of predictable text, a highly structured lesson, markers, and marker boards) position him to follow a set of instructions about literacy learning. Physically, he reads autonomously with energy and enthusiasm from the open expanse of the rug, and he waits for permission and direction to read in his small group at the table. Other embodied aspects of these activities, such as loudly cheering and articulating encouragement during the game and whisper-reading during the lesson, also impact Alex's literate identity. Ironically, it is in the competitive sight word game that he is the most cooperative and supportive of others' own literacy learning and identity work. Looking only at the cognitive, structured reading work might lead one to construct a short-sighted understanding of Alex's literate identity. Attending to the embodied intra-activity involved in students' literacy experiences across contexts, even in the same classroom, can help to mitigate deficit-laden constructions of literacy identities that arise from purely cognitive and discursive understandings of literacy.

Third Grade: Constant Negotiations of Literate Identities

It is independent reading time in a third-grade classroom in a public elementary school situated in a racially, linguistically, and ethnically diverse urban neighborhood. There are two teachers in the classroom, as there are many children who have been assessed as in-need of support, and co-teaching is an officially mandated strategy for such support. During the mini lesson, one of the teachers asked children to notice their book characters but also to record in reading logs the book titles, levels of books, and number of pages read. Children were sent off to their independent reading spots; the two teachers conferred each with a child to scaffold their reading, and Stavroula, a Caucasian, middle-class female international graduate student and non-native English speaker, stood close to a group of desks holding a camcorder that she pointed toward particular children to observe. Stavroula has been in the classroom since the beginning of the year conducting an ethnographic case study: a study relying on participant observation for prolonged periods of time to understand the local particulars of complex phenomena and, specifically, to examine how children performed literate identities at the intersection of mandated curricula and high-stakes testing.

This particular day, Stavroula's camcorder and body are directed toward Butterfly, an African-American girl, and Aurelia, a Latinx girl, who are seated side by side, with their bodies parallel to their desks where their reading logs are placed, each on one side of Aurelia's book bag. Butterfly takes two books from her friend's bag and fills out her reading log. She bends over to pick up a pencil from the floor, sits up, tilts her head to the left and right, cracks her fingers, and glances at the camera Stavroula points toward her, while standing about a meter away. Butterfly looks at the page on which the book is opened: "Broccoli." She flips to the cover: "'Who ate the broccoli?' Ewww!" She looks at her log, her pencil filling in information, and interrupts: "These are H-I books?" her gaze directed to Aurelia, who answers "yes" after the question is heard twice. The teacher announces there are five minutes left for independent reading, to which Butterfly responds, "I read these two," lifting two books up and taking another from Aurelia's bag. She logs the book and flips through pages, suddenly throwing her body back in the chair and waving her hand in front of her nose, "Whew ... this book stinks!" still waving her hand. Her eyes glance at the camera, her hand now jotting notes on the reading log, her body still directed toward her desk.

Vignette Analysis: Our Reading of the Event

A view on Butterfly as an embodied reader foregrounds how her bodily movement, books, gaze, hand, and matter synchronized to produce a recognizable image of a reader. As expected, she pivoted her body toward her desk, read leveled books, gazed at words and pictures as she read independently, filled out her reading log to note titles, levels of books (for which she checked with her peer), and number of pages. This countered her persistent positioning as "at risk," given that an Individualized Educational Plan (IEP) followed her since first grade. Such positioning often meant that she engaged with simplified material, including reading leveled books below her grade level: reading F-G level books was a marker of difference from her peers who read at a higher level, and of deficiency compared to the goal of reaching level O at the end of third grade. Her question to Aurora and her statement that she read two books of H-I level are indications of how she embodied that capable, knowledgeable reader identity at the same time those words traversed her positioning as struggling.

Making sense of Butterfly's embodied reading also necessitates that we consider this particular event in relation to how literacy learning was usually formed in this classroom but also in conjunction with discourses of school literacy, where reading is prioritized as decoding words in print, while measuring children's ability and sorting books according to perceived level regulates what literacy learners can do and be at school. Taking into consideration how human bodies, materials, activities, and the set-up of physical spaces usually came together in this classroom helps us notice how Butterfly's bodily movement, and hence recognition as reader, is controlled by a reading log that is produced by and materializes discourses of print-based, leveled reading, accountability (as in, record to prove that you read) and studentship (as in, comply with the teachers' direction as well as to a ticking clock that regulates reading time and bodies). And these are, in turn, read on Butterfly's body: her fingers where a pencil is always stuck, her hand that is resting on the log, and her gaze and movement across books and the log. Nevertheless, Butterfly's independent reading body is fidgety and always on the move, from bending to glancing to chatting to sensing and smelling a book (note how her "Ewww!" for broccoli shifts to disgust of stinky books). Reading can be smelly, and books do stink; perhaps before and because of an audience and a camera that documents interest. But stinky books and smelly reading reframe readers as not just thinking, individually reading, and recording their progress but as also moving, sensing, and feeling. Whether Butterfly can read books beyond her reading level is thus rendered irrelevant and silent sustained reading livens up, and this becomes a space for rewriting Butterfly as a reader who moves, gazes, acts, and can *[exist]* regardless of leveling and IEPs.

Middle School: Navigating the Push and Pull of Multiple Identities

The weather is cooperating on a Thursday morning in late May for the eighth-grade Poetry Slam. While conducting a qualitative case study, drawing from classroom ethnography and critical research traditions to challenge prevailing assumptions about what is considered knowledge and truth in classroom life, Grace focuses her video camera on Omar, an Arab-American boy in a socio-economically and ethnically diverse urban public middle school. Omar sits on a metal folding chair in the middle of a sunny brick courtyard facing a concrete stage. Leaning in with his forearms on his thighs and his writer's notebook folded in his hands, he fixes his gaze on two classmates who perform spoken word poetry about teenage angst, reading from a notebook while improvising the accompanying dramatic gestures. After several minutes of listening, Omar glances around at the audience of fellow eighth graders, observing their attentive bodies. When his classmates finish their poem, Omar waits to see how others respond, then claps and whoops enthusiastically with them.

As the two boys step down from the stage, one of the teachers, Mr. Davis, asks who wants to go next. When nobody volunteers, the literacy coach, Ms. Brooks, asks Omar if he wants to read his poem. Described by his teachers as a "struggling reader and writer," Omar shakes his head no and looks at the floor, even though he had worked on his poem for over a month and Ms. Brooks had praised his final draft. He had taken a long time to come up with a topic (his cat) and then spent a lot of time doubting whether his poem was "good enough." Both Mr. Davis and Ms. Brooks assured him that "good poetry" could be about any topic at all. As Ms. Brooks encourages him now to read aloud his poem, others join in, saying, "Come on, Omar!" From across the courtyard, one classmate calls out, "I'll read it for you!" while another walks up behind Omar and tips his chair forward, leaving Omar no choice but to stand. He smiles but immediately grabs his chair, sits down, shakes his head no again, and looks back at the floor.

Vignette Analysis: Our Reading of the Event

Designing this case study with classroom ethnography and critical research methods allowed Grace to interrogate constructs of "struggling" literacy learners. To do so, she needed to attend not just to Omar's embodied performances when writing but also to the embodied performances of peers and the expectations for embodied performance conveyed through the discourses flowing within and across classrooms. Using a video camera also allowed Grace to capture data of the complexity and moment-to-moment sociocultural exchanges and intra-actions of a classroom setting—the ongoing background conversations of peers; the shifting of bodies, chairs, notebooks; the direct address of youth by adults; etc. —all of which fueled an incessant push-pull of social positioning and identities.

Framing literacy simply as a cognitive ability, one might assume Omar doubted the quality of his poem because of his positioning as a "struggling writer." Indeed, the discourses about literacy circulating in the school privileged the social confidence and easy flow of ideas that students like his two classmates exhibited whenever they worked with words and texts. Such discourses were reinforced through language such as "good poetry" or topics being "good enough." And yet, the efforts Ms. Brooks and his classmates exhibited to encourage Omar is a tacit acknowledgment that our bodies feel and sense while engaged in literacy work, infusing the poem he had written with his personal histories and experiences of writing and reading aloud, and creating new meaning concerning the poem beyond just what the words on the page conveyed (Enriquez, 2016; Lewis & Dockter Tierney, 2011). Such events were embodied, certainly, but they were also entangled in the circulation of human and non-human activity within the courtyard context. Omar was dealing with the sheer increase of human bodies in the audience, evidenced when he broke concentration on listening to his peers on stage to glance around and observe his peers in the audience. Additionally, the embodied work of stepping on a stage to publicly read aloud one's own writing added another layer to the construction of his identity as a writer. Receiving Ms. Brooks's approval of his poem in the classroom, and his peers' encouragement at the poetry slam, might have bolstered Omar's identity as a writer, but the intra-action of bodies in this context complicated and unsettled what he and others understood about his literate identity. Across the production of his poem, Omar's literate identity fluctuated from "struggling" to capable to resistant. Thus, the physical displacement of his body off the chair was an apt metaphor—a literal example of the intra-action and flows among human and non-human entities that constantly shift our literate identities.

High School: Resisting and Re(Writing) Literate Identities

As a 34-year-old White female researcher, Liz constructed a performance ethnography while hanging out in a tenth-grade English class for over a year, closely collaborating with the teacher and six youth outside of class time. A performance ethnographer uses fieldnotes, interviews, and artifacts with emotions, voices, material objects, and discursive forces like long-held assumptions that determine people's identities, values, and actions to compose scripts or choreograph performances that evoke findings with an audience, different from the traditional ethnographic research publication. Liz, the teacher, and six youth explored the ways they negotiated meanings for pop culture texts like accessories and clothing people use to adorn bodies (e.g., jeans, shoes, headphones, nail polish, and earrings). This approach to studying literate identities depicted participants' embodied experiences with pop culture texts intra-acting with planned pop culture curriculum. Liz prioritized conflicts over meaning as moments when literate identities are palpable, "produced", and possibly interrupted. This means she followed the ways language, gesture, material objects (in this case, a material script), discursive forces, and (in this event, raced) identities produced new identities.

During a March 27 English class, a high school sophomore who self-identified as half Ecuadorian half Dominican (Santo) and a tenth-grade female who self-identified as Black (Lucretia) performed racial identities and positioned or raced one another amid discourses that govern race talk in school. Early in the period, Santo said Lucretia's guitar-shaped earrings made her White. Lucretia interrogated this position in speech (e.g., "*Why'd you say I'm trying to be White?*"), gesture (pointing to get Santo back to their collaborative assignment), silence (ignoring comments), and finally shouted, "...*Oh, would you stop saying about whiteness!*" Santo laughed, rubbed her back, physically imitated *Lucretia* identifying *him* as racist, identified himself as Black, positioned the school PA announcer's voice as White, and performed his own discomfort being misrecognized as White when he did ["nerdy"] things like carry projects to school.

A data collection and analysis method Liz used to prioritize youth perspectives was a 1:1 interactive follow-up interview. During interviews, Liz brought lunch and scripts of scenes like the March 27 back-and-forth between Santo and Lucretia. Liz asked Santo what *he* thought about the script of that day in school. Liz began the follow-up interview naming her identity as a White female researcher conducting research about pop culture texts and literacies youth of color negotiate in school. Liz explained the ethics of qualitative research on youth literacies that compelled her to invite Lucretia's and Santo's interpretations of data given all their aged and raced differences.

Santo's eyes pored over the paper script of the March 27 classroom scene, nonstop, not looking up as Liz spoke and asked questions. When he looked up, leaned back, and wiped his face with his hand, he remarked: "I actually remember that day too... I just remember what I was wearing." As they discussed the script, Santo positioned himself as racist, stupid, childish, dumb, random, and the lunchtime interview closed when the bell cut off his story positioning himself as bipolar.

SANTO: Miss, I'm gonna tell you something right now that I recently found out. It was kind of scary for me cuz I realized that throughout the actions I've done 'til now, my dad has bipolar which means, I'm bipolar! I swear to god. Now that they told me that I noticed that. I was like oh my god, I'm acting just like him.

Vignette Analysis: Our Reading of the Event

In this vignette, language, gesture, raced identities as read and inscribed on bodies, and a material object—the script—are producing new subjectivities.

While Liz asked Santo (through repetition and direct questions) to think about how race circulated in his classroom interactions with Lucretia, he took up a different discourse where he was constructed as a pathologized individual (the stupid, the dumb, the bipolar). Santo effectively reached for a popular narrative to explain shifting selves—a narrative that, while positioned as a mental disorder in need of diagnosis and medical management, could justify or excuse what he assumed Liz perceived to be impossible, bad, or racist behavior in school.

Coupling theories of literate identity performance with ethnographic methodology repeatedly reminds Liz of the ways in which our research tools produce and foreclose literacies and identities. Just like Butterfly's reading log disciplines reading and produces evidence of good reading, Liz, Santo, and a script assembled to produce Santo as bipolar. Tools intra-act with bodies, texts, and discourses to "see", "hear", and mis/recognize literate identities. Liz endeavored to perform the woke White female researcher making space for youth of color—whose bodies are often invisible in schools—to confirm, deny, or revise raced identities. In the literacy research world, this was Liz performing her literate identity. Yet, Liz's research tools (field notes, photographs, and recordings of literate identity performances with material pop culture texts) converged with time (a lunch period), place (a classroom), discourses (school race talk, cross-racial research ethics, psychological disorder), human bodies (Santo), and material objects (a transcript) to render and proliferate a whole new set of identities for Santo (stupid, dumb, bipolar). This reading *and re-reading* of literacy research necessitate that we, as researchers, embrace vulnerability; that we accept an invitation to unknowing and begin to consider the ways "language is coupled with the material world" (de Freitas & Curinga, 2015, p. 254). The transcript of March 27 imbued the everyday with political valence, imposing a stranglehold on past potential. And so, the interview did not end because Santo was offended. The interview did not end because Liz had run out of questions. The interview ended because the lunch bell rang and Santo had to go to class. And if they revisited that transcript today, somewhere else, something new would emerge; new literate identities would become.

Discussion

In this chapter, we read events from an embodiment perspective to demonstrate how the shaping and transformation of literate identities emerge in embodied act: namely, through the acts of material bodies and as discourses are inscribed on and by bodies. As children and youth take up and destabilize those identities through and in their bodies, school literacy and other discourses are both sedimented and transformed. Literacy, therefore, includes not only cognitive skills but also intrinsic feelings, unplanned activities, and contradictions as bodies, things, audiences, and norms for literacy assemble in the mundane moments of school and research practice. Accordingly, what a literate identity is, how it is valued, and who establishes it is not just a matter of discourse but also of what that discourse does to our bodies, and how our bodies respond to, comply with, subvert, and even challenge those discourses. Literacy and literate identities (as with aged, raced, classed identities, and so on) reside in material bodies, subjective feelings, and produced subjectivities—in the loud cheering and whisper-reading of Alex; in the pivoting of bodies and the fixing of gazes on leveled books and reading logs in Butterfly's case; in Omar's denial to move his body away from his chair and onto a stage; in Santo's pathologizing of his body to mitigate and resist racial/racist discourse.

Embodiment does not only look at how discourses and identities are mediated through bodies; rather, recognizing also that embodiment involves affect, performativity, and materiality, we see further possibilities for reading literate identities and literacy practice. First, *literate identities are dispersed across and emerge in the entanglements of children, teachers, tools, artifacts, and physical time-spaces*. In our cases, literate identities emerged when children's bodies, teachers' encouragement of writers and monitoring of the reading process, spinning word games and shared reading materials, reading logs and books that stink, notebooks with cat poems, stages, transcripts, apologetic responses, and shame came together—or, entangled—to form an event. In this sense, different layers of bodies (human bodies, material bodies, and bodies of knowledge) emerge as relevant at different pedagogical moments where durable formations *and* new becomings are *both* possible (Burnett et al., 2020; Ehret & Leander, 2019).

This understanding produces a second realization: that *an embodied view of literate identities helps understand literacy (teaching, learning, research) as boundary (re)making: as a leaky, flowy process of (re)defining what counts as literacy, affirming the recognition of but also risking the "othering" of literacy learners* (Kontovourki et al., 2020). Being a reader, writer, and learner multiplied in the coming-togetherness of Alex, a spinning game, practicing word recognition, and collaborating with peers. And this all happened away from the teacher's gaze, even if the game itself was part of school literacy practice. We read a multiplying reader identity in the entanglement of Butterfly, a reading log, and yet books that stunk or provoked disgust. We also saw flows in the public and the research assemblages of which Omar and Santo, respectively, were part. Omar's still body and Santo's exaggerated response are read as refusals of the positions attributed to them by others who attempted to destabilize positions and discourses; stages and transcripts did not have the assumed effect, even when they were deliberately pulled into the assemblage as means to reconfigure learner and raced identities. And, these assemblages did not conclude; rather, they were interrupted or remained unfinished as new "stuff" (another student, a bell, a ticking clock) entered the assemblage.

The idea that literate identities may be multiple and shifting goes along with the ways in which literacy itself multiplies and is concurrently stabilized. Across the cases we presented, literacy was seen as playing, collaborating, feeling, moving, sensing, celebrating, dressing, touching, and emoting; and those meanings of literacy co-existed with print-based, individualized reading, established genres (reading narrative, writing poem), timed tasks, groupings of children and materials, quantifications of experience, and public displays of ability. In this sense, literacy learning becomes a site where discourses of youth and childhood, of accountability, of pedagogy and discipline are layered up and morphed as they entangle with spaces, materials, and young learners' and teachers' bodies. By looking at children's and teachers' bodies coming together with materials and spaces, we paid attention to discourses of literacy that were maintained and thus stabilized, but we also attempted to identify moments of newness and disruption. In this attempt, our researching gaze, listening ears, standing or sitting bodies in distance or proximity of what we consider worthwhile happenings, the cameras we turn to and the audio devices we stick between material objects and human bodies, and our own aged, gendered, and raced bodies are also all part of assemblages where abled, raced literate identities are stabilized and still remain open to redefinition as new assemblages form.

Conclusion

To conclude, an embodied view of literacy and literate identities creates space for tracing how both are materially and discursively produced, and yet impossible to determine. This is a view of identity where the human is decentered: it alludes to post-structural notions of subjectivity as constructed, even if potentially unfixed (Kontovourki et al., 2020) and can be seen as dispersed across and emerging in entanglements of materials, discourses, and people. Thus, an embodiment lens enables seeing how human and material bodies inscribe what counts as literacy and being literate in bounded spaces like schools, at the same time that it recognizes that boundaries concerning both may be contested and confirmed. In this sense, literacies and identities are seen as being re-formed in entanglements, where exclusions and imbalances may also exist (e.g., Enriquez, 2014; Muhammad & Haddix, 2016).

This view of embodiment contributes to the critical rethinking of literacy and literate identities by considering how bodies are bounded by discourse and power, *as well as* multiply and re-inscribe literacy in ways that are impossible to determine or constrict (Johnson et al., 2021). Accordingly, educators and researchers who are interested in the embodiment of literate identities may become comfortable with being led (by children/youth, materials, and practices), and with the possibility of being re-configured themselves. Like others (e.g., Lenters & McDermott, 2020; Thiel & Jones, 2017), we also think it important to directly examine, contest, and decolonize entanglements that position particular bodies as other, and to reconfigure literacy assemblages to chart possibilities for new becomings.

Discussion Questions

1 What discourses about literate identities (e.g., "good writer," "struggling reader," and "at-risk student") circulate around your pedagogical and/or research practice? What assumptions and expectations about students' bodies are part of those discourses? How are good reading, writing, speaking, and listening supposed to look, feel, or sound?
2 Take 5–10 minutes to observe youth engaged in literacies work, either in or out of the classroom. How do their bodies move, shift, and change during that time? What do you notice about how their bodies come together and intra-act with the other bodies (human and non-human) during that engagement? How might those moment-to-moment shifts and entanglements correspond with different literate identities? How do those identities line up with their "official" literate identities at school?
3 In what ways might you document data about youth bodies engaged in literacies? How do bodies, things, and feelings factor into the lens you use to analyze that data?

References

Burnett, C., Merchant, G., & Neumann, M. M. (2020). Closing the gap? Overcoming limitations in sociomaterial accounts of early literacy. *Journal of Early Childhood Literacy, 20*(1), 111–133. https://doi.org/10.1177/1468798419896067

Carle, E. (1981). *The very hungry caterpillar*. Philomel Books.

de Freitas, E., & Curinga, M. X. (2015). New materialist approaches to the study of language and identity: Assembling the posthuman subject. *Curriculum Inquiry, 45*(3), 249–265. https://doi.org/10.1080/03626784.2015.1031059

Ehret, C., & Leander, K. M. (2019). Introduction. In K. M. Leander & C. Ehret (Eds.), *Affect in literacy learning and teaching: Pedagogies, politics and coming to know* (pp. 1–19). Routledge.

Enriquez, G. (2014). Embodiments of 'struggle': Examining the melancholy, loss, and interactions with print of two adolescent 'struggling readers'. *Anthropology & Education Quarterly, 45*(1), 105–122. https://doi.org/10.1111/aeq.12050

Enriquez, G. (2016). Reader response and embodied performance: Body-poems as performative response and performativity. In G. Enriquez, E. Johnson, S. Kontovourki, & C. Mallozzi (Eds.), *Literacies, learning, and the body: Putting theory and research into pedagogical practice* (pp. 41–56). Routledge.

Godwin, A. P., & Jiménez, R. T. (2020). The science of reading: Supports, critiques, and questions. *Reading Research Quarterly, 55*(S1), S7–S16. https://doi.org/10.1002/rrq.360

González Ybarra, M. & Saavedra, C. M. (2021). Excavating embodied literacies through a Chicana/Latina feminist framework. *Journal of Literacy Research, 53*(1), pp. 100–121. https://doi.org/10.1177/1086296X20986594

Hagood, M. C. (2005). Bodily pleasures and/as the text. *English Teaching: Practice and Critique, 4*(1), 20–39.

Johnson, E., Enriquez, G., & Kontovourki, S. (2021). Children's and youth's embodiments of critical literacy. In J. Z. Pandya, R. A. Mora, J. Alford, N. A. Golden, & R. S. de Roock (Eds.), *The handbook of critical literacies* (pp. 71–81). Routledge.

Jones, S. (2013). Literacies in the body. *Journal of Adolescent & Adult Literacy, 56*(7), 523–529.

Kontovourki, S., Johnson, E., & Enriquez, G. (2020). Embodiment and literacies: Teaching, learning, and becoming in a post-world. *English Teaching: Practice and Critique, 19*(4), 381–388. https://doi.org/10.1108/ETPC-11-2020-191

Leander, K., & Boldt, G. (2013). Rereading "A pedagogy of multiliteracies": Bodies, texts, and emergence. *Journal of Literacy Research, 45*(1), 22–46. https://doi.org/10.1177/1086296x12468587

Lenters, K., & McDermott, M. (2020). Introducing affect, embodiment, and place in critical literacy. In K. Lenters & M. McDermott (Eds.), *Affect, embodiment, and place in critical literacy: Assembling theory and practice* (pp. 1–17). Routledge.

Lewis, C., & Dockter Tierney, J. (2011). Mobilizing emotion in an urban English classroom. *Changing English, 18*(3), 319–329. https://doi.org/10.1080/1358684x.2011.602840

Luke, A. (1992). The body literate: Discourse and inscription in early literacy learning. *Linguistics and Education, 4*(1), 107–129. https://doi.org/10.1016/0898-5898(92)90021-n

Mallozzi, C. M. (2016). Disciplined within a discipline: English teachers are bound to be human bodies. In G. Enriquez, E. Johnson, S. Kontovourki, & C. Mallozzi (Eds.), *Literacies, learning, and the body: Putting theory and research into pedagogical practice* (pp. 57–71). Routledge.

Mohr, C. (2010). *Merry-go-round.* Townsend Press.

Moje, E. B., & Luke, A. (2009). Literacy and identity: Examining the metaphors in history and contemporary research. *Reading Research Quarterly, 44*(4), 415–437. https://doi.org/10.1598/RRQ.44.4.7

Muhammad, G. E., & Haddix, M. (2016). Centering Black girls' literacies: A review of literature on the multiple ways of knowing of Black girls. *English Education, 48*(4), 299–336.

Snow, C. E. (2018). Simple and not-so-simple views of reading. *Remedial and Special Education, 39*(5), 313–316. https://doi.org/10.1177/0741932518770288

Thiel, J. J., & Jones, S. (2017). The literacies of things: Reconfiguring the material-discursive production of race and class in an informal learning centre. *Journal of Early Childhood Literacy, 17*(3), 315–335. https://doi.org/10.1177/1468798417712343

Wager, A. C., & Perry, M. (2016). Resisting the script: Assuming embodiment in literacy education. In G. Enriquez, E. Johnson, S. Kontovourki, & C. Mallozzi (Eds.), *Literacies, learning, and the body: Putting theory and research into pedagogical practice* (pp. 252–267). Routledge.

Zapata, A., Kuby, C. R., & Thiel, J. J. (2018). Encounters with writing: Becoming-with posthumanist ethics. *Journal of Literacy Research, 50*(4), 478–501. https://doi.org/10.1177/1086296X18803707

CONCLUSION

Advancing Identity in the Literacy Field

Katherine K. Frankel, Christine M. Leighton, and Christopher J. Wagner

Introduction

Our purpose in this edited volume has been to provide a broad introduction to the concept of literate identities, overview how this concept has been applied in diverse ways in the literacy field, and explore what can be learned about literacy development, learning, and instruction when literacy is reframed as an identity practice. By bringing together authors who think deeply about literate identities across a range of theoretical and methodological perspectives, this book illuminates both the power and potential of identities to shape how we understand the ways that children and youth engage with literacy in and beyond their classrooms and schools.

In this concluding chapter, we look across the four sections of the volume to synthesize and reflect on how contributing authors conceptualize and study literate identities in their own work. We also discuss the implications of this collective work for future theory, research, policy, and practice. Specifically, we argue for the need to transcend binaries and silos in identity work in literacy to expand theorizations, methodologies, and applications of literate identities and their development to include attention to how literate identities (a) develop across practices involving reading, writing, and other forms of communication; (b) develop across ages, grades, and disciplines; and (c) connect to and problematize broader conversations in literacy related to achievement, assessment, accountability, and equity. Ultimately, we encourage readers of this volume to consider the affordances of literate identities as a framework for reimagining literacy learning opportunities for children and youth.

DOI: 10.4324/9781003271406-22

Theorizing Literate Identities

What Have We Learned About Literate Identities as a Theoretical Concept?

Contributing authors draw on a range of theoretical and epistemological perspectives to conceptualize literate identities. For instance, some authors ground their studies in sociocultural perspectives to situate identities and literacies within social practices (e.g., Learned et al., Chapter 7; Skerrett, Chapter 8) while other authors conceptualize literate identities in relation to more cognitively oriented concepts like motivation and self-efficacy (e.g., Walgermo & Uppstad, Chapter 2). Still other authors draw on concepts like embodiment to explore literacy and identity as entanglements of the material and human worlds (e.g., Enriquez et al., Chapter 12). Additionally, Compton-Lilly (Chapter 10) offers insights into the ways that different theories (i.e., intersectionality, figured worlds, assemblage) can highlight particular aspects of children and youth's literate identities while de-emphasizing others.

Literacy itself is conceptualized in various ways across studies. Some authors, like Moses (Chapter 1), focus on literacy as the reading and writing of predominantly print texts. Other authors, like Lewis Ellison et al. (Chapter 9), draw on theories of multimodality to expand the scope of what is meant by literacy beyond the printed word to include meaning making across modes (e.g., visual, auditory, linguistic) and through the use of digital tools. This diversity in conceptualizations of literacy across studies is important because how researchers understand what literacy entails has analytical as well as instructional implications for how children and youth are positioned by themselves and others as literate beings in light of these understandings.

Finally, it is important to note that conceptual understandings of literate identities also inform, and are in turn informed by, how authors conceptualize development. That is, the theoretical commitments that undergird theories of literacy and identity can also shape how notions of development are constructed and explored empirically. For example, contributing authors demonstrate how literacy and identity practices may look different over time and across contexts—from young children engaging in language and early literacy practices in and beyond their classrooms and schools (Wagner, Chapter 3) to older youth navigating the constraints of testing and tracking within a high school context (Learned et al., Chapter 7). Indeed, children and youth draw on different resources as they construct literate identities across time and space, with older youth able to utilize their relatively more extensive histories, experiences, and related narratives about what constitutes literacy and what that means for themselves and their peers as literacy learners (Hall, Chapter 6). However, this is not to say that younger children are not also informed by past experiences and future expectations as they engage with literacy (Moses, Chapter 1). Therefore we, like many of the contributing authors, aim to understand literate identities as dynamic and continuously constructed as children and youth navigate the diverse contexts of their lives over time.

The diversity in how authors in this volume conceptualize literacy, identity, and development is a strength in the field. It also is a challenge, as it complicates the notion of "literate identities" and is a reminder of the importance of clearly and explicitly grounding studies of literacy and identity within the theoretical and epistemological commitments that underlie these concepts.

What Do We Wonder About?

In light of the diversity of perspectives on literacy and identity represented in this volume, as well as in the literacy field more broadly (Lewis & Del Valle, 2008; Moje & Luke, 2009; Wagner, 2021), we see a need for scholars to be intentional and clear in the ways that they theorize literate identities. It is also important for scholars to consider what might go unaccounted for by relying on a particular theoretical lens. For example, scholars who study young children's literate identities using a theoretical framework grounded in monolingual ideologies about language and literacy will not have a perspective that is complex enough to account for the diversity of ways in which multilingual children enact their identities (Wagner, Chapter 3). Or, scholars studying older youth navigating the myriad constraints of public high schools might not fully consider the systems-level structures that constrain students' literate identities without a theoretical framework that attends to issues of power (Learned et al., Chapter 7).

Most contributing authors ground their work within situated understandings of literate identities as they are taken up and enacted as part of social, cultural, and historical practices. We see a need for ongoing theoretical development—including theory layering, in which researchers utilize two or more theories in complementary ways to illuminate complexities—to better account for the multiple factors at play in the study of literate identities. For example, contributing authors highlight the importance of incorporating additional theories to understand the ways that multilingualism (Wagner, Chapter 3), multiliteracies (Lewis Ellison et al., Chapter 9), cultural relevance (Francois, Chapter 4), and transnationalism (Skerrett, Chapter 8), to name just a few, all contribute to the construction of literate identities and how consideration of these key aspects may complicate or extend current understandings and assumptions.

Relatedly, we see an ongoing need for more explicit and focused attention to questions of power, authority, equity, and justice in the study of literate identities (Lewis et al., 2007). This is a need that contributing authors also note, with several demonstrating the ways that critical theories can add complexity to the study of literate identities. For example, Francois (Chapter 4) explores the affordances of a theoretical perspective oriented to culturally sustaining literacy practices, and Skerrett (Chapter 8) advocates for the incorporation of de/colonial perspectives in the study of literate identities among transnational youth as a way to call attention to how transnationalism can be framed as an asset at the same time that it works to marginalize particular identities.

We also think that the field needs to explore in more depth how to conceptualize literate identities across ages and grade levels in ways that are open to difference while also complicating and deconstructing rigid notions of "childhood" and "adolescence." We wonder what it might look like to ask and answer developmental questions about literate identities while simultaneously troubling and deconstructing linear notions of development. Attending to difference and change in literate identities over time and across ages can be generative, but it needs to be done in ways that are fluid and flexible and that consider young people's literacy experiences and histories in and beyond school. One way to do this is to theorize more robustly and critically what is meant by terms such as "time," "change," and "development," including ways that those constructs might be theorized as multifaceted and nonlinear (e.g., see Kabuto, Chapter 11).

Finally, as a field we must push back on erroneous assumptions about very young learners that position them as less capable of constructing robust literate identities. One way to do this is to ensure that identity theories take a sufficiently broad view of literacy (e.g., beyond what is revealed through oral language and print literacies) to also consider how embodiment, affect, and nonverbal modes of communication might provide key insights into young children's literate identities (e.g., see Enriquez et al., Chapter 12). Another way is to explicitly question and critique whether and how identity theories account for development and growth, and, where necessary, to draw on current understandings of development to modify and extend those theories to more fully capture variations over time.

Ultimately, as we consider the important theoretical contributions of the authors in this volume, which build on the contributions of other literacy and identity scholars, we contend that a commitment to theoretical complexity in the study of literate identities is essential. This may include the layering of theories to make sense of complex questions about literate identities across space and time combined with an active resistance to attempts to simplify the complexity of children and youth's lives and identities.

Studying Literate Identities

What Have We Learned About Studying the Literate Identities of Children and Youth?

In addition to the range of theoretical perspectives and diversity of ages and grade levels represented by the chapters included in this edited volume, most authors drew on a robust array of data sources, including participant observation, interviews with young people and those who know them (e.g., parents, teachers), and the collection and analysis of literacy artifacts (e.g., drawings, written narratives, multimodal compositions) to inform their understanding of children and youth's literate identities.

The different methodological choices made by authors tend to align with their conceptual approaches to literacy, identity, and development. That is, theoretical orientations shape the kinds of research questions authors ask, the data they collect, and their analytic processes. For example, Walgermo and Uppstad (Chapter 2) use constructs like motivation and self-efficacy that can be measured through formal assessment tasks that yield quantitative data. By using these kinds of measures, they are able to consider literate identities in the context of large-scale literacy assessments, exploring questions like, how can formal literacy assessments enhance students' interest and self-concept as readers and writers? In contrast, other authors such as Moses (Chapter 1) and Skerrett (Chapter 8) orient to identity from sociocultural perspectives that prompt different kinds of questions (e.g., how social interactions as they occur as part of children and youth's engagement with literacies impact identity development). The research methods that authors use to answer these questions vary, from Walgermo and Uppstand's larger-scale, quantitative study design to Moses' and Skerrett's qualitative designs that utilize ethnographic and formative methodologies. Regardless of the methods used, all of the contributing authors advocate for the importance of asking complex questions and collecting robust data to avoid essentializing children and youth's literate identities.

Several of the contributing authors in this volume approach the study of literate identities, not simply as researchers but also as educators whose understanding of literate identities shapes their instructional approach. For example, the chapters by Giunco et al. (Chapter 5) and Skerrett (Chapter 8) attend to the ways that the authors' positioning as practitioner-researchers, combined with their understandings of literate identities, shaped their approach to teaching as well as research. Specifically, Giunco and her colleagues explore how attention to literate identities can inform educators' reworking of literacy instruction to be more responsive to students. In a different example, Lewis Ellison et al. (Chapter 9) reflect on the processes of designing their STEAM workshop to be responsive to students' intersectional identities. In each of these cases, the authors highlight the importance of attending to researcher (and educator) positionality in the study of literate identities.

Finally, contributing authors call attention to the valuable insights that are gained from longitudinal research methods that seek to understand children and youth's literate identities over time. For example, both Kabuto (Chapter 11) and Compton-Lilly (Chapter 10) explore the nuances and complexities of longitudinal qualitative methodologies that seek to understand children's identities, literacies, and experiences as they and significant adults in their lives (e.g., parents, teachers) experience and reflect on them over longer periods of time. For Kabuto, this involved data collection with a child and her mother over ten years, beginning when the child was in first grade and continuing until 11th grade. For Compton-Lilly, the longitudinal design included children, mothers, and teachers, and extended across 13 years from when the children were in first grade through 12th grade. A key insight provided by these studies is how fixed and linear notions of ability and development, as they are instantiated in academic theories as well as in educational institutions and practices, fail to capture the richness and complexity of young people's identities across contexts and over time.

What Do We Wonder About?

We see an important need for more expansive approaches to researching literate identities across a range of methodological considerations. Expanding the methodological scope might take many forms. For example, Walgermo and Uppstad (Chapter 2) argue for more robust experimental designs to investigate ways to support literate identities, while other contributing authors suggest the need for more longitudinal theories and methodologies. For instance, multiple contributing authors advocate for the need to engage in research that extends across space (i.e., multiple contexts within and beyond classrooms and schools), time (i.e., across ages and grade levels), and modality (i.e., beyond the linguistic mode) (e.g., Compton-Lilly, Chapter 10; Enriquez et al., Chapter 12; Moses, Chapter 1).

These and other authors also stress the importance of including participants' perspectives on literate identities in robust ways that resist the essentialization of children and youth and their literacies. One way to do this is to prioritize critical, participatory research approaches in which children and adolescents can be involved in the collection and interpretation of data about their own identities. To do this, researchers must orient to children and youth as knowers and doers in their own right such that research studies are designed and conducted *with* participants and communities, which is in opposition to research that is done *to* or *on* participants (Haddix, 2020; Paris & Winn, 2014). Such an approach has the potential to create opportunities for increased diversity in the interpretation of how identities are constructed, analyzed, and represented in research. It also has the potential to provide spaces through which children and youth have more opportunities to exercise their agency and articulate their understandings of their own and others' literate identities, including how those identities are shaped by myriad factors within and beyond school and over time. To do this well, researchers must be increasingly and necessarily aware of their own multiple identities and associated positionalities and attend to critical reflexivity in their work with young people (Milner, 2007).

Finally, we see an urgent need for future research to engage in approaches to studying literate identities that are explicitly grounded in commitments to equity and justice (Baker-Bell, 2020; Jackson, 2020; Lewis et al., 2007; Muhammad & Mosley, 2021). Many of the contributing authors make similar points as they highlight the significance of their findings and call attention to contexts that both constrain and expand students' opportunities to imagine and enact literate identities. Future studies must take these implications for future research seriously by committing to instructional and methodological approaches that are grounded in equity and justice frameworks. This requires researchers to consider both the theoretical and methodological choices that are needed to center diverse ways of knowing and being, including explicit attention to how institutions and broader systems of power shape and constrain literate identities.

Being Responsive to Literate Identities in Policy and Practice

What Have We Learned About Literacy Instruction and Policy-Level Considerations?

The chapters in this edited volume speak to a number of implications for both policy and practice. First, authors highlight the importance—and necessity—of disrupting static identity labels such as "good," "poor," or "struggling" readers (e.g., see Hall, Chapter 6). They critique skills-focused and autonomous approaches to literacy education (Street, 2005) that do not reflect the multifaceted nature of identities as they are understood and enacted across different teaching and learning contexts (e.g., see Enriquez et al., Chapter 12; Walgermo & Uppstad, Chapter 2). At the same time, scholars who bring identity perspectives to bear in their research can and do acknowledge and account for the importance of skills and strategies to literacy learning and development. However, they also draw attention to the ways that a singular focus on skills and strategies captures only one narrow facet of the complexity of literacy and its development over time (i.e., as children grow older and move through elementary, middle, and high school contexts).

Relatedly, some contributing authors highlight how national-, state-, district-, and school-level policies and practices, which tend to focus predominantly on students' acquisition of skills and strategies, often at the expense of the affective and relational elements of literacy, can profoundly influence students' literate identities. In Kabuto's (Chapter 11) study, for example, she traces how one student's ongoing experiences of becoming labeled with disability classifications led to the tethering of her literate identity to experiences of struggle and othering. In Learned et al.'s (Chapter 7) study, the authors show how high-stakes testing and tracking are tied to issues of power and negatively impact students' identities and learning. In both studies, the use of identity theories supports the authors to make visible how young people navigate and resist policies and practices that position them as deficient, in some cases in solidarity with significant adults in their lives (e.g., a parent or teacher). In each of these chapters, the authors call for fundamental changes to classrooms and schools (e.g., heterogeneous classes, alternative assessment options such as portfolios) that may help to disrupt some of the assumptions that underlie uninterrogated educational policies and practices.

They note that these kinds of changes require shifts in how educational stakeholders treat students in their care—not as problems to be solved but as powerful agents of their own lives and learning who help to illuminate and resist the fundamental shortcomings of the educational system itself.

Amid these many challenges, contributing authors also explore how attending to students' literate identities can illuminate ways that classroom literacy practices positively support students' identity development and literacy learning. For example, Moses (Chapter 1) focuses on positive literate identity negotiations in a first-grade classroom. She shows how more inclusive literacy pedagogy (i.e., classroom literacy practices that flexibility extended beyond a focus on skill acquisition to privilege meaning making and social interaction) supported students' learning and positive identity positioning as readers. In a different study, Giunco et al. (Chapter 5) describe how they designed classroom instruction with an explicit focus on students' literate identities, which supported a shift toward more student-centered literacy learning. As these and other authors show, drawing on an identity perspective both to understand and to inform the design of literacy learning environments can positively impact both teaching practices and students' literacy learning.

What Do We Wonder About?

The aforementioned findings and implications index a broad need for a commitment to investing in educators as professionals and their students as active knowers and meaning-makers in their own right. This requires renewed attention to interactions between students, teachers, families, and other educational stakeholders who shape the contexts through which literacy teaching and learning occur. We say "renewed" attention because neoliberal educational policies have largely encouraged a focus on literacy products as a high-level policy lever for attempting to improve reading and writing outcomes. In schools, this focus often leads to various top-down policy mandates, such as requirements to purchase and use prepackaged literacy curricula from among a limited number of approved commercial suppliers; a simultaneous growth of scripted curricula that emphasize fidelity of implementation and ability labeling and sorting over authentic literacy practices and social interaction; and a devaluing of the preparation, training, and expertise of teachers.

These chapters instead highlight the need to center the lived experiences, perspectives, and relationships of children and youth in order to define high-quality literacy learning as fundamentally rooted in social interaction and collective learning and development. This requires investments in teachers' ongoing learning, robust literacy materials and libraries as tools for students' literacy learning, and time for meaningful literacy experiences that respond to and extend the linguistic and cultural assets and interests of young people.

In light of the important policy and practice-focused implications of the studies included in this volume, and inspired by the ongoing work of the contributing authors as well as other identity scholars, we wonder what it might look like to reimagine literacy learning through the lens of literate identities and through the notion of literacy as an identity practice. How might we apply insights gained from the studies reported here to current and future educational policies, curricular design, and instructional practices? To begin to answer this question, we offer the following areas in need of sustained attention:

1. Increased, facilitated communication with teachers, school and district administrators, policymakers, and other educational stakeholders about the complexity of literate identities, their connections to literacy development, and the implications of these complex theoretical understandings of (and empirical findings about) identity for policy and practice that informs literacy learning in and beyond schools.
2. Explicit attention to deconstructing processes of assessment, tracking, and labeling that narrow students' and teachers' understandings of what it means to be literate in and beyond classrooms and schools and that can negatively impact children and youth's conceptualizations and enactments of themselves as readers and writers.
3. A commitment to supporting and extending children and youth's existing multifaceted and intersectional identities as both a process and an outcome of literacy education. This includes making room for student agency and knowledge as a central component of literacy instruction.

As contributing authors show, these efforts are stymied in educational environments where curricula are prescribed and constrained and where effectiveness is measured narrowly, and often solely, through assessments of basic skills. As currently designed and mandated, these kinds of materials cannot capture the complexity of students' literacy processes and practices across contexts and over time.

The three action areas noted above are critical at this particular point in time, when there is increasing, intense focus in the scholarly community, as well as among practitioners and policymakers and in the popular media, on the science of reading and related discussion about what constitutes "effective" literacy instruction (Aukerman & Schuldt, 2021; Goodwin & Jiménez, 2020; U. S. Department of Education, 2016). As noted above, many of these conversations focus on the "right" instructional approach to support students' foundational skills. While we do not dispute that foundational skills like phonological and phonemic awareness, decoding, and fluency are important (and themselves intertwined with students' literate identities), we argue that equal, perhaps more, attention must also consider students' literate identities as integral to the processes and practices of literacy development (Muhammad, 2022).

At its core, the concept of literate identities highlights reading and writing as relational practices. Therefore, to understand students' multifaceted identities and develop instruction that is responsive to and sustaining of those identities, there is an urgent need to move away from a product-oriented perspective on literacy teaching and learning. Instead, we advocate for a shift toward literacy learning that foregrounds young people and their developing identities as readers, writers, and people across contexts and over time.

References

Aukerman, M., & Schuldt, L. C. (2021). What matters most? Toward a robust and socially just science of reading. *Reading Research Quarterly, 56*(S1), S85–S103. https://doi.org/10.1002/rrq.406

Baker-Bell, A. (2020). *Linguistic justice: Black language, literacy, identity, and pedagogy*. Routledge.

Goodwin, A. P., & Jiménez, R. T. (2020). The science of reading: Supports, critiques, and questions. *Reading Research Quarterly, 55*(S1), S7–S16. https://doi.org/10.1002/rrq.360

Haddix, M. (2020). This is us: Discourses of community within and beyond literacy research. *Literacy Research: Theory, Method, and Practice, 69*(1), 26–44. https://doi.org/10.1177/2381336920937460

Jackson, D. (2020). Relationship building in a Black space: Partnering in solidarity. *Journal of Literacy Research, 52*(4), 432–455. https://doi.org/10.1177/1086296X20966358

Lewis, C., & Del Valle, A. (2008). Literacy and identity: Implications for research and practice. In L. Christenbury, R. Bomer, & P. Smagorinsky (Eds.), *Handbook of adolescent literacy research* (pp. 307–322). Guilford.

Lewis, C., Enciso, P. E., & Moje, E. B. (2007). *Reframing sociocultural research on literacy: Identity, agency, and power*. Routledge.

Milner IV, H. R. (2007). Race, culture, and researcher positionality: Working through dangers seen, unseen, and unforeseen. *Educational Researcher, 36*(7), 388–400. https://doi.org/10.3102/0013189X07309471

Moje, E. B., & Luke, A. (2009). Literacy and identity: Examining the metaphors in history and contemporary research. *Reading Research Quarterly, 44*(4), 415–437. https://doi.org/10.1598/RRQ.44.4.7

Muhammad, G. (2022). Cultivating genius and joy in education through historically responsive literacy. *Language Arts, 99*(3), 195–204.

Muhammad, G. E., & Mosley, L. T. (2021). Why we need identity and equity learning in literacy practices: Moving research, practice, and policy forward. *Language Arts, 98*(4), 189–196.

Paris, D., & Winn, M. (Eds.). (2014). *Humanizing research: Decolonizing qualitative inquiry with youth and communities*. Sage.

Street, B. V. (2005). At last: Recent applications of New Literacy Studies in educational contexts. *Research in the Teaching of English, 39*(4), 417–423.

U. S. Department of Education. (2016). *Using evidence to strengthen education investments*. https://www2.ed.gov/policy/elsec/leg/essa/guidanceuseseinvestment.pdf

Wagner, C. J. (2021). Literacy and identities. In G. Noblit (Ed.), *Oxford research encyclopedia of education*. Oxford University Press. https://doi.org/10.1093/acrefore/9780190264093.013.990

INDEX

Pages in *italics* refer to figures and pages in **bold** refer to tables.